The Mountain Pierces The Blue Sky

山，
刺破青天

The Mountain
Pierces The Blue Sky

First Collection of Poems

詩 詞 初 集

1960-2005

A Chinese-English Bilingual Text

漢 英 對 照

Br. Peter Zhou Bangjiu, O.S.B.

周邦舊　著

January 2017

2017年1月

Seventh Updated Edition

第七次修訂本

St. Andrew's Abbey, USA

美國聖安德肋大修院

Printed In Taiwan

台灣印刷

版　　權：聖安德肋大修院
　　　　　　（2008年、2009年，2011年和2017年）。
審 訂 者：德肋撒・瑪利亞・莫洛女士。
編　　排：永望文化事業有限公司。
七　　版：2017年1月。
封面照片：1986年10月30日，教宗若望保祿二世在宗座宮廷接見筆
　　　　　者時，定睛看著他在中共獄中所賦的關於聖父的詩詞。
封面裡照：雷內・加西亞的兄弟拍攝於2016年7月17日。
扉頁照片：2001年5月2日，筆者在宗座宮廷向教宗若望保祿二世呈
　　　　　上他的三本書。
封底裡畫：本院前修士辣法額爾(尤金)・薩蘭德拉繪製於2008年。
封底照片：1986年10月30日，筆者在宗座宮廷拜謁教宗若望保祿二
　　　　　世時的一個情景。照片下方附有三段引文，分別來自羅
　　　　　杰・馬洪尼樞機主教、本院方濟各・本篤大院長和本院西
　　　　　滿・奧多尼爾神父為本書所寫的「前言」。
出 版 者：聖安德肋大修院（美國加利福尼亞州化野漠）。
初　　版：由愛德華・利特爾若翰和本院多默・巴布西施修士審訂，
　　　　　吉姆・莫勒的《寧靜》於1995年9月在美國出版。
二　　版：由本院西滿・奧多尼爾神父審訂，朱立德神父的《九八
　　　　　編輯委員會》於2006年9月在台灣出版。
三 四 版：由本院西滿・奧多尼爾神父審訂，由聖安德肋本修院先
　　　　　後於2006年11月和2008年1月在台灣出版。
五 六 版：由德肋撒・瑪利亞・莫洛女士審訂，由聖安德肋本修院
　　　　　先後於2009年10月和2011年1月在台灣出版。
作　　者：周邦舊。
書　　名：山，刺破青天(中文書名由黃美之女士於1995年6月惠為
　　　　　題簽和蓋章)。
國際書號：1-881614-01-8（平裝)(1995年英文初版本於美國)。
美國國會圖書館目錄編號：94-012045。
10987654321。
9781881614018。
國際書號：978-986-7173-75-1 (平裝)(2008年漢英對照本於台灣)。
承 印 者：永望文化事業有限公司。
　　　　　台灣台北市師大路170號3樓之3, (02)2368-0350
9789867173751。

Copyright ©2008, 2009, 2011 and 2017 by St. Andrew's Abbey.
Editor: Theresa Marie Moreau.
Layout: Yeong Wang Cultural Enterprise Company Ltd.
Seventh Edition: In January 2017.
Cover Photograph: On October 30, 1986, during an audience with
 Br. Peter in the apostolic palace, Pope John Paul II fixes his eyes
 upon Br. Peter's poems composed about His Holiness in a
 Chinese Communist jail.
Inside Front Cover Photograph: Rene Garcia's brother on July 17, 2016.
Title Page Photograph: Br. Peter presents Pope John Paul II with
 his three books in the apostolic palace on May 2, 2001.
Inside Back Cover Art: Our Br. Raphael(Eugene) Salandra in 2008.
Back Cover Photograph: A scene of the audience of Br. Peter with
 Pope John Paul II in the apostolic palace on October 30, 1986,
 with three quotations from the three Forewords respectively by
 Cardinal Roger Mahony, our Abbot Francis Benedict, O.S.B., and our
 Fr. Simon J. O'Donnell, O.S.B.
Publisher: St. Andrew's Abbey, P.O. Box 40, Valyermo,
 CA 93563, USA, (661)944-2178.
First Edition: Edited by Edward Littlejohn and our Br. Thomas Babusis;
 published by Jim Moeller's Serenity in the USA in September 1995.
Second Edition: Edited by our Fr. Simon J. O'Donnell, O.S.B.; published
 by Fr. Matthew Zhu Lide's September Eighth Editorial Board in
 Taiwan in September 2006.
Third and Fourth Editions: Edited by our Fr. Simon J. O'Donnell,
 O.S.B.; and published by our St. Andrew's Abbey in November 2006
 and January 2008, in Taiwan.
Fifth and Sixth Editions: Edited by Theresa Marie Moreau; and
 published by our St. Andrew's Abbey in October 2009 and January
 2011, in Taiwan.
Author: Br. Peter Zhou Bangjiu, O.S.B.
Title: The Mountain Pierces The Blue Sky. (The Chinese title was
 graciously written and sealed by Mrs. Mimi H. Fleischman in June
 1995.)
ISBN: Softbound 1-881614-01-8 (First Edition in 1995 in the USA).
Library of Congress Catalog Card Number: 94-012045.
10 9 8 7 6 5 4 3 2 1.
9781881614018.
ISBN: Softbound 978-986-7173-75-1 (Updated Edition in 2008 in Taiwan).
Printer: Yeong Wang Cultural Enterprise Company Ltd.
 3F. 3. No 170 Shih Ta Road, Taipei, Taiwan.
9789867173751.

獻　詞

敬獻給聖瑪利亞天主之母

救主耶穌爾愛子，祂乃上智生命光。
上智之座童貞母，聖德善良世無雙。

天使前來報喜訊，答語神奇驚四方；
親切愉悅訪表姊，唱出讚歌多激昂。

基督誕生又奉獻，失而復見於聖堂；
凡此種種情和景，珍藏心裡常思量。

愛主熱情滿胸懷，平凡家務成輝煌。
如詩似畫爾生平，千秋萬代永流芳。

主愛經訓和芳範，深思謹遵望扶將。
滄海人生助孩渡，俾頌聖子於天堂！

賴爾支援勝豺狼，坐牢受辱又何妨！
畢恭畢敬詩集獻，表明忠誠謝慈祥！

Dedication

To Holy Mary, Mother Of God

Jesus, our Savior, is your beloved Son;
He is the Wisdom and the Light of life.
Ever Virgin Mother, Seat of Wisdom,
Matchless in virtue, in goodness.

You gave your wonderful answer
To the Annunciation of the Angel;
You sang a fervent song of praise
To your cousin during your joyful Visitation.

Christ's birth, His presentation
And His finding in the Temple:
You treasured all these scenes and things
In your heart for constant meditation.

With your heart
Full of love for the Lord,
Your ordinary housework became glorious.
Your life was like a poem, a painting,
Leaving a sweet scent throughout the ages.

Help us to meditate on the love of God,
To practice the Biblical teachings,
To follow your exceptional example.
Tide us, your children, over the wide ocean of life,
So as to praise your Son in Heaven!

Relying on your support,
I defeated the Wolf.
Imprisonment and insults,
what then do they matter?
I dedicate to you with reverence
This collection of poetry
To express my fidelity,
In gratitude for your kindness!

目　錄

Contents

美國出版者的話

吉姆・莫勒

美國加州歐普蘭寧靜
1995 年 7 月 5 日

　　幾年前我見到一張問候卡片，片上說過像是這樣的話：「**有些人進入了你的生活中，而在那次的相晤後，你的生活將絕不會再是一如既往。**」

　　周修士就是那種罕見的人。許多人談論他們的天主，做的卻很少，只有少許人才想度與天主儘多儘好地交往的生活。在編輯他的自傳《**東方黎明在望**》期間，他給了我機會來觀察他持以生活的人生哲學。當自己和周修士在一起時，我感受到天主的愛是經由他而臨於我身。我常常發覺自己在注視著他，在他不知道的情況下注視著他，我可以見到他的嘴唇在移動，在祈禱。我注意到他的舉動，他與別人的相互交往，似乎每個姿態都是愛的姿態，愛的表情。

　　這第二本書《**山，刺破青天**》，可讓讀者再次獲得與周修士相交相處的機遇。它在表面上是一冊詩集，但其語言卻遠遠地有所超越。在《**東方黎明在望**》中他領我進入了他的仁愛忠恕的哲學，而本書則引導我去同天主進行真實的交往。當你閱讀他的詩詞，聆聽他的話語，感受到他的思想激動人心的力量時，我想你也會像我一樣，發現他和天主是常相往還，頻繁接觸。

Note
The American Publisher
Jim Moeller

Serenity, Upland, CA, USA
July 5, 1995

Some years ago I read a greeting card that said something like this, "There are people who come into your life, and after that meeting, your life will never be the same again."

Brother Peter is one of those rare people. Many people talk about their God, and do little else, but there are a few who have chosen to live their lives totally in connection with God. During our work on his autobiography, *Dawn Breaks in the East*, he allowed me to "hitchhike" and see his philosophy as he lived it. When I am with Br. Peter, I feel the love of God coming through him. Often I find myself watching him, unbeknownst to him, and I can see his lips moving in prayer. I watch his movements and interactions with others, and every gesture is a gesture of love.

This second book, *The Mountain Pierces The Blue Sky*, allows the reader to again "hitchhike" with Br. Peter. It may appear to be a book of poetry, but the words go far beyond that. In *Dawn Breaks in the East* he introduced me to his philosophy of total love and total forgiveness. This book introduces me to a true communication with God. As you read his poetry, hear the words and feel the emotional power of his thoughts, I think you will also discover, as I did, his great communion with God.

中國出版者的話
朱立德神父

台灣彰化

2006 年 5 月 23 日

　　法國哲學家帕斯卡（1623－1662）在他的《**思想錄**》中寫道：「**我只相信那些殉教證道者的故事。**」他的看法反映出了最初幾個世紀裡天主教作家的思想。例如，公元四世紀埃及亞歷山大主教聖亞大納削就曾這樣說過：「**殉道者以鮮血所作的見證，比任何言辭都更加強大有力。**」

　　今天是 2006 年 5 月 23 日，適值本篤會周邦舊修士的英文書《**東方黎明在望**》的初版中文本於台灣問世五個月的值得紀念的日子，我十分高興地獲悉，他的第二本書也將很快在這裡刊行。本編輯部深感榮幸，能再次協助他出版這冊中英文對照的詩集。

　　在本書《**山，刺破青天**》裡共有詩詞 211 首。這些詩詞是賦於兩個不同的時期，因而也就出自兩種不同的心情和兩種不同的筆調。最初的五十七首，描述了他在囹圄為信仰奮戰，著重表明了他對上主的忠貞和熱愛。這是凌駕一切，甚而是超越生死的崇高的情操；這可視如當前的中國苦難教會的真實寫照。當 1960 年 8 月 10 日聖老楞佐殉道節，周修士在四川省南充縣省一監赤膊挺胸，迎戰共黨獄吏時，他哼出了他的第一篇詩作。的確，他在二十六載的鐵窗生活的日日夜夜，總是謹飭慎重地

Note
The Chinese Publisher
Fr. Matthew Zhu Lide (Chu Li-Te)

Zhanghua, Taiwan
May 23, 2006

Blaise Pascal (1623-1662), a French philosopher, wrote in his *Thoughts (Pensees)*: "I only believe the stories of those who have been martyred." His views reflect the thoughts of Catholic writers of the early centuries. For example, St Athanasius, Bishop of Alexandria in Egypt in the fourth century, said: "The witness of the blood of the martyrs is much stronger than any words."

Today is the 23rd of May, 2006, a memorable day marking the five-month anniversary of the publication in Taiwan of the first edition of the Chinese text of the English book, *Dawn Breaks in the East*, of Br. Peter, a Benedictine monk. I am very glad to learn that his second book will also appear here very soon. Our Editorial Board is greatly privileged one more time to help with the publication of this collection of poems in a Chinese-English text.

In this book, *The Mountain Pierces the Blue Sky*, there is a total of 211 poems. These poems were composed during two different periods of time and hence in two varying frames of mind and in two differing tones or styles. The first fifty-seven poems describe his struggle in prison for the Faith and emphatically indicate his allegiance to and love for the Lord. This is a noble sentiment excelling all and transcending even life and death. This can be regarded as a real portrayal of the present suffering Church in China. On August 10, 1960, on the Feast of St. Lawrence, Martyr, when Br. Peter, stripped to the waist, with his chest thrown out, went to meet head-on the Communist jailer, he hummed his first poem in the No. I Provincial

持身，兢兢業業地抗魔，以向主示忠，對主報愛。他曾在本書第 15 首詩中這樣地向上主傾訴了他的衷曲：「**幾時鐐銬離？何日慈顏晤？惟望旨承行，不計身心苦！**」隨後的一百五十四首詩詞，則是在喜悅和自由的氣氛中寫出。1985 年 6 月 29 日，為紀念自己返回美國修院後矢發修會大願，他曾在第 88 首詩中向主獻上耿耿丹心時說道：「**忠心百煉獻蒼穹！長夜夢非空！**」1986 年 10 月 30 日，當他個別覲見教宗若望保祿二世時，他曾在第 127 首詩中表達了他的特殊感受：「**聖宮進謁喜洋洋……擁抱，再回接見父慈祥……情景，永生永世亦難忘！**」他當時是激動得感恩的淚止也止不住，心裡的話說也說不完。

周修士是在 1955 年下獄，初判二十年，後又兩次加刑，每次都是五年。1981 年，當地法院接受了他的申訴，覆審了他的第二次加刑案，指出了該案屬於意識形態的範疇，應以再教育而不是以科刑的方式來處理；因而給他撤銷了第二次加刑的原判，並且宣佈將他立即釋放。1981 年 7 月 25 日出獄時，他有過這樣的激情：「**懷著對上主的一片忠誠，勝利地、愉快地跨出了監牢的鐵門。**」（《**東方黎明在望**》132 頁）。第二天由蓬安到了南充，他又以如是的詩句來表明當時的感觸：「**舉目望藍天，一切向主獻；心寧趨寧靜，無憂又無怨。**」（同上 133 頁）。

面對大陸教會當前的形勢，《**九八編輯委員會**》和《**中國教會殉道史資料室**》懇切地呼籲和勉勵全大陸所有忠於聖座的主教、神父、修士、修女和信友，不分地上或地下，都用本書作者許多年前所說的話向上主宣誓說：

「**主啊！祢在十字架上的痛苦早已達到了極限。我怎能再用任何忘恩負義和變節叛教的言行，來將祢手上足上的鐵釘打**

Prison of Nanchong County, Sichuan Province. Indeed, during his prison life of twenty-six years, day and night, he always acted cautiously and fought the Devil conscientiously to show his fidelity to the Lord and to return His love. In the 15th poem of this book he poured out his feelings to the Lord in this way: "When will the fetters and handcuffs leave me? When, O when will I see Your loving face? If only Your Will be done, I shall not be concerned with my sufferings in body and mind!" The following one hundred and fifty-four poems were written in a joyful and free atmosphere. On June 29, 1985, in commemoration of his Solemn Monastic Profession after his reunion with his American monastery, he presented his fealty to the Lord in a poem (No. 88), saying: "A time-tempered loyalty has been dedicated to Heaven! The dream throughout a long night--by no means empty!" On October 30, 1986, when he had a private audience with Pope John Paul II, he expressed his special feelings in a poem (No. 127): "Full of joy, I enter the apostolic palace...The Holy Father embraces me; he is kind to grant another audience...The scene--unforgettable for ever and ever!" At that time, he was so excited that he could not stop his eyes from shedding grateful tears nor say all that was on his mind.

Br. Peter was imprisoned in 1955, originally sentenced to twenty years' imprisonment and later given additional sentences twice, five years each time. In 1981, the local court accepted his appeal, reviewed the case of his second additional punishment and indicated that this case came under an ideological category and accordingly should be handled only by re-education, not by condemnation. Therefore, the Court rescinded his original sentence of the second additional imprisonment and declared his immediate release. On July 25, 1981, he left the jail in such a fervor: "I triumphantly and cheerfully passed through the iron gates of the prison, carrying in my heart all my allegiance to the Lord." (*Dawn Breaks in the East*, P. 131). The next day,

入得更深些？我絕不能只是為了『苟全性命於亂世』而拿真理作交易。我已下定了決心，要為祢至死戰鬥，要為祢隨時準備投身於戰鬥，投身於以自己的生命作代價的戰鬥。」（同上 79－80 頁）。

having arrived from Peng'an in Nanchong, he expressed his feelings in these poetic verses: "Lifting up my eyes to the blue sky, I offer my all to the Lord; now in my calmed heart worries and complaints disappear." (Ibid. p. 133).

Facing the current situation of the Church on the Mainland, our September 8th Editorial Board and our Information Center of the History of the Chinese Martyrs earnestly appeal to and encourage all the bishops, priests, monks, sisters and faithful of the entire Mainland, loyal to the Holy See, whether on the ground or under the ground, to swear to the Lord in the words of the author of this book spoken many years ago:

"Lord, on the Cross Your agony reached its extreme limit quite early. How could I by any word or act of ingratitude and betrayal drive still further the nails into Your hands and feet? I could never barter away the truth just 'to save my life to live dishonorably in this troubled world', in the the words of Zhuge Liang (183-234). I have determined to fight until death for You, to be ready at all times to throw myself into the battle for You even at the cost of my life." (Ibid. p.77).

序　一

西滿・奧多尼爾神父

美國加州聖安德肋大修院
2006 年 3 月 1 日聖灰禮儀

　　周修士在他的化野漠修院現已度過了 22 年，比起他在獄中所度過的只少 4 年。他隨身帶來的，僅僅是他在中國的經歷，但這些經歷卻是多麼豐富呀！他生長在天主教家庭，他的信德得到了很好的培植、深切的撫育；聖寵把他塑造成了基督的好門徒。他被接納為本篤會的一名少年學生，他來到了一口充沛的水井，這水井是由他企圖加入的比利時修士的會院所興建的。隨著二十世紀中葉的兇暴的巨變，他所選擇的修院被驅散，被逐出了他們心愛的中國。他這下是孤苦零丁了，但他卻狠下決心要做一名修士，要全力以赴地活於真理，講出真理，而且，如果是天主的旨意，還要死於真理。

　　然而，什麼才是這樣的真理呢？它不是別的而是對基督的愛的認識。那使他經受住考驗和囚禁，經受住好多孤苦和好多誤解的，正是這種認識。他擁有這真理，他的一思一慮、一言一行也就受其指揮。他深知徹悟：沒有天主教會，那對基督的愛的充分認識就會迷失方向。他因而成了那個教會的一名戰士。他不願意教會被撕裂，被從根割斷，卻希望教會能自由地擁有基督，擁有福音，擁有聖事。他無法設想：自己堅持真理的心靈會沒有教會的慰藉。他也不能想像：自己可愛的中國不會榮獲機遇，來傾聽基督的福音，領受基督的慈愛，慶祝基督

Foreword I
Fr. Simon J. O'Donnell

St. Andrew's Abbey, CA, USA
March 1, 2006
Ash Wednesday

Brother Peter has now passed 22 years in his monastery at Valyermo, only 4 years shorter than he spent in prisons. He brought with him only his experiences in China. But how rich were these experiences! Raised in a Catholic household, his faith was well planted and nourished deeply. He was formed by grace to be a good disciple of Christ. As a young Benedictine student he came to a rich well, built by the community of Belgian monks whom he sought to join. With the big tumultuous changes of mid-twentieth century, his chosen community was scattered in exile from their beloved China. Alone now and fiercely determined to be a monk, he strove with all his energies to live the truth, to speak the truth, and, if God had willed it, to die for the truth.

And what is this truth? It is nothing else than the knowledge of the love of Christ. It was this knowledge that kept him going through trials and imprisonments, through so much isolation and so many misunderstandings. His possession of this truth dictated his every thought and his every move. He knew in the core of his being that without the Catholic Church, the fullness of the knowledge of the love of Christ would be lost. And so he became a champion of that Church. He did not want it to be torn apart, nor severed from its roots. He wanted the Church to be free in its possession of Christ, the Gospel, and the Sacraments. He could not imagine his heart holding on to the truth without the consolation of the Church. He could not imagine his beloved China without a graced opportunity to hear the Gospel, to

在聖事中的鑒臨和工作。

　　首先，他的長征意味著他與自己修院的分離。而其次呢，他的長征則把他領回到了自己的修院，但他卻爲此付出了被迫而離鄉背井的重大代價。在放逐波浪的衝擊中，他盡心竭力地堅持住他從前蒙受過的一切教誨、生活過的一切信念。他成了一名孑然一身的獨居修士，他在生活中儘無同院會友的即時安慰，卻有著來自他所擁有的基督的穩妥可靠的撫綏。他的獨居處所是他遭囚禁的牢獄，是他難以謀生、漂泊無定的街頭，甚至還是他自己的對其所追求者似乎深感疑懼的原來的老家。在陷入那些有著叛變的徵兆的包圍的四面楚歌中，他既已知道那位獨一無二者是絕不會背離他的，他也就因之寧願爲了基督的愛而捨棄一切了。

　　他要與之作鬥爭的，既是他自己身內的妖魔鬼怪，也是在中國橫行霸道的牛鬼蛇神，更是那些不容許教會生存，不容許教會自由地生活，不容許教會傳佈基督贈與人類的救恩的禮品的魑魅魍魎。他正在主所置於其前的坎坷艱難的征途上進行著改造。因之，他的勇氣不會餒洩，他的希望不會低沉，他的心臟不會停止同基督愈益親近的願望一起跳動，而基督曾爲他和全人類心甘情願地死難，並且還死在十字架上。

　　所有這些經歷，現在成了禮物，裝入包裹，於 1984 年到達化野漠，而此包裹正是周修士本人。他老早就已將自己的經歷儲存在他的腦海裡和他的心靈中，但那些並不是單純地留駐在他身上的經歷而已。他的富有詩意的心靈創作了成百上千首詩詞，來慶祝他的痛苦和他的損失、他的喜悅和他的憂傷，來記錄他對主的信仰和熱愛、對主的忠誠和感激。這些純樸的詩篇

come to the love of Christ, and to celebrate Christ's presence and work in the holy sacraments.

First, his journey meant separation from his community. And, second, his journey led him back to his community but at the cost of severance from his beloved homeland. Awash in the effects of exiles, he clung with all his might to everything he had been taught, to everything he had lived. He became the monk-hermit, living without the immediate consolation of his brothers but secure in the consolations coming from his possession of Christ. His hermitages were the prisons where he was incarcerated, the streets where he was forced to make a meager living, even his family which seemed to doubt his pursuits. Surrounded with signs of betrayal, he knew the One who would never betray him--and he preferred nothing whatever to the love of Christ.

He fought with his own demons and with the demons working in China--especially those who would not allow the Church to exist, to exist freely and to proclaim Christ's gift of salvation. He was being transformed on the rough and hard ways the Lord had placed before him. So, his courage would not flag, his hope would not diminish, his heart would not cease to pulsate with his desire to draw closer to Christ who willingly suffered death, even death on a cross for him and for all mankind.

All of these experiences, now become gifts, came in the package that arrived at Valyermo in 1984 and the package was Brother Peter himself. Within his mind and heart he had stored his experiences. But they were not to be experiences that simply resided in him. His poetic soul created hundreds and hundreds of poems to celebrate his pains and his losses, his joys and his sorrows, and to record his faith and his love for the Lord, his loyalty and his gratitude to the Lord. These simple poems became the new psalter played on the strings of his

，成了彈撥在他心弦上、哼唱在他嘴唇邊的新穎的聖詠。這些禮物不應當成為無聲的語言而秘藏心中，卻應當作為有聲有字的詩篇而為眾刊行公佈。這些詩篇是他經歷的見證，是可資好心善意者閱讀和反思的贈禮。而在閱讀和反思中，我們不得不驚奇上主的美好，讚嘆祂引領我們行進的道路。同時，這些詩篇還可用來測試我們信德的深淺。周修士的言辭現刻對我們變成了挑戰：在我們沿著通往生命的羊腸小道前進時，我們務必使自己的信德不斷地深化。

　　當前，周修士的話語和信息，還是第一次可以從他的母語中文獲得。這應當感謝所有使之成為可能的人士。我很高興地證實，周修士為令此事得以功成業就，曾經做出過艱苦的努力。這對於他該是多大的歡樂、多大的愉悅：叫自己的話語以英文、以法文，時下更以中文現身於世，見知於眾。

　　讓他的言辭成為基督的賜人生命的話語，在一個中國人的心靈中是如何深居長住的跡象。讓他的言辭對每位親愛的讀者都是一項請求：對中國教會不要輕率行事，卻要為之祈禱，使其在唯一的天主教會內成為一個十足的、有生命的地方教會。在過去的六十年中，那兒發生了好多好多事件，但願在未來的幾十年裡，只會有一個與基督的整個奧體完全共融的中國教會。

　　組成周修士的信仰的一個充滿活力的部分，是他的本篤會的遺產。當他一生中從這座修院到那座修院、從這個國家到那個國家遷來遷去時，聖本篤會規的詞句總是給以激勵。聖保祿的名言「**基督的愛催促著我們**」，反映在了全部會規中。本篤的門徒相信：基督的愛是滲透一切的，是到處都在的。正是這愛驅策著我們去愛基督。聖西彼廉對此講得很好：「**你為了基**

heart and chanted upon his lips. These gifts would have to be rendered not in silent words of the heart, but in the words of poems published for all. These become the testimony to his experiences, these become gifts for all good hearts to read and reflect upon. And in the reading and reflecting we cannot but marvel at the goodness of the Lord, and wonder at the roads he guides us over. At the same time these poems serve to test the depths of our faith. The words of Brother Peter have now become challenges for us to see to it that our own faith deepens as we progress along the narrow way that leads to life.

Now, too, for the first time the words and message of Brother Peter have become available in his native Chinese. A debt of gratitude is owed to all who made this possible. I am happy to attest to the laborious efforts Brother Peter made to see this work done. How happy it has made him to have his words available in English, in French, and now in Chinese.

Let his words be a sign of how deeply in one Chinese soul Christ's words of life have come to reside. Let his words be an invitation to each dear reader not to act rashly but to pray for the Church in China--that it may be a full and living local Church in the one Catholic Church. So much has happened in the last sixty years, may the next decades find only a Chinese Church in full communion with the whole Body of Christ.

A vital part of Brother Peter's faith is his Benedictine heritage. The words of the Holy Rule inspired Brother Peter as he moved through life in different monasteries and in different countries. St. Paul's famous words "the love of Christ urges us" are reflected throughout the Rule. The follower of Benedict is convinced that the love of Christ is all pervasive--it is everywhere. And this love inspires us to a love for Christ. St. Cyprian has said it so well: "Prefer nothing to Christ for He has preferred nothing to you! Cling tenaciously to His

督應該寧願捨棄一切，因為祂為了你已經甘願捨棄了一切！你當頑強地堅持住祂的愛！」這種相互間懇摯的愛支持著修士，儘管他知道自己已走上的征程只不過是凹凸粗劣，有時還會是嚴酷無情的。但他也明白，只要執著地堅持住這愛，他就可經由耐心的忍受，而確能使自己洗心革面，煥然一新。

本篤還早已清楚，忠實於福音的生活方式，也就是對福音的生活方式的忠誠，會最終領往對天主的無畏無懼、完善美滿的愛，生活的確會變得更輕鬆愉快。而這正是本篤給予的保證。現刻，輕鬆愉快是心靈的事，是在培養心靈的真實渴望。而歸根到底，這最大的渴望應該是對永生本身。到達了這樣的境界，修士會再次隨同聖保祿，將自己的心思絕不集中於塵世，卻只集中於天上。這項認識會掌控他，會策勵此忠實的心靈邁步走向基督為我們所贏得的全勝。

我們應同基督一起共享圓滿的天國生活。可驚奇的是：那些堅定地注視著天國的修士都已捐獻出了自己的塵世生活。注視天國並不是抹掉了塵世，但這卻改變了我們怎樣去察看一切事物的觀點。如此一來，渺小的就成了顯要的，軟弱的就成了主要的，被遺棄了的又被擁抱了起來，得不到愛的又得到了愛。在他們當中基督被發現了，在他們當中基督受到了服侍。如果我們想做基督永生的伴侶，我們就得在塵世生活中發現祂。周修士的經歷和詩詞證明了：基督能這樣被發現，基督能這樣得到服務，與基督也能這樣交往。祝願上主將我們大家都領入永生吧！

love!" This mutual, affective love sustains the monk even though he knows that he has set out on a path that cannot but be burdensome and sometimes harsh. But clinging steadfastly to this love, the monk knows that it is by patient endurance that he is truly made new and transformed.

Benedict also knew that fidelity to the Gospel way of life would ultimately lead to the perfect love of God which casts out fear. Life becomes easier, delightful, indeed. And this is Benedict's assurance. Now the ease and delight is a matter of the heart, the cultivation of true spiritual longings. And ultimately, the greatest yearning must be for eternal life itself. Again, with St. Paul, the monk focuses never on the terrestrial but only on the celestial. This knowledge takes hold and spurs the faithful heart on to the full victory won for us by Christ.

We are to become partakers with Christ in the fullness of kingdom living. It is amazing that monks, whose gazes are so firmly fixed on heaven, have become such contributors to life on earth. The heavenly gaze does not erase the earthly. It changes how we see everything. The little become important, the weak become central, the abandoned become embraced, the loveless become beloved. In them is Christ found, in them is Christ served. If we are to be Christ's companions in eternal life we must find him in earthly life. Brother Peter's experiences and poetry attest to this discovery of Christ, this service of Christ, this companionship with Christ. May the Lord bring us all together to eternal life!

序　二

錢志純　主教

台灣花蓮

2006 年 5 月 17 日

　　周邦舊修士爲紀念他出牢 25 週年，最近增訂了他在十一年前於美國出版的詩詞初集。他這次是要使其以漢英對照的新顏來與世見面。去年聖誕節前夕，他在台灣刊行了他在上世紀九十年代初葉即已於美國問世的英文書《**東方黎明在望**》的中文本。在那本書裡，他記述了他三十三年爲教會奮戰的事跡。憑藉超人的記憶力，他在腦海裡保存了許多賦於獄中的反映著對當年一些戰鬥事件的點滴感受的詩篇。1984 年 11 月由共產中國來到美國後，他在友人的協助下將那些詩篇中的一小部分譯成英文，付梓面世。

　　周修士是一位精神鬥士。他願以自己的經歷，鼓勵在中共的壓迫下受著各種各樣的艱辛的教友堅持住他們的完整信仰，並且勸誡自由世界裡的好心善意者別讓自己被中共政府的虛假的宗教自由所欺騙，以致忽視了地下教會實際的存在。他還想提醒他們，不要忘記那些忠於教宗的天主教徒所遭受的苦難，更不要否認忠貞的天主教徒仍然在同殘暴專制的共黨政府進行著鬥爭和對抗。

　　教廷方面近年來認爲中國只有一個天主教會，而所謂的「**愛國教會**」也已只是名存實亡了。新任樞機香港主教陳日君更指出，「**愛國教會**」內百分之八十五的主教，已求得了教宗若

Foreword II
Bishop Andrew Qian Zhichun
(Tsien Tchew-Choenn)

Hualian, Taiwan
May 17, 2006

To commemorate the 25th anniversary of his release from jail, Br. Peter recently updated the first collection of his poetry published in the United States of America eleven years ago. This time he intends to give it a new appearance in a Chinese-English bilingual text for all the world to see. Last year, on Christmas Eve, he published in Taiwan the Chinese edition of his English book, *Dawn Breaks in the East*, which had come out in the USA as early as in the beginning of the nineties of the last century. In that book he narrated the deeds of his valiant struggle of thirty-three years for the Church. With an exceptionally good memory, he preserved in his mind many poems composed in prisons and reflecting his feelings in those days on certain fighting events. Having come to the USA from Communist China in November 1984, with the help of his friends, he translated a small part of those poems into English and published them.

Br. Peter was a spiritual warrior. With his own experiences he would like to encourage the faithful subjected by the Chinese Communist oppression to a variety of tribulations to persist in their integral Faith. He wants to warn the people of good intention in the liberal world not to allow themselves to be deceived by the Chinese Communist government's false religious freedom to such a degree as to neglect the real existence of the Underground Church. He also wants to remind them not to forget the misery of the Catholics loyal to the Pope, nor to deny that faithful Catholics still struggle against and resist the Communist despotic government.

望保祿二世的認可，已成爲天主教的成員。「**愛國教會**」的「**天主教愛國會**」和「**天主教主教團**」這兩個組織，已不再有什麼作用了；兩個表面上的首領，或已死兩年，或久病不起，現在的執行秘書劉柏年先生，也僅僅是遵照中共訓示而發號施令的形式上的主管罷了。

如果我們說中國只有一個天主教會，這絕不意味著在目前就已經是事實，而只是一種希望，只是橋樑教會歷年奮鬥的目標。而這目標就是在促成**官方教會**和**地下教會**的對話，以便就雙方的合一，至少也是就彼此的和睦共存達成協議，或者取得諒解。

教宗本篤十六世對那些生活在沒有宗教信仰自由的國家裡遭受到許多限制和各種痛苦的天主教團體，最近曾深表關懷和支持。他絕對不是一位對真理會讓步、會妥協的人。因此，十分顯然的是：解決**官方教會**和**地下教會**之間的「合一」的問題，絕對不是暗示或者容許後者向前者投降。但教宗卻願意激勵後者向對方顯示出最大的誠意、堅持、耐心和愛德。

周修士的這冊詩集《**山，刺破青天**》，是繼他去年歲尾出版的那本自傳《**東方黎明在望**》之後的又一信仰見證。他曾在本書的〈**自序**〉中寫道：「**我的詩詞增加了我爲信仰鬥爭的力量和勇氣，強化了我對上主的忠貞和熱愛。它們既給了我加刑、受辱、戴銬、繫鐐、遭批鬥、關小牢的考驗和磨難，但也同時給了我戰勝這一切的忍耐、毅力和信心。**」

周修士希望他的故事有益於其他尚在受信仰考驗的人。他年事已高，仍然孜孜不倦地搦管直書；這顯示出他關心教會在中國的發展和自己同胞的得救的一片熱忱。他的熱忱令人敬佩！

The Vatican in recent years holds that there is only one Catholic Church in China and that the so-called Patriotic church exists in name only. The newly-appointed Cardinal Joseph Chen Rijun (Zen Ze-kiun), Bishop of Hong Kong, also pointed out that eighty-five percent of the Patriotic bishops have already received the approval of Pope John Paul II and hence have become members of the Catholic Church. The two organizations of the Patriotic church, The Chinese Catholic Patriotic Association and The China Catholic Bishops College, have been unable to play any role. One of the two apparent leaders died two years ago and the other has been sick for a long time. At present, Mr. Liu Bainian, the general secretary, is the only one formal leader who issues orders according to the Chinese Communist instructions.

If we say that there is only a single Catholic Church in China, it would never mean that this is a fact at this moment, but rather merely a hope and a fighting goal of the Bridge church over the years. This objective is to help bring about a dialogue between the Official church and the Underground Church so that an agreement or an understanding can be reached on their unity or, at least, on their harmony and coexistence.

Pope Benedict XVI recently showed his loving thoughtfulness and support for the Catholic communities living in countries with no religious freedom and encountering many restrictions and all sorts of distress. He is absolutely not a man of concession nor a compromiser of the truth. Therefore, it is very evident that the way to settle the issue of "unity" between the Official church and the Underground Church can never hint at nor allow the surrender of the latter to the former. But the Pope would urge the latter to manifest her great sincerity, persistence, tolerance and charity for the other side.

Br. Peter's collection of poems, *The Mountain Pierces the Blue Sky*, is another witness to the Faith following his autobiography, *Dawn*

這個集子是由他親口哼出的中文原詩和親手草擬的英文譯作所組成，是他離開黑牢返回修院後多年來心血的結晶，也是他所作出的殫精竭慮、焚膏繼晷的努力的成果。想來會符合國人的期待，會受到公眾的歡迎！

Breaks in the East, published at the end of last year. In the Preface to this book he wrote: "My poems increased my strength and bravery to fight for the Faith and strengthened my fidelity to and love for the Lord. They gave me trials and tribulations of an additional penalty, insults, handcuffing, shackling, criticism, struggle against and solitary confinement, but at the same time they offered me the endurance, willpower and confidence to overcome them all."

Br. Peter wishes his story to benefit other people undergoing the ordeal of Faith. Despite his advanced age, he still engages in taking up the pen to write arduously. This reveals his earnest enthusiasm concerning the development of the Church in China and the salvation of his compatriots. His zeal is worthy of admiration! This collection is formed by Chinese original poems, hummed on his own lips, and the English translations, drawn up in his own hand. It is the crystalization of his many years of painstaking labor after departing the dark prison and returning to his monastery. It is also the fruit of his utmost effort, exhausting his energies and consuming his time. I know that it will be in keeping with his compatriots' expectations and that it will be well received by the public!

序　三

曾慶導　神父

台灣輔仁大學
2006 年 4 月 16 日復活節

　　每次讀周邦舊修士的詩詞，我都會感動得流淚，這並不是因爲自己特別的感情豐富，而是因爲在這些詩詞的字裡行間所顯示出來的勇氣豪情，的確是太感人了！

　　在中國大陸所謂的「文化大革命」期間，人人都要讀毛語錄、背毛詩詞。很具諷刺性的是：本集子的書名卻正是取自那些詩詞中的一首。詩詞本身就很有感染力和鼓動力。毛詩確曾毒害過許多人，特別是年青人。可見好工具放在壞人手中所造成的傷害和破壞會是極大的。但現在周修士已把這好工具拿回來了，恢復了詩詞應有的導人向上的好名聲。

　　聖經裡就有一百五十首來自靈感的詩篇。這些詩篇是在聖神的指導下，記錄了舊約子民在其悠久歷史中的喜怒哀樂，興衰起落，成敗利鈍，是主耶穌所喜愛的聖經詩歌。周修士的詩詞與聖詠是有些類似，是天主默感了他在共黨獄中的那些煢煢子立、漫漫長夜裡而賦出、而記住了的，應是我們基督徒所愛好的勵志佳什。

　　可以說，周修士的詩詞對算做中國千百年來有韻文學的巨大遺產的唐詩宋詞，是神妙的增補。作爲一個基督徒，我甚至還會說周修士的詩詞比許多古代詩詞都更鏗鏘、更強勁、更動人、更有啓發性。這道理很簡單：天主、基督和聖母在他的作

Foreword III
Fr. Augustine Zeng Qingdao
(Tsang Hing-To)

Fu Jen Catholic University, Taiwan
April 16, 2006
Easter Sunday

Every time I read Br. Peter's poems I am so touched that I cannot help shedding tears. This is not because I am too sentimental but because the heroic courage and spirit manifested between the lines of these poems are truly moving and inspiring.

During the so-called Great Cultural Revolution on Mainland China everyone had to read Mao's quotations and learn his poems by heart. Ironically, the title of this anthology is taken from one of those poems. Poetry has an infectious and agitating power of its own. Mao's poems had indeed poisoned many people, especially the youth. It is evident that a good tool in the hands of an evil man can cause great damage and destruction. But Br. Peter has taken back the good tool and has restored to poetry the good name of guiding people to a higher level.

In the Bible there are also one hundred and fifty inspired psalms which under the guidance of the Holy Spirit record the pleasure and anger, the sorrows and joys, the rise and decline, the ups and downs, the successes and failures, the smooth and the rough of the people of the Old Covenant in their long history. We know that our Lord Jesus loved those Biblical songs. Br. Peter's poems are somewhat similar to those sacred psalms. I am sure that it was God who inspired him in those long lonely nights in Communist prisons to compose and to memorize his many poems. Followers of Christ will love these inspiring poems.

Br. Peter's poems can be regarded as a wonderful addition to the

品中的臨幸是清晰可見。

　　基督憑藉十字架救贖普世，周修士在他的「**復活節頌**」（見第三首）中歌頌道：

> 「**復活力量大，**
> **化頑育賢良；**
> **勇飲十架杯，**
> **登天謁君王！**」

　　基督走過逾越奧跡，祂吩咐我們也要跟著做。周修士感受到基督在十字架上的大愛之後，決心以愛還愛。他酌飲了十字架的爵杯，無畏地捍衛了天主教信仰和天主教會。他為此多年來所受的苦難定會與基督所受的融合在一起，成為引導眾人，包括那些給他製造過多年的痛苦生活的迫害者在內的得救的途徑。他的榜樣激勵著我們，激勵著他的讀者去效法他，像他效法基督一樣，激勵著我們大家去走逾越奧跡的路。

　　衷心感激周修士多年來不辭辛勞地慘淡經營，使我們現在就能見到他的這冊既有英文又有中文的詩集。這是文學和精神瑰寶，可供我們珍賞熱愛，可使我們意氣高昂。但願周修士不要就此止步，卻當再接再勵，好讓第二和第三集接踵而至。

great heritage of Chinese poetry from the Tang and Song dynasties and for centuries afterword. As a Christian, I would even say that Br. Peter's poems are still more sonorous, more powerful, more moving and more edifying than many ancient poems. The reason is simple: God, Christ and the Blessed Mother are clearly present in his works.

It was by the Cross that Christ redeemed the world. This Br. Peter sings in celebration in his poem, *"In Praise of Easter"*:

> *"The power of the Resurrection is unlimited:*
> *Converting the stubborn,*
> *Strengthening the wise,*
> *Fostering the virtuous.*
> *Drinking bravely the chalice of the Cross,*
> *We shall ascend to Heaven and see the King!"*
>
> (No. 3)

Christ has passed through the Paschal Mystery, and He bids us to do the same. After experiencing the unfathomable love of Christ on the Cross, Br. Peter resolved to return this love with love. Drinking the chalice of the Cross, he fearlessly defended the Catholic Faith and the Catholic Church. His sufferings of many years because of that will join those of Christ and will become the channel of redemption for all, including even those persecutors who made his life miserable for so many years. His example inspires us, his readers, to imitate him who imitates Christ so well and to pass, each one of us, through the Paschal Mystery.

Thanks to Br. Peter's untiring efforts of many years, we now have this collection of his poems in both English and Chinese. It is a literary and spiritual gem for us to treasure and to be uplifted by. We only hope that Br. Peter would not stop here but that a second and third collection would be forthcoming!

自　序

美國加州聖安德肋大修院
2006 年 7 月 25 日出牢 25 週年

　　隨著拙書《**東方黎明在望**》的中文初版於 2005 年聖誕節前夕在台灣的面世，我這才有了時間來重審在 1995 年 9 月於美國出版的詩集，來使其以漢英對照的新面貌在本年內於台灣和美國同時問世。從而，與世共享自己為教戰鬥、為主作證和同人交往的悠悠歲月裡的充滿焦慮和憂傷、充滿希望和喜悅的悃愫和激情。

　　我檢查了原來的 171 首詩詞，並增加了 40 首新的。這些新的或賦於離開大陸前的四個寒冬中，或吟於最近的十個陽春裡。

　　我遠非擅長賦詩填詞，更未對詩詞有過深入的研究。我所讀過、所熟記的著名的騷客詞人的作品，為數也十分有限。我現在還記得，還能瑯瑯上口的不多的詩詞，也只是自 1966 年 6 月以來就一直記住的毛澤東的那 37 首，在 1983 年曾予強記過的《**白香詞譜**》所選百闋詞中的一些，以及來自《**唐詩三百首**》和其他幾種詩詞選集中的少許而已。實際上，自己對詩詞的不解之緣，當時是形成於對其音韻抒情的濃厚興趣，對己傾訴衷腸的迫切需要。坦率地說，自己所賦詩詞只是形式上大抵合於傳統的詩詞格律，合於《**平水韻**》；而在意境方面則完全談不上，我僅僅是用來記事、敘物、言志和抒懷罷了。

　　黃美之女士是一位筆耕了四十多年的華人作家。早在 1995 年 6 月，當本詩集的英譯文初版即將問世時，她曾應我本人和我的出版者吉姆·莫勒先生與肯·莫勒先生的邀請，在那本書

Author's Preface

St. Andrew's Abbey, CA, USA
The 25th Anniversary of My Release from Jail
July 25, 2006

With the publication of the first Chinese edition of my book, *Dawn Breaks In The East*, in Taiwan on Christmas Eve of 2005, I have had the time to review the poetry published in September 1995 in the USA. I would like to publish this poetry with such a new face in a bilingual Chinese-English text this year both in Taiwan and in the United States of America. With this I will be able to share with the world my sincere feelings and intense fervor of many worries and sorrows, many hopes and joys during my long years of struggling for the Church, witnessing to the Lord and associating with others.

I went through the original 171 poems and have added 40 new ones which were composed during a stretch of four cold winters before leaving the Mainland and in the period of the last ten warm springs.

I am far from good at composing poems nor have I made a deep study of poetry. I have read and memorized the poems from works of past famous poets very limited in number. I now remember and can still recite clearly and sonorously 37 poems of Mao Zedong memorized since June 1966, a few from *Baixiang Ci Pu*, a collection of 100 poems (Ci), once committed to memory in 1983, and a few from the *Three Hundred Tang Poems* and from some other poetic collections. In fact, my indissoluble bond with poetry arose at that time from my great interest in their rhythmic expression and from my urgent need for pouring out my heart. Frankly speaking, my poems have followed only formally and generally the traditional poetic rules and forms and the rhyme scheme of *Pingshui Rhym*. For my poems

的封面和扉頁上題寫了五個俊秀的中文字的書名，並加蓋了她的刻著中文名字的私章。在這次的新版本中，仍然保留著她原來的題名和印章。為此，我謹向她再致謝忱。

在這段覆查詩集的時期裡，西滿・奧多尼爾神父慨然助我審訂了所有新舊詩詞、所有《自序》和所有新《序》的英譯文，並且還為本書寫了一篇《序》。錢志純主教鈞座和輔仁大學神學教授曾慶導神父也曾惠然審閱本書，慨賜《序言》。原詩集英文本的出版者吉姆・莫勒先生承擔了為新的英譯文打字，為本書作了一些編排。朱立德神父料理了本書在台灣的出版，還寫了《編者的話》。永望文化事業有限公司為中文原稿和所有其他中文譯件打了字，為全書作了編排和印刷。黃慧玲女士和其夫君彌額爾・科特先生，基督蒂娜・金女士和她的兩個女兒詹妮弗、阿曼達，斐理伯和弗洛拉・赫凱塔伉儷，杰拉德・若瑟・克里斯托弗・米拉尼先生、他的太太菲利絲・德登・米拉尼和他的母親瑪格麗特・安娜・倫多・米拉尼，杰姆和奧德麗・阿伯雷拉伉儷，以及安吉・溫斯頓女士等贊助了這次的出版。許多好友都曾給本書提供照片，或者給以其他各式各樣的幫助。對所有上述的尊長和朋友，也對其他一切未在這裡提到的援助者和支持者，敬致最衷心的謝意。

由於《漢語拼音》體系已經為國際社會所普遍接受，為舉世全球所廣泛採用，為了讓所有不同國籍和不同民族的讀者易於閱讀和了解，本書乃用以拼寫所引用的全部中國人名和地名，並以之作為其統一的音譯詞。

我的詩詞帶給了我各種各樣的效果。它們增加了我為信仰鬥爭的力量和勇氣，強化了我對上主的忠貞和熱愛。它們既給

literary rhythmic conception is totally out of question. I have used them merely to record events, narrate facts, talk about ideals and express personal feelings.

Mrs. Mimi H. Fleischman is a Chinese writer for over forty years. As early as June 1995 when the first English edition of this poetry was about to appear, at my invitation and that of my publishers, Mr. Jim Moeller and Mr. Ken Moeller, she exquisitely rendered and sealed with her Chinese name on the front cover and the title page the five Chinese characters for the title of the book. Her original inscription and seal are still kept in this new edition. I want to thank her once again for her kindness.

During this period of reviewing my poetry, Fr. Simon O'Donnell affably helped me with the editing of the English texts of all the new and old poems, all the Prefaces and all the new Forewords. He also wrote a Foreword to the book. His Excellency Bishop Andrew Qian Zhichun and Fr. Augustine Zeng Qingdao, S.J., professor of theology at Fu Jen Catholic University, graciously went through the book and kindly wrote their Forewords. Mr. Jim Moeller, the publisher of the original poetry in its English edition, undertook the typing of the new English text and the layout of the book. Fr. Matthew Zhu Lide took care of the publication of the book in Taiwan and wrote a Note for it. The Yeong Wang Cultural Enterprise Company, Ltd., helped to type the Chinese original text and all the other Chinese documents, to layout and to print the book. Ms. Elaine Huang Huiling and her husband, Mr. Michael L. Cotter, Ms. Christina Kim, her daughters, Jennifer and Amanda, Mr. Philippus H. Herkata and his wife Flora, Mr. Gerard Joseph Christopher Milani, his wife Phyllis Deden Milani and his mother Margherita Anna Rando Milani, Mr. and Mrs. Jaime J. Abrera, and Ms. Angie E. Winston sponsored this publication. Many friends provided the book with pictures or assisted in other ways. To

了我加刑、受辱、戴銬、繫鐐、遭批鬥、關小牢的考驗和磨難，
但也同時給了我戰勝這一切的忍耐、毅力和信心。它們還經常
向我提供極大的安慰和愉悅。我企望、我祈禱：它們藉著這次
的出版發行，也能對旁人的心靈和精神有所裨益。假如慈愛的
天主藹然延長我的風燭殘年，並且繼續賜以清醒的頭腦和旺盛
的精力，或許在不久的將來會有詩詞第二集與讀者諸君見面。
祝願好天主降福你們大家！

2016 年 9 月 8 日

聖母誕辰

　　在這次的新版本中，只有一點點改動；而這點改動，則全
由德肋撒・瑪利亞・莫洛女士惠為審訂。

all the above-mentioned dignitaries and friends and to all the other helpers and supporters not referred to here I extend my deepest and heartiest gratitude.

Because of the Hanyu Pinyin system already universally accepted by the international community and widely employed by the whole world, it is used here to transliterate all the Chinese names of persons and places in this book and to unify their transliterations. This will facilitate all readers from different countries and nationalities to read and to understand.

My poems have brought me results of all kinds. They increased my strength and bravery to fight for the Faith and strengthened my fidelity to and love for the Lord. They gave me trials and tribulations of an additional penalty, insults, handcuffing, shackling, criticism, struggle against and solitary confinement, but at the same time they offered me the endurance, willpower and confidence to overcome them all. They often bestowed upon me great consolations and joys. I hope and pray that they also make a little contribution to the minds, hearts and spirits of others through this publication. If the loving God will amiably prolong my years, old and ailing like a candle fluttering in the wind, and continuously grant me a sober mind and exuberant vigor, a second collection of my poetry may meet with my dear readers in the near future. May the good God bless you all!

September 8, 2016
Birth of the Blessed Virgin Mary

In this new edition there were only a very, very little changes, and the changes were graciously edited by Theresa Marie Moreau.

英文本初版序一

洛杉磯總主教
羅杰・馬洪尼樞機

加州洛杉磯
1995 年 4 月 16 日復活節

　　本人很高興與諸位讀者共享，化野漠聖安德肋大修院周修士所吟詠的這冊詩詞初集《**山，刺破青天**》。這在他非平凡的人生中是一種可愛的舊和新的交融。在化野漠與周修士在中國西南四川省的出生地和他所進入的西山本篤會修院之間的距離，不僅可理解爲若干英里，而且還可理解爲個人傳奇。這個傳奇涵蓋著他的被捕遭關和他在其本省四川成都、南充與蓬安三座城市的下獄坐牢。而給他加上的所謂罪行，則是他對羅馬天主教會、對教宗本人的忠貞不渝。他爲此遭受了二十六年的牢獄和折磨。

　　1929 年由比利時聖安德肋大修院派遣到中國的屬於聖母領報分會的歐洲籍本篤會修士，於 1952 年被監禁了，並隨即被驅逐出了共產中國。因著天主上智的安排，他們終究於 1956 年在我們洛杉磯總主教轄區內羚羊峪化野漠重建了他們的修院。1992 年 8 月 2 日，我將大院長的祝福榮幸地授予了化野漠新近升格爲大修院的首任大院長方濟各・本篤。自從來到本總主教轄區以來，這些修士就從事著多種多樣的使徒工作，藉以讓在俗的男男女女共享他們的具有特殊風格的修道院的祈禱。他們在「化野漠青少年之家」接待了我們那些前往度過退省時光的

Foreword I
To The First English Edition
Cardinal Roger Mahony
Archbishop Of Los Angeles

Los Angeles, CA.
April 16, 1995
Easter Sunday

It is a personal joy for me to share with you, the reader, this first collection of poems, *The Mountain Pierces The Blue Sky*, composed by Brother Peter Zhou, O.S.B., of St. Andrew's Abbey, Valyermo. It is a delightful mixture of the old and new in his extraordinary life. The distance between Valyermo and Sichuan Province in southwest China where Brother Peter was born and entered the Benedictine Monastery of Xishan is understood not only in terms of miles but of a personal saga. This saga embraces his arrest and his imprisonment at three different cities, Chengdu, Nanchong, and Peng'an--all in his native Sichuan Province. His so-called crime was his unbending loyalty to the Roman Catholic Church and to the person of the Pope. For this he was imprisoned and tortured for twenty-six years.

Sent to China in 1929 by the Abbey of St. Andre, Belgium, the European Benedictine Monks of the Congregation of the Annunciation were imprisoned and then expelled from Communist China in 1952. They eventually, through God's Providence, re-established their Priory at Valyermo in Antelope Valley, within our Archdiocese of Los Angeles, in 1956. On August 2, 1992, it was my privilege to impart the Abbatial Blessing on Abbot Francis Benedict, O.S.B., the first Abbot of the new Abbey in Valyermo. Since their arrival in this Archdiocese the monks have engaged themselves in a variety of ministries through which the special character of monastic prayer is shared with women and men living in society. This ministry embraces the large groups of our young people who spend time on retreat in the Valyermo Youth Center. The monastery guest house has provided a haven for those wishing to make a private retreat or in groups. The monks also engage

由年輕人組成的大型團隊，在修院客房向那些想作個人或集體
退省者提供了避世和靜修的場所。修士們有在大學和神學院兼
課的，也有協助本地堂區神父和專職司鐸工作的。他們的夏季
研討會和專題講座已成了可珍愛的傳統。不過，他們的主要工
作卻是祈禱，周修士正是這些常行祈禱的人中的一員。

　　他是這座本篤會修院裡的唯一依然健在的中國修士。原以
為已死去的他，卻終究在 1984 年 11 月 27 日來到了洛杉磯。他
的調寄《**浣溪沙**》的詞《**來美一年書懷**》，不僅表露了他的喜悅，
而且還表露了他對所蒙受的恆心和自由的恩賜的不勝感激：

　　　　「歷史長河僅瞬間，
　　　　戰龍赤縣卅三年！
　　　　凱歌再唱滿心歡。

　　　　師長同窗來四面，
　　　　一堂聚首盡開顏。
　　　　思源飲水謝蒼天！」（見第 100 首）

　　他在共黨監牢的 26 個歲月裡，為了使自己忠貞常在、心神
健旺而採取的唯一方法是：每天神望彌撒，唸經默想，按照古
典詩詞的格律，賦詩兩千多首，並將其儲存於腦海裡。在這本
詩集中，你們和我都能有幸分享他的內在生活。1960 年 8 月 11
日，當他在南充監獄被戴上手銬後，他曾以調寄《**生查子**》的
《**食如獸**》的詞來表達了他那時的感受：

　　　　「驕陽照飯場，反銬連雙手。
　　　　俯首口來銜，進食如禽獸！

in teaching part-time at universities and seminaries. They assist in the local parishes and chaplaincies. Their summer conferences and workshops have become a treasured tradition. However, their principal work is prayer and one of these men of prayer is Brother Peter.

He is the only surviving Chinese monk of this Benedictine Community. Presumed dead, he finally arrived in Los Angeles on November 27, 1984. His poem, *Some Feelings Since Arrival In The United States One Year Ago,* expresses not only his joy but his profound gratitude for the gifts of perseverance and freedom:

> *"But a drop*
> *In the great river of history –*
> *My thirty-three years*
> *In the fight against the Dragon in China!*
> *Full of joy,*
> *I sing a song of victory once more.*
>
> *Teachers and classmates from all quarters,*
> *We gather here together,*
> *Rejoicing and laughing.*
> *While drinking water,*
> *Thinking of its source,*
> *I express my gratitude to Heaven!"*   (No. 100)

For twenty-six years in Communist prisons, his only method of remaining steadfast and sane was to participate mentally each day in the Mass, mentally pray the psalms, meditate and compose over two thousand poems which he committed to memory through the use of classical Chinese tunes. In this book of poems you and I are privileged to share in his inner life. Handcuffed in Nanchong Prison on August 11, 1960, he expresses how he felt in his poem, *Taking Food As An Animal:*

赤身十架懸，主為吾儕救。

報愛示忠誠，變獸何羞有？」（見第 2 首）

　　如此的遭遇和他的予以接受，顯示出了他為著諧和天主聖意而完全棄絕自己的精神，而這正是自我解脫道路的頂點，就像馬米翁大院長（1858-1923）在其《**基督是修士的典範**》書中所寫的那樣。耶穌接受了苦難。為了這個緣故，當基督快要進入世界時，祂便對天主說：

「**犧牲和素祭，已非你所要，**

　卻給我預備了一個身體；

　全燔祭和贖罪祭，已非你所喜。

　於是我說：看，我已來到！

　關於我，書卷上已有記載：

　天主！我來是為承行你的旨意。」

（希 10：5－7）

　　以某種神秘的方式，周修士和所有步武耶穌後塵的我們大家都被召喚去受苦，以「**補充基督的苦難所欠缺的。**」（哥 1：24）這樣的安排能使看起來毫無意義的化為有意義的，而終結也總是常有的，正如艾略特（1888-1965）所曾淳樸地描述過的那樣：

「**我們所稱作的開始，常常是終結，**

　而消滅終結，卻是在製造開始；

　終結就在我們所由之開始的地方。」

"The burning sun shines on the dining ground,
Cuffs bind my two hands behind my back.
I bow my head
To take food with my mouth,
As do birds and beasts!

Hanging naked on the Cross,
The Lord saved us.
To repay His love,
To show my allegiance,
What is the shame
Of becoming an animal?"
(No. 2)

Such an experience, and his acceptance of it, demonstrates his spirit of total abandonment to God's will, which as Abbot Marmion (1858-1923) wrote in his volume, *Christ The Ideal Of The Monk*, is the crowning point of the way of detachment. Jesus embraced suffering. For this reason, when Christ was about to come into the world, He said to God:

"You do not want the sacrifice and offering of animals.
But you have prepared a body for me.
You are not pleased with the offerings of animals burned
Whole on the altar,
Or with sacrifices to take away sins.
Then I said, 'Here am I, O God,
To do what you want me to,'
Just as it is written in the book of the Law."
(Hebrews 10:5-7)

In some mysterious way Brother Peter and all of us who follow the way of Jesus are called to suffer in order to "fill up those things that are wanting of the sufferings of Christ." (Colossians 1:24) Such a disposition can make sense out of what appears to be nonsense. But there is always an end. As T. S. Eliot (1888-1965) so simply wrote:

（《四重奏》）

　　對周修士來說，曾經有一個坐牢的終結，也有一個同我們在加利福尼亞州這兒的開始。我珍視他生活在我們中間，這可繼續提醒我們也該是忠心耿耿。「**我們祖先的信仰，神聖的信仰！我們有誓死效忠於你的決心和膽量。**」：是一首可珍愛的讚美詩。在我們當中就有一位曾經忍受過「**地牢、烈火和刀劍。**」在孑然一身的時刻，我們也要記起那支持我們的天主的慈愛，就像主對朱莉安娜・諾威治（1343-1443）所說的那樣：

　　　　「我將使一切好轉，
　　　　　我要使一切好轉，
　　　　　我會使一切好轉，
　　　　　我能使一切好轉，
　　　　　你自己就要看到
　　　　　一切將會好轉。」
　　　　（《記述》十五章）

　　中國教會仍在受苦受難，在為紀念福音傳佈中國正進入第七個世紀而向中國本地教友和神職界發出的聯合牧函中，中國大陸八位主教說道：「**我們必須擦乾眼淚，療好創傷，滿懷新的精神，來見證主愛，實踐主愛，來歡欣鼓舞地奔赴傳揚福音的戰場。**」周修士曾是那個戰場上的一名戰士，他如今則以常行祈禱者的身分繼續從事著那場戰鬥。這些中國主教在其牧函的結尾處宣稱：「**所有天主教徒都必須認識到：如果沒有與聖統制和普世主教團的首腦，換言之，沒有與教宗和與之合一的主教**

"What we call the beginning is often the end
and to make an end is to make a beginning.
The end is where we start from."
(Four Quartets)

For Brother Peter there was an end to imprisonment and a beginning with us here in California. I treasure his presence which is a continual reminder that we too must be loyal. *"Faith of Our Father, Holy Faith, we will be true to thee till death,"* is a cherished hymn. We have in our midst one who endured *"dungeon, fire and sword."* In moments of desolation we too will remember the love of God which sustains us. As the Lord said to Juliana of Norwich (1343-1443):

"I will make all things well,
I shall make all things well,
I may make all things well
And I can make all things well
And you will see that yourself
That all things will be well."
(Showings Ch. XV)

The Church in China still endures its sufferings. In a joint pastoral letter of eight bishops in mainland China addressed to the local Chinese Catholics and clergy commemorating the seventh centenary of the beginning of evangelization in China, they said: "We must dry the tears, heal the wounds, and , filled with a new spirit bearing witness to and carrying God's love, we must run joyfully to the battlefield of evangelization." Brother Peter was part of that battlefield. He continues that battle by being a man of prayer. The Chinese bishops ended their letter by stating "all Catholics must realize that there can be no ministry of bishops which is not in communion with the hierarchy and the head of the universal College of Bishops, in other words, with the Pope and the bishops in communion with him." Brother Peter remained loyal and he expresses

團的共融，就不可能有主教的聖職。」1986 年 10 月 30 日，赤膽忠心的周修士在羅馬晉謁教宗時，曾以《**個別覲見教宗若望保祿二世**》為題的《**定風波**》詞，表達了他當時的感受和心情。其詞曰：

> 「日出東方放彩光，
> 　聖宮進謁喜洋洋。
> 　樓上小堂洵壯麗，
> 　聖祭，
> 　虔誠莊重獻穹蒼。
>
> 　傾聽留神看譯稿，
> 　擁抱，
> 　再回接見父慈祥。
> 　和煦秋陽窗上映，
> 　情景，
> 　永生永世亦難忘！」（見第 127 首）

　　在履行自己的司祭職責的初期，能為北加利福尼亞州的華人團體服務，這對我來說是一份恩賜。多年來就一直保留著對那項工作的熱愛。就在最近，我曾呼籲柯林頓總統，停止驅逐那些聲稱為避免強迫墮胎和絕育而逃離故國的中國難民。中國還在受著苦難。我和他一起為中國同聲祈禱，也和他一起為保持信仰而感到喜悅。我祝願他像聖本篤所勸導的那樣，「**在心靈洋溢著不可言喻的愛的喜樂中，常常奔馳在天主誡命的道路上。**」（《**會規**》序 49）。

his feelings on meeting the Pope in Rome on October 30, 1986, in his poem *"A Private Audience With His Holiness John Paul II:"*

> *"The sun is rising from the east*
> *With splendor;*
> *Full of joy,*
> *I enter the apostolic palace.*
> *In the chapel upstairs,*
> *Truly magnificent,*
> *The Holy Sacrifice is offered*
> *To Heaven devoutly, solemnly.*
>
> *Listening attentively,*
> *Glancing at my manuscript,*
> *The Holy Father embraces me;*
> *He is kind to grant another audience.*
> *The warm autumn sun*
> *Is mirrored on the windows:*
> *The scene –*
> *Unforgettable for ever and ever!"*   (No. 127)

In my early days of priesthood it was a grace for me to minister to the Chinese community in Northern California. That love has remained over the years. Only recently I appealed to President Clinton to halt the imminent deportation of Chinese refugees who say they fled their country to escape forced abortion and sterilization. China still suffers. I join my prayers with Brother Peter for China and I rejoice with him in keeping the faith. May he always, as St. Benedict advises, "run on the path of God's commandments, our hearts overflowing with the inexpressible delight of love." (Prologue 49).

英文本初版序二
方濟各・本篤大院長

加州化野漠聖安德肋大修院
1995 年 2 月 2 日

　　我感到榮幸，來向諸位讀者介紹周修士的詩詞初集。這些詩詞的寫作，或出自對牢獄生活的體驗，或在獲釋和返回其修院以來，出自對一些事件，對一些與許多認為他本人和他當前的出現是天主的一份大恩者的交往的反思。周修士與我們相處的這十多年，是他為寫回憶錄和詩集而勤奮工作的歲月。他在心靈深處受到了鞭策，來為他人敘述和錄下，天主要他給二十世紀這最後的九十年代的教會和世界傳遞的信息。

　　我見到《聖經》和《聖本篤會規》中的許多章節，都在周修士身上得到了生動活潑的體現和實踐。「**我此刻的談話是給你說的，不拘你是誰，只要完全棄絕私意，並且矢志為主基督、為真君作戰，那你就拿起這最堅強、最光輝的聽命的武器去從事戰鬥吧。**」(《會規》序 3)周修士的很多獄中詩詞都引起了我對他為忠實於信仰而進行的戰鬥的懍然敬畏。他的戰鬥力是由天主的聖寵所授予，他所秉賦的堅強決心也沒有被威力所擊潰，儘管那威力曾經驅逐過他的修院，並且還逮捕過那些公開地效忠於普世教會和其最高牧者的天主教徒。

　　在他與自己修院的分離期間，淒涼孤苦的監牢便成了他的「**修院**」，在那兒得到履行的卻是《會規》的精神：「**我們要以忍耐分擔基督的苦難，以便在將來共享祂的天國。**」(《會規》序

Foreword II
To The First English Edition
Abbot Francis Benedict

St. Andrew's Abbey, Valyermo, CA.
February 2, 1995

It is an honor to introduce to you the first collection of Brother Peter's poems written from his prison experience and, since his liberation and restoration to his monastic community, from reflection on events and his relationship with the many people who hold his person and his presence as one of God's greatest gifts. Brother Peter's more than ten years among us have been years of diligent work on his memoirs and poems. In his inmost being he is impelled to recount and record for others the message which God invites him to give to the Church and to the world of this last decade of the twentieth century.

I see alive, enfleshed, and fulfilled in Brother Peter many passages from Sacred Scripture and from St. Benedict's Rule. "This message of mine is for you, then, if you are ready to give up your own will, once and for all, and armed with the strong and bright weapons of obedience to do battle for the true King, Christ the Lord" (Prologue 3). So many of Brother Peter's poems from prison elicit in me an awe for the battle he waged to be true to his faith. His struggle was empowered by God's grace and his natural dogged determination not to be overcome by those forces which exiled his monastic community and arrested those openly faithful to the universal Church and her Chief Shepherd.

In his separation from his community, his "monastery" became the prison of solitude, where the spirit of the Rule "we shall through patience share in the sufferings of Christ that we may deserve also to share in his kingdom" was fulfilled (Prologue 50). His poem, number

50）他在這冊詩集的第 50 首極其美妙地說道：

> 「促膝談心於主前，
> 孤牢身繫又何妨！
> ……
> 冀望記憶猶強勁，
> 保舊吟新增主光！」

　　這座修院團體同周修士一起都認為，他在 26 年囚禁後的倖存和他從共產中國的解脫使他有理由從事專職寫作。我希望他的見證，將會給許多處於損害、創傷或者心靈痛苦中的人們帶來慰藉和激勵。他的詩詞曾經成為一種神奇療法，舒緩過他為基督所遭受的打擊，曾經使他有能力超越迫害者所給予的負面影響，有能力生活在只有天主才能提供的那種平安中。他對天主的熱愛，在第 86 首詩中即可清楚地見到：

> 「……
> 懦懦無榮傾碧血，
> 區區有幸慕群芳。
> 漫長考驗言難述，
> 深厚神恩僕未忘。
> ……」

　　認識和愛護周修士的我們大家在他身上見到的比言語，甚至比他自己的言語所能描述的還要多得多。他受磨受苦的孤寂

50 in this collection, says so beautifully,

> *"Since I can sit side by side,*
> *And talk intimately with my Lord,*
> *I might as well live in a solitary cell!...*
> *I wish my memory to remain strong*
> *To keep the old poems and compose new ones*
> *For the greater glory of the Lord!"*

This monastic community has believed with Brother Peter that his survival of 26 years imprisonment and his deliverance from Communist China warrant his full time occupation in writing. It is my hope that his witness will encourage many who are in a period of loss, trauma, or interior trial. His poetry became a divine therapy cushioning the blows he endured for Christ. His poems enabled him to transcend the negative impact of his oppressors and to live in that peace which only God could provide. His zealous love for God is clearly seen in poem number 86:

> *"...In my weakness,*
> *I was not given the honor*
> *Of shedding my blood;*
> *In humility,*
> *I now have the good fortune*
> *Of admiring the fragrant flowers.*
>
> *Words fail to describe*
> *My prolonged trials,*
> *But I cannot forget*
> *The profound divine kindness..."*

歲月和他在我們中間的幽靜祈禱與勤奮寫作，已經使他由通過聖本篤的十二級謙遜，而「**到達了無恐無懼全心愛主的完美境界。以前由於畏懼而遵守的一切誡命，如今則是出於這愛主之情，毫不費力地便能做到，彷彿習慣成了自然，已不再是由於怕下地獄，而是出於熱愛基督、良好習慣和喜愛修德。**」（《會規》七章 67－69）。

　　請讀者諸君品嚐周修士的詩詞吧！這些詩詞曾經是他的起過拯救作用的藥物，是他的成年累月的伴侶，是他的傳送給世界的信息。還請在那裡面發現他與天主的關係，他對信仰的激情，他對天主啟示給他的真理的不屈不撓的赤膽忠心。隱蔽在他證言中的不是別人，而正是作為他的生命的靈魂和生活的中心的主耶穌基督。他免於殉道烈士的死難，或許是為了在我們的時代就像在過去的每個時代一樣，成為天主聖言的活生生的見證。

All of us who know and cherish Brother Peter see more in him than words can describe, even his own. His lonely years of suffering and his solitary diligence of prayer and writing among us have brought him through St. Benedict's twelve steps of humility to "arrive at that perfect love of God which casts out fear. Through this love, all that he once performed with dread, he will now begin to observe without effort, as though naturally, from habit, no longer out of fear of hell, but out of love for Christ, good habit and delight in virtue." (Rule, ch. 7: 67-69).

Please savor the poetry which has been Brother Peter's saving remedy, his constant companion, and his message to the world. Find in it his relationship with God, his passion for faith, his unbending fidelity to the truth that has been revealed to him by God. Hidden in his testimony is none other than the Lord Jesus Christ, the soul and the heart of Brother Peter's life. He was spared the martyr's death to become a confessor to the Word of God alive in our day as in every age.

英文本初版自序

加州化野漢聖安德肋大修院
1995 年 5 月 2 日

　　下獄坐牢對於一個人來說，並非總是一件不幸的事；當他是為了上主而深幽囹圄時，這尤其是千真萬確的。我對詩詞原本一無所知，可是，多年的鐵窗生涯，卻向我提供了讀詩的機遇，作詩和學詩的志趣，特別是在共黨監獄所度過的悠悠寒暑，更給了我吟風弄月的素材和激情。由是，一首首詩詞，自一九六六年夏季以來就從自己火熱的心靈，不斷地向外迸發，在自己生命的火花中蔚為大觀。天父的這項分外恩賜，甚至延續到了此時此地，使我不能不對祂的慈愛而美妙的安排讚嘆再三。我也總是感念那位鐵窗知己盲囚趙漢業，他曾讓我借閱一冊毛澤東詩詞，使我得以自學自修，從而大膽地賦詩填詞，冒昧地涉足詩壇聖地。

　　不論是在紅色監牢的囚禁年代，還是在出獄後返回遂寧縣老家的三年期間，全都無法將所吟詩詞抄錄於紙。直到來美兩月後的 1985 年 1 月，我才有了可能著手錄下這些作品；從 1 月 4 日到 2 月 10 日，850 多首記得比較清楚的詩詞乃得躍然紙上。由於翻譯上的困難，自中文原稿譯成英文者，還不到此數字的十分之一；而這些詩的英譯初稿，除了六首是由曾慶導修士和葉素貞修女擬就外，餘則全部出自本人的拙手拙筆。

　　蒐入這冊集子的賦於獄中的詩詞只有 57 首，其餘 114 首除 4 首外，全是來到美國後的新作。這些新作的數量是後來居上，其中 54 首是關於自己 1986 年秋的比利時和羅馬之行。在本集

Author's Preface
To The First English Edition

St. Andrew's Abbey, Valyermo, CA.
May 2, 1995

It would not always be a misfortune for a person to be in jail. This is especially true when he is imprisoned and isolated for the Lord. Originally, I knew nothing about poetry. Yet, many years of life behind bars afforded me the opportunity to read poems, to aspire to compose my own, and to learn to do so. The long winters and summers in Communist prisons gave me, particularly, the material and enthusiasm for writing poems of my own. In this way, my poems, one after another, have come forth without ceasing from my burning heart since the summer of 1966, and they have presented a splendid sight in the flames of my whole being. This special favor from the Heavenly Father continues even to this place and moment. I cannot help but praise over and over His loving and wonderful design. Also, I always keep gratefully in mind the blind inmate Zhao Hanye, a close friend during my imprisonment, who loaned me a copy of the poems of Mao Zedong to read from which I taught myself to boldly compose poetry and to rashly set foot in the sacred place of the poetic world.

It was utterly impossible to write down my poems on paper either during my captivity in the Red prisons, or during the following three years after I had left jail and returned to my old home in Suining County. Not until January 1985, two months after I arrived in the United States, was I able to begin to copy down these compositions. From January 4 to February 10, over 850 poems kept clearly in my memory, flowed vividly onto my paper. Because of the difficulty of translation, fewer than one-tenth of this number have been translated into English from the original Chinese. The first rough translations of

子裡，我的新舊詩詞同時顯露頭角，我的悲歡離合也一併脫穎而出，儼如飽經滄桑的人生五味——甜、酸、苦、辣、鹹——宛然在目！

1985 年 3 月 21 日，在本院當時的副院長而今的大院長方濟各‧本篤神父的要求和扶掖下，我開始將頌復活節的三首詩譯成英文。從那時起直到去冬，我不斷地審查舊詩，吟賦新的，從事英譯，進行修改。在這長達十年的審稿過程中，我得到了下面這許多友好在審閱、修改、打字、再打字、影印、提供照片和資金等方面的極大幫助：斐理伯‧愛德華茲神父、凱琳‧魏爾赫米修女、彭妮‧法赫蘭德太太、耶肋米‧德里斯科爾神父、若翰‧德斯蒙德先生、肯‧帕克先生、若‧杜奎特先生、帕特‧費勒太太、吉恩‧德‧貝蒂尼小姐、維多利亞‧布朗太太、愛德華‧利特爾若翰先生、多默‧巴布西斯修士、德米安‧維倫修士、洛蕾‧哈蒂爾小姐、李聖淑小姐、特麗‧湯普森小姐、瑪莉安納‧帕普女士、安納‧麥克法登女士、德波拉‧威廉斯女士、陳薰女士、毛永昌先生、潘愛桃先生、張倩兮小姐、良‧格林伍德先生、艾米‧格林伍德太太、雨果‧福爾斯伉儷、阿古斯蒂娜‧西西莉婭‧赫凱塔小姐、賈維茲夫婦、阿伯雷拉伉儷、瑪多納‧埃德加太太、若瑟‧佈倫南神父、蕭恩‧克羅寧神父和埃倫‧利特爾若翰太太。

我深知自己對中國舊體詩詞僅僅是一知半解。中文原作既非典雅，英文譯著更匪優美。這些詩詞，雖經飽學鴻儒一再審閱，多次匡正，似乎仍未完全抒情達意。但願其精神猶在，期能對在奔赴永生的征程上的讀者增強力量，給以激勵，去迎擊各種挑戰，面對各種困難。假如這個集子能歌頌主愛，傳播真

these poems, except six by Br. Augustine Zeng Qingdao, N.S.J., and Sr. Grace Ye Suzhen, S.D.S.H., were all done by myself.

Only 57 poems I composed during my imprisonment have been included in this collection. The remaining 114 poems, except 4, are all new and written since my arrival in the USA. Among the new ones, the late-comers outnumbering the old-timers, 54 concern my trip to Belgium and Rome in the autumn of 1986. In this collection, my poems, new and old, show their faces in public at the same time; my sorrows and joys, partings and reunions emerge together and display themselves as if the five flavors -- sweet, sour, bitter, pungent and salty -- were present in all the vicissitudes of life!

On March 21, 1985, at the request and with the assistance of Fr. Francis Benedict, then Subprior and now Abbot of our monastery, I began to render the three poems in praise of Easter into English. From then on until last winter, I had never ceased to examine the old poems, to compose new ones, to do the English translations and to make revisions and corrections. During this long course of ten years of revision, I was greatly helped by the following many friends in reviewing, editing, typing, retyping, photocopying or providing pictures or funds: Fr. Philip Edwards, Sr. Karen Wilhelmy, Mrs. Penny Fahland, Fr. Jeremy Driscoll, Mr. John Desmond, Mr. Ken Parker, Mr. Joe Duquette, Mrs. Pat Feller, Miss Jean DeBettignies, Mrs. Victoria C. Brown, Mr. Edward Littlejohn, Br. Thomas Babusis, Br. Damian Whalen, Miss Lori Hartill, Miss Suky Lee, Miss Terry Thompson, Ms. Marianne Papp, Ms. Anne McFadden, Ms. Deborah D. Williams, Ms. Joan Chen, Mr. James Mao Yongchang, Mr. Pan Aitao, Miss Isabella C. Zhang (Chang), Mr. Leo Greenwood, Mrs. Amy Greenwood, Mr. and Mrs. Hugo Foertsch, Miss Agustina Sicilia Herkata, Mr. and Mrs. Gilbert Chavez, Mr. and Mrs. Jaime Abrera, Mrs. Madonna M. Edgar, Fr. Joseph Brennan, Fr. Sean Cronin and Mrs. Ellen Littlejohn.

理，嘉惠世人，或雅或拙，其又何傷?!

　　本稿的標題是取自毛澤東於 1934 年至 1935 年間以「**山**」為題所填的三首短詞《**十六字令**》中的兩句詩。說實在話，頗具諷刺意味的是：我的全部詩詞，竟然濫觴於被當作樣板的他那三十七首詩詞！在長年累月的監禁期中，我往往陷入沉思：毛澤東既然可以憑藉鏗鏘詩句去宣揚謬論，蠱惑人心，毒化思想，危害國家，奴役百姓，為什麼我不應該利用詩詞來捍衛信仰，表明忠貞，頌揚主愛，傳佈救恩呢？

　　有鑒於此，這標題或許具有一定的現實意義。它既可被看作是中國哲學家韓非（公元前 280-233）所說的「**以子之矛，攻子之盾**」；也可以被理解為中國另一位哲學家朱熹（1130-1200）所謂的「**即以其人之道，還治其人之身**」。這會使毛和其追隨者狼狽周章嗎？他們會感到啼笑皆非嗎？

　　仰仗上主至高無敵的神力，我歷時三十三載抗擊了紅色天空裡的狂風暴雨。這些詩詞顯示著我對祂的赤膽忠心，記錄著自己曩昔鬥爭的情景，反映著自己當前喜悅的心境。惟願它們有如山嶽，刺破青天，逕達天宮，博得我們**慈父**的歡心，從而惠及教會，益於世界！「**山，刺破青天**」：形像鮮明動人，美妙壯麗。毛賜佳句，無任感激！

　　羅杰·彌額爾·馬洪尼樞機主教鈞座和極可尊敬的方濟各·本篤大院長答應了我的請求，給本書分別寫了「**序**」。他們的言辭將常常響在我的耳邊，對我自己和我的眾位讀者定會是諄切訓諭和激勵。黃美之女士惠為揮毫潑墨，使中文書名躍然於封面和扉頁，她並且還為之蓋上了自己的私章。吉姆·莫勒先生、肯·莫勒先生和辛西婭·克拉克女士，曾為本書的編排和

I know well that I have only a smattering of knowledge of classical Chinese poetry. The Chinese original is not refined, nor is the English translation. Though the poems have repeatedly been examined and corrected by the learned, they do not totally express my thoughts and feelings. If only their spirit remains to strengthen and inspire the reader facing all kinds of challenges and difficulties in his way toward eternal life! If this collection can praise divine love, disseminate the truth and benefit others, what harm is there in its form, polished or clumsy?!

The title of this manuscript is taken from two verses of the three short poems composed by Mao Zedong during the years 1934 to 1935, after the style of *Song of Sixteen Characters* on the subject of the Mountain. To tell the truth, all my poems were ironically born of those thirty-seven of his poems adopted as my example. Time after time, during my many years behind bolt and bar, I used to be lost in thought. Since Mao Zedong could resort to sonorous verses to propagate his fallacies, confuse man's minds, poison their thoughts, jeopardize the country and enslave people, why should I not use poems to defend the Faith, show my loyalty, sing praises of the Lord's love and spread the grace of salvation?

In view of this, the title may have practical significance. It might also be interpreted as "setting your own spear against your own shield," in the words of Chinese philosopher Han Fei (280-233 B.C.), or as "dealing with a man in the manner in which he has dealt with others," in the words of another Chinese philosopher Zhu Xi (1130-1200). Will this make Mao and his followers scared out of their wits? Will they find themselves between laughter and tears, unable to laugh or cry?

Relying on the supreme power of the Lord, I resisted the violent wind and rain of the Red sky for thirty-three years. These poems show

出版作出過極大的努力。

　　如果沒有天主的扶掖，沒有聖母的支援，沒有眾多朋友的協助，這冊詩集是無法完成，無法出版的。爲此，理所當然，非做不可的是：對天主、對聖母感恩戴德，向所有上面已經提到和並未提到的、曾給本書的出版以各種各樣幫助的尊長和友好申謝致敬。我祈求好天主降福他們，並降福一切親愛的讀者！

my fidelity to Him, record the scenes of my past struggles and reflect my present joyful frame of mind. May they, like mountains, pierce the blue sky, soar straight up to the heavenly palace and win our loving Father's delight and favor for the profit of the Church and the world! *"The Mountain Pierces The Blue Sky,"* a striking and beautiful image. I am deeply grateful to Mao for it!

His Eminence Cardinal Roger Michael Mahony and the Right Reverend Abbot Francis Benedict responded to my request and wrote their Forewords to this book. Their words will always ring in my ears, and surely be earnest instruction and inspiration both to me and to my readers. Mrs. Mimi H. Fleischman wielded her writing brush and plash-ink and made the Chinese title of the book appear vividly on the front cover and the title page which she also sealed with her own proper seal. Mr. Jim Moeller, Mr. Ken Moeller and Ms. Cynthia Clark made a great effort to do the layout and publication of this book.

If there had been no support from God, no assistance from Our Lady and no help from many friends, this collection of poetry could not nave been completed and published. Therefore, it is natural and necessary to bear a debt of profound gratitude to God and to Our Lady, and to extend my deep appreciation and pay homage to all of the dignitaries and my friends, above-mentioned or unmentioned, who were contributors to the publication of the book in ways of all kinds. I pray the good God bless them and also all my dear readers!

1. 緊銬從天降！

念奴嬌
中國四川省南充縣省一監
1960 年 8 月 10 日
聖老楞佐執事殉道節

炙陽斜照，
吏傳喚、
赤膊挺胸前往。
審訊躬親來股長，
無懼昂然迎上。
問及**舒君**，
令書材料，
堅決忠心抗。
救人榮**主**，
軍團焉得誣謗？

「**曾否犯罪**？」三詢，
「**罪無**！」三對，
氣壯言豪爽。
立被緊將前臂銬，

1.   Tight Handcuffs Come From Heaven!

To the Tune of Nian Nu Jiao
(Charming Girl Nian Nu)
No. 1 Provincial Prison
Nanchong County, Sichuan Province, China
August 10, 1960
Feast of St. Lawrence, Deacon and Martyr

As the scorching sun sets,
The official sends for me.
Stripped to the waist,
With my chest thrown out,
I go to meet him.
The section chief himself
Is going to interrogate me.
I step forward, upright and unafraid.
He inquires about Sister Lucia Shu
And orders me to write
The required material concerning her;
I resolutely refuse to do so.
For its work
In saving mankind, glorifying God,
Why should the Legion of Mary be slandered?

Three times he asks:
"Have you committed a crime?"
With a heroic spirit and straightforward words,
I answer three times: "No crime!"
My forearm is immediately, tightly cuffed.

考驗從天而降！
聖母慈親，
老楞英烈，
助戰支援望！
魔威徒逞，
低頭**神將**休想！

註：舒德君修女於五十年代曾在成都為教會
　　頑強地戰鬥過。軍團指聖母軍。

A trial comes from heaven!
Our Lady, merciful Mother,
Saint Lawrence, heroic martyr,
Please come and help me in the struggle!
In vain, Devil,
You show your power!
Do not imagine
The Divine General will bow his head!

Note: In the 1950s Sr. Lucia Shu Dejun struggled tenaciously
in Chengdu for the Church.

2. 食如獸

生查子
南充監獄
1960 年 8 月 11 日

驕陽照飯場，
反銬連雙手。
俯首口來銜，
進食如禽獸！

赤身十架懸，
主為吾儕救。
報愛示忠誠，
變獸何羞有？

2.   Taking Food As An Animal

To the Tune of Sheng Zha Zi
(Fresh Berries)
Nanchong Prison
August 11, 1960

The burning sun shines
On the dining ground,
Cuffs bind my two hands
Behind my back.
I bow my head
To take food with my mouth,
As do birds and beasts!

Hanging naked on the Cross,
The Lord saved us.
To repay His love,
To show my allegiance,
What is the shame
Of becoming an animal?

3. 復活節頌

五言詩
南充監獄
1965 年 4 月 18 日

主死息天怒，
萬物何悲傷？
天使已降現，
守卒盡逃亡。

復活鐵事實，
新紀此濫觴！
三日出地腹，
重建敬父堂。

瑪利見主樂，
佳音急傳揚；
聞訊門徒驚，
困惑攪愁腸。

若望先馳抵，

3.   **In Praise Of Easter**

In the Poetic Style of Wuyan Shi
Nanchong Prison
April 18, 1965

The death of the Lord
Has calmed the wrath of Heaven.
Why have you continued to grieve,
All you creatures?
The angels have descended and appeared,
The guards have all taken flight.

The Resurrection — an undeniable reality,
Begins a new era!
He came out of the belly of the earth
On the third day
To rebuild the Temple to worship His Father.

Overjoyed to see the Lord,
Mary hurried to proclaim the Good News;
Hearing her message,
The disciples were all astonished,
Feeling puzzled in their saddened hearts.

Running ahead, approaching first,

俯身塋探望；
伯鐸隨後至，
入墓去端詳。

厄村往蒙陪，
聆教二徒昂；
進餐分餅時，
認出主容光。

門徒晚會中，
憂疑滿胸膛；
目擊主顯容，
欣喜竟若狂。

多默未目睹，
暫疑又何妨？
見傷立作證，
厥證永流芳！

向徒頻顯容，
情景永難忘；
聖山駕雲彩，

John bent down to peer into the tomb;
Peter arrived soon after,
Entered the tomb and looked all around.

On the way to the village of Emmaus,
Accompanied by the Master,
Two disciples were excited
Listening to His teaching.
At the breaking of the bread,
They recognized
The glorious Face of their Lord.

During the evening gathering,
The disciples' hearts were burdened
With sorrow, with doubt;
Seeing the Lord appearing before them
With their own eyes,
They were overcome with joy.

Thomas not seeing with his own eyes,
What did it matter
That he doubted for a time?
He bore witness when he saw the wounds,
Leaving a sweet scent for eternity!

So often did He manifest Himself
To His disciples.
Those scenes shall never be forgotten.
Riding the clouds on the holy mountain,

勝利返天堂。

就座於父右，
萬聖頌慈祥；
十日遣聖神，
真理傳四方。

復活力量大，
化頑育賢良；
勇飲十架杯，
登天謁君王！

Victoriously He returned to Paradise.

His seat is at the right hand of the Father;
His mercy is praised by all the saints.
He sent the Holy Spirit on the tenth day,
Spreading the fullness of truth
To the four corners of the earth.

The power of the Resurrection is unlimited:
Converting the stubborn,
Strengthening the wise,
Fostering the virtuous.
Drinking bravely the chalice of the Cross,
We shall ascend to Heaven and see the King!

4. 聖若瑟
聖母淨配讚

鷓鴣天
南充監獄
1966 年 3 月 19 日

守誠遵規自幼年，
虔誠典範妙姻緣。
關懷**聖母耶穌**育，
至死全心使命肩！

聞**主命**，
夜闌珊，
立時照辦不遲延。
梓人致聖卑而貴，
祈助吾儕**天國**攀！

4.   Praise To St. Joseph, Husband Of The Blessed Virgin Mary

To the Tune of Zhegu Tian
(Partridges in the Sky)
Nanchong Prison
March 19, 1966

From childhood
You had observed
The commandments and precepts.
Your dedication was exemplary,
Your marriage beyond compare.
To care for the Blessed Mother,
To foster Jesus,
You fulfilled these missions
Until your dying day!

Hearing the orders of the Lord
In the stillness of the night,
You obeyed immediately without delay.
From carpenter to saint,
From lowliness to nobility,
You, we beseech:
Help us ascend to the Kingdom of Heaven!

5. 頌聖本篤

鷓鴣天
南充監獄
1966 年 3 月 21 日

遁跡深山尋主虔，
苦修勤禱閱三年。
早成大器光芒放，
若谷虛懷奇蹟繁。

修院建，
會規編，
西方會祖益塵寰。
門徒濟濟躋於聖，
教導楷模代代傳！

5.   Ode To St. Benedict

To the Tune of Zhegu Tian
(Partridges in the Sky)
Nanchong Prison
March 21, 1966

You withdrew to the remote mountains,
Seeking the Lord with devotion.
You disciplined yourself severely
And prayed unceasingly
For three years.
A man of large mind,
You matured early,
Illuminating all around you.
You had a heart as open as a valley,
Your humility won you frequent miracles.

Founding monasteries,
Writing the Monastic Rule,
As the Patriarch of Western monasticism,
You have brought great benefits to the world.
Many of your disciples
Are among the saints.
Your teachings and example
Will be handed down
From generation to generation!

6. 復活節：
救主離棄墳

七律
南充監獄
1967 年 3 月 26 日
復活節

三日復甦真救主，
化吾悲痛作歡欣。
表明慈愛生由婦，
顯示神通出自墳。
征服死亡驚守卒，
贏來生命是仁君。
光輝復活乾坤照，
天使歡呼顫鬼群！

6.   For Easter:
Our Savior
Abandons His Tomb

In the Poetic Style of Qilu
Nanchong Prison
March 26, 1967
Easter Sunday

He who rises again on the third day —
Truly our Savior!
He changes our mourning into great joy.
In mercy and love
He is born of woman;
In power and might
He rises from the tomb.

Conquering death,
He astounds the guards;
Winning life,
He becomes our loving King.
His glorious Resurrection
Shines through sky and earth:
Angels acclaim Him;
Demons tremble!

7. 復活節吟

七律
南充監獄
1967 年 3 月 26 日
復活節

聞報佳音拭淚珠，
縱情歌唱又歡呼。
歡呼人子終全勝，
歌唱救星今復甦！
人子捨身除世罪，
救星克敵贖群奴。
五傷燭火燃堂內，
照亮前程為信徒。

7.   A Song Of Easter

In the Poetic Style of Qilu
Nanchong Prison
March 26, 1967
Easter Sunday

Hearing the Good News,
We wipe away our tears;
We are singing, applauding
To our hearts' content.
We are acclaiming—
The Son of Man has won finally, completely;
We are singing—
The Savior lives again!

The Son of Man gave up His life
To blot out the sins of the world.
The Savior defeated His enemies
To redeem all His servants.
The candles of His Five Wounds
Are burning in the churches,
Illuminating the way,
The future
For His believers.

8. 聖伯多祿宗徒讚

浪淘沙
南充監獄
1967 年 6 月 29 日

從主獻身堅，
爾棄漁船；
熱情熾愛映於言。
慧眼認清天主子，
磐石名傳。

休愧叛三番！
悔淚餘年，
身懸十架顯忠肝。
有鑰有權天國啟，
助進望焉！

註：本詞中文連同巴黎外方傳教會方濟各・巴利剛神
　　父的法譯文，曾轉載於他們的《巴黎外方傳教會》
　　期刊的 2011 年 7-8 月 463 號的 67 頁。

8.   Praise To St. Peter, Apostle

To the Tune of Lang Tao Sha
(Wave-Washed Sands)
Nanchong Prison
June 29, 1967

To follow the Lord resolutely,
To dedicate your life to Him,
You left your fishing boat.
Your enthusiasm and love for Him
Were mirrored in your words.
Your eyes full of Heavenly wisdom
Recognized the Son of God.
Your name, the Rock, began to spread.

Let not your three betrayals of the Lord
Be imputed to you as shame!
Tears of repentance
Accompanied your remaining years;
You hung on a cross,
To witness your profound loyalty.
You have the keys, the power
To open the Kingdom of Heaven,
We hope you
Help us to enter it!

Note: The Chinese text of this poem with its French
translation by Pere Francois Barriquand, MEP,
was reprinted on page 67 in their periodical,
Missions Etrangeres de Paris, No 463
juillet-aout 2011.

9. 禱獻升天母

浪淘沙
南充監獄
1967 年 8 月 15 日
聖母蒙召升天節

主母別塵寰，
德備功全，
身靈齊上九重天。
就座君王基督右，
助御坤乾。

教會信條頌，
十七年前，
紅旗如火正燎原。
早逐赤精兒女救，
再懇慈萱！

9.   Prayer To Our Lady Of The Assumption

To the Tune of Lang Tao Sha
(Wave-Washed Sands)
Nanchong Prison
August 15, 1967
Assumption of the Blessed Virgin Mary

Mother of Our Lord,
You bade farewell to this world,
Reaching the perfection of virtue and merit.
You ascended the highest heaven
Both in body and soul.
You are seated
At the right hand of Christ the King,
Helping to rule the universe.

The Church proclaimed this dogma
Seventeen years ago,
When the Red flag was spreading in the world,
Like a fire blazing in the prairie.
Save your sons and daughters,
Come quickly and drive away the Red monster —
This is once more my prayer to you,
O loving Mother!

10. 始胎無原罪聖母讚

念奴嬌
南充監獄
1967 年 12 月 8 日
聖母始胎無原罪節

欽差天使，
報佳音、
賀以神恩充滿。
「無玷始胎」明曉示，
露德當年容顯。
列入信條，
歡呼教會，
鬼怪齊驚顫！
頌歌嘹喨，
普天寰宇傳遍。

主母有寵無愆，
位尊德備，
玉體升天燦。
慶幸蛇頭遭踏碎，

10.   **Praise To Our Lady Of The Immaculate Conception**

To the Tune of Nian Nu Jiao
(Charming Girl Nian Nu)
Nanchong Prison
December 8, 1967
Solemnity of the Immaculate Conception
of the Blessed Virgin Mary

The Angel, envoy of the Heavens,
Is visiting you, Mary,
To bring Good News,
To give you felicitations
On your fullness of divine graces.
"I am the Immaculate Conception!" —
This, your clear declaration in the days
Of your manifestations at Lourdes.
This faith is counted a dogma,
Everywhere acclaimed in the Church:
It frightens, shakes all evil forces!
The songs of praise are loud and full,
Ringing out far and wide,
Everywhere, everywhere in the world.

As the Mother of God,
You had no sin, only grace;
Your place is unique, your virtue complete.
Lifted into the Heavens,
Your glorified body shines there.
Rejoicing at the trampling of the Snake's head,

人類沾恩非淺。
萬代千秋，
五洲四海，
兒女同聲讚！
心靈祈淨，
俾能**基督**朝見！

11. 奇哉聖誕節：天主成為人

七律
南充監獄
1967 年 12 月 25 日
聖誕節

天主造人還降生，
工程贖世妙難名。
貞娘孕娩驚寰宇，
賢哲來朝震**聖城**。
父意遵行傾**寶血**，
福音傳佈救生靈。
今朝**聖誕**歌天地，
惟願吾儕享太平！

Mankind has benefited deeply, deeply indeed!
Through every generation and all ages,
In all corners of land and sea,
Your children are praising you
Together in one voice!
We implore you:
Purify our hearts,
Then grant us audience with Christ!

11.   How Wonderful Christmas Is –
God Became A Man

In the Poetic Style of Qilu
Nanchong Prison
December 25, 1967
Christmas

God, the Creator of mankind, was made flesh;
The works of Your Redemption—
Too wonderful to describe!
The Virgin Mother conceived You, bore You,
Shaking all the world;
The wise men came to pay You homage,
Quaking the Holy City.
You fulfilled Your Father's will,
Shedding Your precious Blood;
You spread the Gospel
To save mankind.
Today while heaven and earth are singing
The praises of Your Holy Birth,
May we enjoy Your peace!

12. 聖誕節賀天主母

七律
南充監獄
1967 年 12 月 25 日
聖誕節

天主造人誠壯麗，

人生天主更神奇！

榮蒙閨秀娘親號，

仍保萱堂處女姿。

貞母臨盆無苦惱，

聖嬰入目有歡怡。

乾坤皇后烝民救，

領往天鄉頌子慈！

12.   Congratulations To The Mother Of God At Christmas

In the Poetic Style of Qilu
Nanchong Prison
December 25, 1967
Christmas

Truly magnificent:
God creates mankind.
But still more magnificent:
Mankind gives birth to God!

On you, Mary, a virgin,
Is gloriously bestowed the title "Mother";
Yet you, the Mother, keep your virginity still —
The virginity of a maiden.

Though a virgin mother in labor,
You experience no distress:
You know great joy
Gazing on your Holy Baby.

Queen of heaven and earth,
Save us, your people,
By leading us to the Heavenly homeland
To praise the mercy of your Son!

13. 爲盲獄友引路

生查子
南充監獄
1968 年 12 月 8 日

五囚久失明，
持棍探途走。
引路亦需人，
遇便伸援手。

一心為主榮，
不問盲知否。
基督似冬陽，
普賜溫黔首！

13.   Leading
The Blind Fellow Prisoners

To the Tune of Sheng Zha Zi
(Fresh Berries)
Nanchong Prison
December 8, 1968

Losing their sight long ago,
Five prisoners hold their sticks
To feel their way.
They also need people to lead them.
Whenever opportunity offers,
I stretch out to them a helping hand.

I aim to give glory to the Lord,
Irrespective of
Whether the blind know or not.
As the winter sun,
Christ spreads warmth
Universally to all people!

14. 獄中喜迎聖誕節

滿庭芳
南充監獄
1970 年 12 月 24 日

顯示慈祥，
稟承父命，
主來拯救人靈。
降胎神妙，
白冷馬槽生。
養父貞娘欣喜；
歌高唱、
天使歡騰。
來朝拜，
深更半夜，
羣牧喜盈盈。

奇瓊，
千古震：
人形主取，
神性人承；

14.   Joyously Welcoming Christmas In Prison

To the Tune of Man Ting Fang
(Fully Fragrant Court)
Nanchong Prison
December 24, 1970

To show Your mercy,
In obedience to Your Father's will,
You, our Lord, have come
To rescue our souls.
Conceived miraculously,
You are born in a manger in Bethlehem.
Your foster father and Virgin Mother
Are rejoicing;
Singing Your praises loudly in the Heavens,
Your angels are jubilant.
To pay homage to You,
In the depth of night
The shepherds are coming
Fuff of joy.

A marvelous and magnificent spectacle
Earthquaking through the ages:
God takes a human form
And mankind is granted a divine nature;

聖子塵寰蒞，
天國人登。
新紀公元肇始：
眾得救、
前景光明！
愚頑化，
信徒堅定：
囚禱繾中嬰！

The Son comes down to the earth
And man ascends into Heaven.
The Christian era, a new age, begins:
The prospects for salvation
Are bright for all!
For the enlightenment of the ignorant,
For the conversion of the stubborn,
For the perseverance of the faithful,
I, a prisoner, appeal to You,
Infant, wrapped in swaddling clothes!

15. 生日述懷

生查子
南充監獄單獨囚禁中
1971 年 8 月 26 日

行年卅五焉，
依舊囚囹圄。
半載錮孤牢，
向主衷情訴：

「幾時鐐銬離？
何日慈顏晤？
惟望旨承行，
不計身心苦！」

15.   Opening My Heart
On My Birthday

To the Tune of Sheng Zha Zi
(Fresh Berries)
Solitary Confinement at Nanchong Prison
August 26, 1971

At the age of forty-five
I am still in jail.
For half a year confined in a solitary cell,
I pour out my feelings to the Lord:

"When will the fetters and handcuffs leave me?
When, O when will I see Your loving face?
If only Your Will is done,
I shall not be concerned
With my sufferings in body and mind!"

16. 再見，
親愛的小監！

浪淘沙
南充監獄
1971 年 10 月 7 日

相處意綿綿，
二百餘天，
詩詞三百表心肝。
聖母來援今與別，
淚下潸然。

勞役待身邊，
不再安閒，
如何繼續賦詩篇？
地久天長恆愛主，
重聚非難！

16.   Farewell,
My Dear Solitary Cell!

To the Tune of Lang Tao Sha
(Wave-Washed Sands)
Nanchong Prison
October 7, 1971

With an unbroken affection
For over two hundred days
We have lived together;
In three hundred poems
I have opened my heart.
Thanks to the help of Our Lady,
I am to leave you now,
Tears trickling down my cheeks.

Forced labor is awaiting me,
I will no longer have leisure.
How shall I continue to compose my poetry?
My love for the Lord will endure
As long as the universe.
Never will our reunion be difficult!

17. 銬乎，
為何爾突別？

玉蝴蝶
南充監獄
1971 年 10 月 7 日

多回離合悲歡，
心緒似江翻！
禱主賦詩篇，
衷情爾審焉！

同居非盡苦，
功建賴支援。
恩惠記心間，
冀望君早還！

17.   Handcuffs,
Why Should You Depart
Unexpectedly?

To the Tune of Yu Hudie
(The Jade Butterfly)
Nanchong Prison
October 7, 1971

Time and again—
Partings and reunions, griefs and joys.
My mood seethes,
Like a boiling river!
Praying to the Lord,
Composing poems—
My inner feelings are known to you!

My life with you
Has never been only pain;
With your support
I have achieved much.
I keep your kindness in mind;
Your early return is expected!

18. 臨別贈鑱言！

減字木蘭花
南充監獄
1971 年 10 月 7 日

叮噹步步，
勵我勇行天國路。
異夢同床，
長伴寒宵雪上霜！

僕猶耿耿，
君卻怏怏而辱命。
如不甘休，
靜待歸來報爾仇！

18.   Parting Words To My Fetters!

To the Tune of Jian Zi Mulan Hua
(The Magnolia)
Nanchong Prison
October 7, 1971

Your clatter followed my every step,
Encouraging me to walk bravely
The way to the Heavenly Kingdom.
We shared the same bed,
But dreamed different dreams.
You kept me company
On so many cold nights,
Adding frost to snow!

I remain loyal,
But you are disheartened and sigh,
Failing to accomplish your mission.
If you are unwilling to give up,
I peacefully await your return
To avenge yourself on me!

19. 獄友李希孔，
枉然爾來譴！

玉蝴蝶
南充監獄
1971 年 10 月 10 日

君嘗希孔希賢，
大志繫牢遷。
晚會譴徒然，
毛書拒讀堅。

無期刑未減，
瞻馬首堪憐！
風燭古稀年，
何嚴人責焉？

19.   In Vain You, Fellow Prisoner Li Xikong, Condemn Me!

To the Tune of Yu Hudie
(The Jade Butterfly)
Nanchong Prison
October 10, 1971

Once you, Mr. Li, hoped to be
A man like Confucius,
A man of virtue.
Put in jail,
You began to change your ideals.
But for nothing—
Your condemnations of me at evening meetings,
I still firmly refused
To read Mao's book.

Your life sentence was not reduced;
In vain—
You have followed the Party lead!
Aged seventy,
A candle fluttering in the wind,
Why should you censure others so severely?

20. 告別南充監獄

水調歌頭
前往蓬安勞改營途中
1971 年 10 月 11 日

夏日炎炎到，
秋水碧而離。
前途展望興奮，
往事緬懷怡。
銅銬摧殘八月，
鐵鐐折磨五載，
兩度小牢羈。
帶鐐誓詞吐，
臂爛拒頭低！

駁讕言，
彰赤膽，
誦雄詩。
加刑、批鬥，
惟教典範舉監馳。
生命讚歌暗唱，
舊體詩詞勤賦，
頌謝**主**仁慈。
十一冬相處，
牢友別依依！

20.   Farewell To Nanchong Prison

To the Tune of Shui Diao Ge Tou
(The Song of the Water Music)
On the way to Peng'an Labor-Reform Camp
October 11, 1971

I came to you, my prison,
Under a scorching sun;
Now I am leaving in autumn,
When the waters appear blue.
Excitedly I look forward to the prospect
While joyfully recalling past events.
I was tortured by bronze cuffs
For a total of eight months,
Tormented by iron fetters
For a total of five years;
Twice I was confined in a solitary cell.
While being shackled,
I swore an oath;
As my right forearm rotted from cuffing,
I vowed not to bow my head!

To refute slanders,
To show my loyalty,
I recited my poem in my group meeting!
Your additions to my sentence,
Your public criticism could do nothing,
But spread my example within your walls.
I sang my *Song of Life* in secret,
I composed my classical poetry diligently
To praise and thank the Lord for His mercy.
Having lived for eleven winters
Within your compound,
My prison and my friend,
I am sorry to say goodbye!

21. 再調另一勞改營

漁家傲
蓬安勞改營
1971 年 10 月 11 日

數十官兵囚百幾，
東方欲曉征程啟，
十部專車魚貫駛。
顛簸屬，
暈車嘔吐嘗多次。

午抵蓬安勞改地，
夜觀電影《紅燈記》；
先烈楷模追矢志！
蒙激勵，
願將肝腦塗於地！

21. My Second Transfer To A Labor-Reform Camp

To the Tune of Yu Jia Ao
(Fisherman's Pride)
Peng'an Labor-Reform Camp
October 11, 1971

Scores of officials and men
As well as more than one hundred prisoners,
Worried and fearful,
Started on a journey,
While dawn is breaking in the east.
Ten special trucks traveled
One after the other like fishes.
Jolted badly,
I was carsick, vomiting repeatedly.

At midday
We arrived at the labor-reform place in Peng'an.
Watching at night
The movie, *The Red Lantern*,
I vow to follow
The example of the Christian martyrs!
Inspired by them,
I am ready to die the cruelest death!

22. 凝望獨禁囚室

定風波
蓬安勞改營
1971 年 10 月 12 日

昨夜新來難入眠，
今晨仔細四圍看。
牆角崗樓何必咒，
猶有，
孤牢十七外垣邊！

宛若長蛇諸斗室，
威力，
秋風落葉慴南冠！
料得來朝同爾戰；
宏願，
淫威不滅不師班！

22.   Gazing At Solitary Cells

To the Tune of Ding Feng Bo
(Calming Storm)
Peng'an Labor-Reform Camp
October 12, 1971

Last night — sleepless
For me, a new transfer;
This morning
I look around carefully.
No need to curse
The watchtower at the corner of the two walls.
There is something more:
Seventeen solitary cells
Close to the outside wall!

Strung along the wall as a long snake,
The cells are so menacing
As to fill prisoners with fear,
Like an autumn breeze
Sweeps away fallen leaves!
I will one day do battle with you.
My great ambition:
Never to withdraw
Until your arrogance is crushed!

23. 憤聞聯合國大會
接納中共政權

浪淘沙
蓬安勞改營
1971 年 10 月 29 日

聯大辯論完，
決議頒焉：
北京接納逐台灣！
聽播廣場寒夜裡，
憤滿心間。

二十有三年，
赤縣黎元，
含辛茹苦待聲援。
舉世誤從毛暴政，
誠可悲嘆！

23.   Indignation On Learning That The United Nations General Assembly Has Admitted The Chinese Communist Regime

To the Tune of Lang Tao Sha
(Wave-Washed Sands)
Peng'an Labor-Reform Camp
October 29, 1971

Having concluded the debate,
The U.N. General Assembly decided:
To admit Beijing and expel Taiwan!
Listening to the radio in the square in the cold night,
I was full of indignation.

During twenty-three years
The Chinese people
Have endured all kinds of hardships,
Waiting for support.
The world has been misled by Mao's tyranny—
Truly a lamentable situation!

24. 毛《語錄》，
永別乎？

浪淘沙
蓬安勞改營
1971 年 11 月 21 日

命令隊中頒，
早膳剛完：
毛書《語錄》盡交還。
緣故紛紛私下議，
眾犯茫然！

誦讀未今天，
《語錄》何言？
免於斥責我心歡。
五載深嚐騷擾苦，
永訣望焉！

24.   Part Forever, Mao's *Quotations*?

To the Tune of Lang Tao Sha
(Wave-Washed Sands)
Peng'an Labor-Reform Camp
November 21, 1971

Just after breakfast
The company issued an order:
All Mao's books, the *Quotations,*
Should be handed back.
In private among the prisoners,
The reason, speculated!
Utter ignorance reigns!

Quotations,
You have not been read today.
What do you have to say?
Having been spared another denunciation,
I feel comforted.
For five years
I have suffered deeply
From your harassment.
We now part forever!

25. 毛《語錄》，
為何爾歸來？

西江月
蓬安勞改營
1971 年 11 月 26 日

辭別匆忙詭秘，

今歸沈默頹唐。

《前言》儘已入墳場，

爾卻掩藏真相！

林或奪權喪命，

毛惟戀棧斜陽！

汝和主子即偕亡，

何必如牛氣壯？

註：《毛主席語錄》的《再版前言》原為林彪所寫，五天
　　前被營部幹事撕去。後來獲悉的原因是：林彪剌
　　毛事敗，乘飛機外逃，該機於 1971 年 9 月 13 日
　　墜毀於蒙古。

25.   Why Do You Come Back, Mao's *Quotations*?

To the Tune of Xi Jiang Yue
(Moon over the West River)
Peng'an Labor-Reform Camp
November 26, 1971

When we parted
You were hasty and secretive;
Now, on your return
You are silent and dejected.
The *Preface* has gone to a graveyard.
But you conceal
The actual state of affairs!

In attempting to seize power,
Lin must have met his death.
Though determined to hold on to his supreme office,
Mao is but a setting sun!
You, *Quotations*, and your master
Will surely die together!
Why should you act as a spirited bull?

Note: The *Preface* to the Second Edition of the *Quotations of Chairman Mao* was
originally written by Lin Biao. It was torn out by camp officials five days before.
We learned later the reason was that having failed to assassinate Mao, Lin fled the
country by plane, which crashed in Mongolia on September 13, 1971.

26. 不理睬高指導員

定風波
蓬安勞改營
1971 年 11 月 29 日

晚會來巡指導員
適逢群犯逼發言。
默不作聲遭眾吼，
高某，
當場干預問由緣。

誦讀毛書聞我拒，
伊怒，
色聲俱屬斥忠肝。
接受安能毛謬論？
忠藎，
喧囂何懼震雲天！

26.   Defying Political Instructor Gao

To the Tune of Ding Feng Bo
(Calming Storm)
Peng'an Labor-Reform Camp
November 29, 1971

During the evening meeting
The Instructor came to inspect our group;
The inmates had been trying to force me to speak.
They protested loudly
At my silence.
As for Instructor Gao,
He intervened then and there,
Asking what was the resson.

Learning of my refusal to read Mao's book,
He became angry.
Sternly and fiercely
He lectured me
For my faithfulness to the Lord.
How can I accept Mao's fallacies?
For a loyal soul,
What is there to fear,
Even if the uproar shakes the heavens!

27. 獄友蘇子梅，
緣何爾伐忠?

水調歌頭
蓬安勞改營
1971 年 12 月 11 日

九夏渝牢繫，
果獄十冬關。
君遷此地兼月，
刑滿在今年。
聖母軍團骨幹，
共黨監牢囚犯，
無恥有榮焉；
受壓身心苦，
俯首乞平安！

聞高見，
知冤屈，
為心酸！
今如桀犬，
猖猖會上吠忠肝。

27.   Why Should You, Fellow Prisoner Su Zimei, Lash Out At A Loyal?

To the Tune of Shui Diao Ge Tou
(The Song of the Water Music)
Peng'an Labor-Reform Camp
December 11, 1971

You were put in prison
At Chongqing for nine summers,
At Nanchong for ten winters.
You were transferred here two months ago.
Your term of imprisonment
Will expire this year.
From being a backbone of the Legion of Mary
To a prisoner in a Communist jail,
In this there is no disgrace
But honor!
Under great pressure,
You felt great pain in body and mind,
And bowed your head
For ease and comfort!

Listening to your opinions,
Realizing the injustice you have suffered,
I grieve for you!
Now
Like the tyrant Jie's dog,
You barked at a fellow faithful soul
During study meetings.
You cast away your integrity

君棄節如敝屣，
僕愛忠踰生命，
相去志天淵！
萁豆同根出，
何急釜中煎？

註：1951 年 12 月 24 日，蘇子梅因被指控為聖
　　母軍的一名領導人而於四川省重慶被捕。
　　我們在同一小組相處了兩週。

Like a pair of worn-out shoes,
While I prefer allegiance
To a consecrated life.
My principles and goals
Are as far apart from yours
As the high heaven from the deep sea!
Beanstalk and bean,
Come both from the same root.
Why should you, the burning beanstalk,
Cook me, the bean, so violently in the cauldron?

Note: On December 24, 1951, accused as a leader of the Legion of Mary, Su Zimei
was arrested in Chongqing, Sichuan Province. We have been in the same group for
two weeks.

28. 總評動員會

菩薩蠻
蓬安勞改營
1974 年 2 月 9 日

去年改造全盤審，
動員大會氛圍凜。
眉睫現難關，
決心衝上前。

任憑批揍銬，
堅拒書材料。
依靠主神通，
成功信念濃。

28.   A Mobilization Meeting For The General Appraisal

To the Tune of Pusa Man
(Strange Goddess)
Peng'an Labor-Reform Camp
February 9, 1974

For the general appraisal
Of last year's reform
A mobilization meeting is held
In an apprehensive atmosphere.
A barrier lies ahead
Close to the eyelrow,
I am determined to break through it.

No matter
How I am criticized, beaten, handcuffed,
I will flatly refuse
To write the required material.
With the invincible power of the Lord,
I am confident of success.

29. 庫房畔
聞王國盛神父自白

浪淘沙
蓬安勞改營
1974 年 2 月 27 日

「拜倒自童年，

法帝尊前。

洋書讀畢福音傳。

犯罪根源深挖掘，

評審過關！」

似箭刺心肝，

入耳王言！

兇鷹信種竟吞焉！

誓獵猛禽除世害，

緊把槍端！

註：王神父係四川省渠縣人。該縣原屬重慶
　　教區，重慶教區當時是在巴黎外方傳教
　　會法籍傳教士的管理下。

29.   Hearing Of Fr. Wang Guosheng's Remarks Near The Storehouse

To the Tune of Lang Tao Sha
(Wave-Washed Sands)
Peng'an Labor-Reform Camp
February 27, 1974

"Since boyhood I grovelled
At the feet of the French imperialists.
After my foreign studies,
I preached the Gospel.
Analyzing deeply
The ideological roots of my guilt,
I scraped through the appraisal!"

Fr. Wang's remarks reached my ears
As a sword piercing my heart!
The ferocious Hawk has actually swallowed
The seeds of Faith!
To rid the world of a scourge,
I pledge to hunt this savage bird.
A shotgun ready fast in my hands!

Note: Fr. Wang is from Qu Xian, Sichuan Province. Originally, the county belonged to the Chongqing Diocese, which was entrusted to the care of French missionaries from the Paris Foreign Mission Society.

30. 王國盛神父刑滿

漁家傲
蓬安勞改營
1974 年 4 月 24 日

順應「革新」期避難，
公仍被捕徒刑判，
鬥銬還遭塵滿面。
留狴犴，
投奔無處今刑滿。

冷浴每晨成習慣，
年逾花甲身猶健，
夢想或非長壽願。
牢記盼：
天年唯主知長短！

30. Fr. Wang Guosheng's Sentence Expires

To the Tune of Yu Jia Ao
(Fisherman's Pride)
Peng'an Labor-Reform Camp
April 24, 1974

To escape calamity
You conformed to the Religious Reform,
Yet you were arrested and sentenced.
You suffered "struggle" and handcuffing,
As if your face had been covered with dust.
You are to stay in prison
Even now at the expiration of your sentence,
Having no place to go for shelter.

Taking a cold bath every morning —
Your usual practice;
Over sixty years old
You are still in good health.
Your hope of longevity
May not be a fond dream.
I hope you always bear in mind:
Only the Lord knows
The length of our allotted span!

31. 1973 年度總評
終結大會

漁家傲
蓬安勞改營
1974 年 4 月 27 日

新搭講臺威力顯，
機槍兩挺如弦箭，
二卒隨時能應變。
標語滿，
會場恐怖全瀰漫。

繩綁腰彎十二犯，
含冤茹苦加刑判，
交困身心蒼白面。
長慨嘆：
何時共黨方完蛋？

31.   A Final Assembly For The General Appraisal Of 1973

To the Tune of Yu Jia Ao
(Fisherman's Pride)
Peng'an Labor-Reform Camp
April 27, 1974

Just put up,
The platform demonstrates its power.
Two machine guns are ready,
Like an arrow on the bowstring;
Two soldiers can meet an emergency
At any time.
Flooded with slogans,
The meeting ground is gripped with terror.

Bound with ropes,
Forcibly bowed down,
Condemned to additional sentences,
Twelve prisoners suffer injustice and pain.
Their afflictions, physical and mental,
Are reflected in their pale faces.
With deep feeling,
I sigh:
When will the Communist Party be finished?

32. 挽回七十年代
初期挫折

菩薩蠻
蓬安勞改營
1974 年 4 月 27 日

年終評審長三月，
檢查拒撰心堅決。
逼鬥儘頻攻，
戰而終奏功。

三遭嘗敗走，
迎擊今降寇。
戰馬不停蹄，
曙光英勇馳。

註：在 1970、1972 和 1973 年的總評期間，
我曾勉強地寫出過簡短的自我檢查。

32.   Recovering From The Setbacks Of The Early Seventies

To the Tune of Pusa Man
(Strange Goddess)
Peng'an Labor-Reform Camp
April 27, 1974

For as long as three months
I have been firm in my decision
To refuse to write the self-examination
During the year-end general appraisal.
Despite under frequent attacks of compulsion and criticism,
I have fought
And achieved success at last.

After three defeats in the past,
Now I vanquish the enemies
When rising to meet them head-on.
Without hesitation,
The war-horse will gallop bravely
Toward the dawn.

Note: During the general appraisal time of 1970, 1972 and 1973,
I reluctantly wrote brief self-examinations.

33. 獄友唐潤朝
逃跑未遂

浣溪沙
蓬安勞改營
1974 年 6 月

毛像毀傷未敬珍，
輕輕年紀進牢門。
不容託故病為因！

朝夕思家方越獄，
捕回捯綁銬加身。
同情淚灑見含辛！

33.   Fellow Prisoner Tang Runchao Fails To Run Away

To the Tune of Huan Xi Sha
(Yarn Washed in the Stream)
Peng'an Labor-Reform Camp
June 1974

Breaking a statue of Mao,
Instead of venerating and treasuring it,
This man is put behind bars
At his young age.
His illness is no excuse!

Missing his family day and night,
He tries to escape.
When recaptured,
He is beaten, bound and handcuffed.
Seeing him suffering,
I weep in sympathy!

34. 女獄友
認罪於全監大會

西江月
蓬安勞改營
1974 年 7 月 6 日

言進定為「右派」，
案翻關入監牢。
教師七載搏狂濤，
鬥銬毆誣嚐飽。

遵命發言今夜，
竟然認罪哀號！
夏空熱浪湧滔滔，
窒息豪情多少？

34.   A Woman Fellow Prisoner Admits Her Sins To The Entire Jail Assembly

To the Tune of Xi Jiang Yue
(Moon over the West River)
Peng'an Labor-Reform Camp
July 6, 1974

Because she dared to give advice,
This teacher was declared Bourgeois Rightist;
Accused of reversing her original judgment,
She was thrown into prison.
During the struggle of seven years
Against the raging waves,
Deeply, she suffered
Criticisms, handcuffing, beatings and slanders.

Instructed to speak tonight,
She finally acknowledges her guilt,
And even weeps piteously!
The heat wave rises to the summer sky,
How many high aspirations
Have been smothered?

35. 殺人大會！

鷓鴣天
蓬安勞改營
1974 年 8 月 27 日

批孔批林運動狂，
停工開會忽班房。
官員共黨淫威逞：
十一囚徒罹禍殃。

繩緊綁，
面如霜，
苦嚐身痛斷肝腸；
一人處決餘加判。
暴政何時方滅亡？

35.   A Killing Assembly!

To the Tune of Zhegu Tian
(Partridges in the Sky)
Peng'an Labor-Reform Camp
August 27, 1974

To criticize Lin Biao and Confucius —
A frenzied campaign.
In the prison, suddenly labor is interrupted,
An assembly is held.
The Communist officials
Demonstrate their arrogance:
Eleven prisoners meet with disaster.

Bound tightly with ropes,
Their faces are pale like frost;
They experience hardships:
Their bodies in pain, their hearts broken.
One condemned to death,
The others given additional sentences.
When will this tyranny be destroyed?

36. 老獄友遭處決

浣溪沙
蓬安勞改營
1974 年 8 月 27 日

毛被徒孫奉若神，
像常刊報害人民，
誰如污損禍臨身。

昔日警官毛像玷，
控遭處死作冤魂！
問天「正義幾時伸？」．

36.   An Old Fellow Prisoner Is Sentenced To Death

To the Tune of Huan Xi Sha
(Yarn Washed in the Stream)
Peng'an Labor-Reform Camp
August 27, 1974

Mao is worshiped by his followers as a god.
The newspaper always carries his picture,
Doing people harm.
But whoever harms the picture invites calamity.

Alleged to have defiled Mao's picture,
A former police officer will be a soul killed innocently,
Accused and sentenced to death!
I ask Heaven:
"When will justice be done?"

37. 悼念蔣中正總統

念奴嬌
蓬安勞改營
1975 年 4 月 7 日

駕崩凶耗，
報章載、
驚悉愁腸將斷。
五十年來戡亂勇，
齎志精神堪讚。
北伐梟雄，
西追**赤卒**，
豪氣長虹貫。
扶桑來犯，
率民八載迎戰。

抗日漁利毛收，
國人受騙，
痛未狂瀾挽！

37. Mourning For President Jiang Zhongzheng (Chiang Kai-Shek)

To the Tune of Nian Nu Jiao
(Charming Girl Nian Nu)
Peng'an Labor-Reform Camp
April 7, 1975

The sad news of your death, O President,
Was published in the newspaper.
Upon learning I was shocked,
My heart broken.
You had the courage during fifty years
To suppress rebellions.
Despite unfulfilled purposes,
Your spirit is worthy of praise.
Making a Northern Expedition
Against powerful forces,
Pursuing the Red Army in the west,
Your strength was
Like the rainbow spanning the sky.
In eight years of struggle
Against the aggression of Japan
You led the people.

Mao benefited unfairly
From the War of Resistance Against Japan,
The compatriot was also deceived.
You were pained
Having failed to stem a raging tide!

嘗膽臥薪長奮勉，

寶島繁榮耀眼！

基督信誠，

教廷交好，

悲化為歡忭。

永安恭祝，

早降**魔怪**猶盼！

註：中華民國總統蔣公中正，兩日前崩殂臺北，享壽
　　八十有八歲。勞改營當局今日收到了昨天的《**四**
　　川日報》，旋即下令於午飯時向犯人宣讀這則消
　　息，欲以破滅其「變天復辟」的希望！

As if by sleeping on the ground,
By tasting gall,
Strengthening your resolve,
You worked hard to make the country strong.
And now
The Precious Island is a brilliant scene of prosperity!
You have believed sincerely in Christ,
And had good relations with the Vatican;
My sorrow is to be turned into joy.
Wishing you eternal rest,
I look forward
To an early surrender of the Devil!

Note: The venerable Mr. Jiang Zhongzheng, President of the Republic of China, died in Taipei two days before at the age of 88. Today the labor-reform camp authorities received the *Sichuan Daily* of yesterday and ordered this news to be read to prisoners during lunchtime to shatter their hopes of political restoration!

38. 獄友王麟，
爲何爾落井下石？

菩薩蠻
蓬安勞改營
1976 年 3 月 3 日

晚間大會遭批鬥，
拒遵吏命吾昂首。
嚎叫爾如狼，
饗愚三耳光！

辱毆批銬咒，
君已頻頻受。
洩忿復邀功，
庸斯爲隱衷？

38.   Why Should You, Fellow Prisoner Wang Lin, Hit A Person Who Is Down?

To the Tune of Pusa Man
(Strange Goddess)
Peng'an Labor-Reform Camp
March 3, 1976

During the evening assembly
Criticized and browbeaten,
I resist the order of the official,
Holding up my head.
Howling like a wolf,
You slap my face three times!

Insults, beatings, criticism,
Handcuffing and curses,
You yourself have suffered
Again and again.
To work off your resentment,
To earn credit—
Do these express your inner feelings?

39. 飛蟲

浣溪沙
蓬安勞改營
1976 年 7 月 9 日

大會晚間開獄中，
電燈閃爍舞飛蟲，
飛來扇上息從容。

種類繁多姿色麗，
自由自在叫嗡嗡，
隨聲歌頌好天公。

39.   **Winged Insects**

To the Tune of Huan Xi Sha
(Yarn Washed in the Stream)
Peng'an Labor-Reform Camp
July 9, 1976

At night
A mass meeting is convened in the jail.
Around the sparkling electric lights
Winged insects dance.
Some of them flit to my fan
Resting quietly.

Of great variety and beauty,
They buzz around contentedly.
Joining with them,
I sing the praises
Of the good Ruler of Heaven.

40. 雨過天晴

西江月
蓬安勞改營
1976 年 7 月 16 日

四日連綿雨降，
九霄陰晦心煩。
終於日出又今天，
愁悶雲消霧散。

風雨瀟瀟已息，
辛酸耿耿將完？
瞻望前景信心堅，
斟飲神杯再勉！

40.   The Sun Shines Again After The Rain

To the Tune of Xi Jiang Yue
(Moon over the West River)
Peng'an Labor-Reform Camp
July 16, 1976

It has rained
Continuously for four days;
Under the gloomy sky
I was sick at heart.
Today at last
The sun comes out again;
My worries vanish,
Fading like clouds and mists.

The whistling wind and pattering rain
Have stopped.
Will the suffering of a loyal heart
Come also to an end?
Looking far into the future,
Filled with firm confidence,
I make another determined effort
To drink from the Divine Cup!

41. 蓬安勞改營診所

減字木蘭花
蓬安勞改營
1976 年 8 月 30 日

培修診所，
觀察內情機會遇。
新式平房，
原係**蓬安天主堂**。

依坡而建，
故貌今朝猶可見。
慨問皇天：
「**聖祭何時重獻焉？**」

41.   Peng'an Labor-Reform Camp's Clinic

To the Tune of Jian Zi Mulan Hua
(The Magnolia)
Peng'an Labor-Reform Camp
August 30, 1976

Going to repair the clinic,
I have an opportunity to observe inside.
These modern single-story houses were
Originally the Catholic chapel in Peng'an.

Built along the hillside,
Its original form is still visible.
Sighing, I ask High Heaven,
"When will the Holy Sacrifice
Be offered here again?"

42. 爾死矣，毛澤東！

念奴嬌
蓬安勞改營
1976 年 9 月 9 日

追隨馬列，
井岡竄、
割據延安偏邑。
慣用黨軍欺「鬥」諜，
得勢烽煙抗日。
高唱和平，
猛攻城鎮，
謀逞神州赤。
長施暴政，
遭災黎庶十億。

毀節害教反神，
身心齊戮，
淫亂汙巾幗。
擁有位權榮妾壽，

42.   You Are Dead, Mao Zedong!

To the Tune of Nian Nu Jiao
(Charming Girl Nian Nu)
Peng'an Labor-Reform Camp
September 9, 1976

A follower of Marx and Lenin,
You escaped to the Jinggang Mountains.
You set up a separatist regime
In Yan'an, a remote city.
Consistently using
The Party, army, fraud, "struggle" and spies,
Taking advantage
Of the War of Resistance Against Japan,
You were in power.
Talking glibly about peace,
Attacking fiercely cities and towns,
You succeeded
In your schemes of sovietizing China.
Exercising a tyranny
Over a long period of time,
You brought catastrophe
To a billion people.

Destroying moral integrity,
Persecuting religions,
Opposing God,
You slaughtered both bodies and hearts.
By debauchery
You defiled womankind.
Having a throne,
Power, honor,

享盡人間春色！
甫圮唐山，
今亡國賊，
死訊誰聞泣？
未吞台港，
料難瞑目安息！

註：1976 年 7 月 28 日，離北京約一百四十英
　　里的唐山，發生了七點八級強烈地震，造
　　成該工業城市的整個毀滅，導致從五十萬
　　到百萬人的重大傷亡。毛澤東於今晨零時
　　十分去世，但這消息卻到半下午才予發
　　佈；勞改營廣播站隨即將之轉播給了犯人。

Concubines and longevity,
You have enjoyed to your heart's content
All the spring color of man's world!
Tangshan has just collapsed,
A traitor to the country, you now perish.
Who will weep at the news of your death?
Having been unable
To annex Taiwan and Hong Kong,
It is difficult for you
To close your eyes,
To rest in peace!

Note: On July 28, 1976, there was an intense earthquake in Tangshan about 140 miles away from Beijing. The shock was of 7.8 magnitude. This earthquake caused the destruction of the whole industrial city and inflicted heavy casualties of from half to a million people. This early morning at 00:10 hours, Mao Zedong died. But the news was not released until the mid-afternoon. It was soon relayed to prisoners by the broadcasting station of the labor-reform camp.

43. 三囚孤牢

臨江仙
蓬安勞改營單獨囚禁中
1976 年 9 月 16 日

毛已身亡屍待瘞，
徒孫徒子居喪，
驚惶萬狀逞猖狂。
夜巡姜幹事，
逼我吐衷腸。

拒向組囚公報誦，
堅持信仰昂揚，
孤牢關入又何傷?!
黃泉毛甫下，
吾豈赴刑場?!

43.   My Third
Solitary Confinement

To the Tune of Lin Jiang Xian
(Immortal by the River)
Solitary Confinement
At Peng'an Labor-Reform Camp
September 16, 1976

Mao has passed away,
Leaving his body to be buried.
His followers, great and small,
Have gone into mourning.
Seized with great fear,
They show off their malevolent power.
Official Jiang comes for inspection this evening,
Forcing me to pour out my heart.

I refuse to read out the press bulletin
To the prisoners of my group.
I uphold the Faith
With a high spirit.
Being put into this solitary cell—
What harm can come to me?!
Mao has just entered the nether world,
Shall I go to the execution ground?!

44. 聽時事報告

清平樂
蓬安勞改營
1976 年 10 月 30 日

何歡何悶？
大會聞音訊：
「**反黨四人牢獄進，**
華主席賢明蓋！」

爭權走卒毛亡，
搶班內助招殃，
粉墨登場華慶。
何時掃盡豺狼?!

註：所謂的「**四人幫**」，係指王洪文、張春橋、
　　毛妻江青和姚文元。

44. Listening To The Report On Current Events

To the Tune of Qing Ping Yue
(The Qing Ping Song)
Peng'an Labor-Reform Camp
October 30, 1976

Is the news worth any response,
Whether of joy or depression,
When it is heard at the mass assembly?
"The anti-Party Gang of Four
Have been imprisoned.
Chairman Hua is virtuous, wise and loyal!"

After the death of Mao
Among his high-ranking followers
There is a scramble for power;
Seeking to succeed him,
His wife invited calamity.
Hua rejoices over
Embarking upon a political venture,
Making himself up and going on the stage.
When will all these wolves be destroyed?

Note: The so-called Gang of Four refers to Wang Hongwen, Zhang Chunqiao,
Jiang Qing – Mao's wife, and Yao Wenyuan.

45. 好犯示關懷

采桑子
蓬安勞改營單獨囚禁中
1976 年 11 月 1 日

「成天靜坐床沿上，
　煩倦寒僵！
　留意安康，
　午睡望君切勿忘！」

　唐囚路過良言吐，
　未諗衷腸。
　惟曉穹蒼：
　祈禱吟詩吾志昂！

註：唐道安是另一中隊囚犯，他是奉派來此看
　　守他本隊的也遭到禁閉的犯人。

45.   Concern Of A Good Inmate

To the Tune of Cai Sang Zi
(Picking Mulberries)
Solitary Confinement
At Peng'an Labor-Reform Camp
November 1, 1976

"All the day long
You sit on the bedside quietly;
You must be anxious, tired, cold and numb!
Pay attention to your health!
Don't forget to take a noontime nap!"

Prisoner Tang speaks these kind words
While passing by.
He cannot read my heart.
Only Heaven knows:
Praying and composing poetry,
My morale is high!

Note: Tang Dao'an is a prisoner from another company. He is sent here
to guard his company's prisoners who are also in confinement.

46. 獄友苟少雲來勸降

卜算子
蓬安勞改營單獨囚禁中
1976 年 11 月 8 日

「天冷小監關，
　手足齊僵凍。
　認罪離牢視野寬，
　暖與他人共！」

「對主僕當忠，
　君命難遵奉。
　照管孤囚受濕寒，
　知爾心情重！」

46.   Fellow Prisoner Gou Shaoyun Tries To Induce Me To Capitulate

To the Tune of Pu Suan Zi
(The Fortune Teller)
Solitary Confinement
At Peng'an Labor-Reform Camp
November 8, 1976

"During cold weather
Confined in a cell,
Your hands and feet are numb.
If you admit your guilt,
You will leave the cell
And have a wide field of vision;
You will share the same warmth with others!"

"To the Lord
I must remain loyal.
I cannot comply with your demand.
In caring for me, a solitary prisoner,
You suffer also from dampness and chill.
I know how heavy your heart is!"

47. 獄友王麟
銬而求饒

菩薩蠻
蓬安勞改營單獨囚禁中
1976 年 11 月 22 日

鄰囚挨鬥重遭銬，
歸來邊泣邊饒告。
號哭震牢房，
聲聲斷我腸！

五回交代苦，
迄未難關渡。
毀志復傷身，
兇殘赤獄真！

47. Fellow Prisoner Wang Lin Begs For Mercy After Being Handcuffed

To the Tune of Pusa Man
(Strange Goddess)
Solitary Confinement
At Peng'an Labor-Reform Camp
November 22, 1976

Struggled against,
My neighbor and fellow prisoner
Is handcuffed once more.
Back in his cell,
He weeps and asks for mercy.
His cries reverberate in my cell,
Each one of his sobs
Almost breaks my heart!

Though enduring
The suffering of confessing five times,
He has not yet passed through the gate.
His determination is undermined,
His health is ruined.
The Red jail is truly evil!

48. 獄友陳登邁自縊

西江月
蓬安勞改營單獨囚禁中
1976 年 11 月 29 日

陳犯心憂意憤，
投繯寒夜身亡。
清晨柴屋見懸樑，
獄吏毫無驚慌。

絕望囚徒自盡，
赤牢便飯家常！
屠心逼命惡昭彰，
共黨何時淪喪？

48.   Fellow Prisoner Chen Dengmai Hangs Himself

To the Tune of Xi Jiang Yue
(Moon over the West River)
Solitary Confinement
At Peng'an Labor-Reform Camp
November 29, 1976

Worried and angry,
Prisoner Chen hanged himself and died
During the cold night.
In the morning
Finding the body in the firewood room
Hanging from a beam,
The prison official gave no alarm.

A despairing prisoner commits suicide —
A common occurrence in the Red prison!
The Communist Party
Gives evidence of its brutality:
It kills the hearts of the people,
Hounding them to death!
When will it perish?

49. 獄友李三合，
為何爾厭惡？

減字木蘭花
蓬安勞改營
1976 年 12 月 11 日

「孤牢三月，
頑固依然將處決！
免受株連，
毋與相親毋與言！」

夜觀電影，
聞李告鄰吾窘境。
生死皆歡，
定奪非人乃好天！

49.   Why Should You, Fellow Prisoner Li Sanhe, Detest Me?

To the Tune of Jian Zi Mulan Hua
(The Magnolia)
Peng'an Labor-Reform Camp
December 11, 1976

"After a three-month solitary confinement
He remains as stubborn as before,
Being on the verge of execution!
To avoid getting involved in his case,
You should not approach him,
Saying nothing to him!"

While watching a movie at night,
I hear Li telling his neighbors
Of my predicament.
No matter whether living or dying,
I always rejoice.
Who will determine my destiny?
No one,
But the good Heaven!

50. 小監三月

七律
蓬安勞改營單獨囚禁中
1976 年 12 月 16 日

促膝談心於主前，
孤牢身繫又何妨！
蚊寒濕譴空騷擾，
情志寧欣常激昂。
兩度疴侵令體弱，
二千詩背使神傷。
冀望記憶猶強勁，
保舊吟新增主光！

50.   Three Months In A Solitary Cell

In the Poetic Style of Qilu
Solitary Confinement
At Peng'an Labor-Reform Camp
December 16, 1976

Since I can sit side by side,
And talk intimately with my Lord,
I might as well live in a solitary cell!
Mosquitoes, cold, dampness and reproaches
Harass me in vain,
While my mood, determination, peace and joy
Run always high.

Twice, bouts of illness
Have caused my body to weaken;
Recitation of the two thousand poems
Has strained my nerves.
I wish my memory to remain strong
To keep the old poems and compose new ones
For the greater glory of the Lord!

51. 欣悉選出
新教宗若望保祿二世

清平樂
蓬安勞改營
1978 年 10 月 28 日

《人民日報》，
　細閱欣知曉：
　選出**教廷**新領導。
　為**教**歡呼叫好！

　棧堅羊眾身強，
　亡還盜悔狼降。
　赤犯天涯祝願，
　敬呈**善牧**東方！

51.   Happily Learning
Of The Election
Of The New Pope John Paul II

To the Tune of Qing Ping Yue
(The Qing Ping Song)
Peng'an Labor-Reform Camp
October 28, 1978

Reading the *People's Daily* carefully,
I am happy to learn:
The Vatican has elected a new leader.
I cheer and applaud for the Church!

May the fold be firm,
The sheep numerous,
Their bodies strong;
May the lost sheep come back,
The robbers of the sheep be repentant,
And the wolves surrender.
As a "Red prisoner,"
From the ends of the earth,
I am sending best wishes respectfully
To the good Shepherd from the East!

52. 痛悉
王國盛神父罹難

清平樂
蓬安勞改營
1979 年 3 月 18 日

山崩夜裡，

巨石工棚毀。

王守石場隨以逝，

正待雞鳴夢碎！

驚聞信息黃昏，

懇求主救亡魂。

目擊前車傾覆，

臨深履薄殘身！

52. Sad At Learning Of The Accidental Death Of Fr. Wang Guosheng

To the Tune of Qing Ping Yue
(The Qing Ping Song)
Peng'an Labor-Reform Camp
March 18, 1979

Last night in a landslide
A big rock destroyed the shed.
Watching over the quarry,
While waiting for the cock-crow
To shatter his dreams,
Fr. Wang became a victim of the rock!

Hearing the news at dusk,
I was shocked,
I entreated the Lord to save his soul.
Seeing the overturned cart ahead,
A maimed person, like me,
Should be alert,
As if approaching an abyss,
Or treading on thin ice!

53. 喜聞教宗若望保祿二世
　　訪問波蘭

六么令
蓬安勞改營
1979 年 6 月 20 日

九天歸訪，
成果真豐滿。
千名報人報導，
電視新聞燦。
六百萬人瞻仰，
盛況誰曾見？
長虹氣貫，
山河語壯，
頑震孩欣善良勉。

長鬥豺狼故國，
戰績輝煌建。
膽識才德非凡，
榮獲三重冕。

53.   Joyously Hearing Of The Visit Of Pope John Paul II To Poland

To the Tune of Liu Yao Ling
(The Six Shortest Strings)
Peng'an Labor-Reform Camp
June 20, 1979

Your nine-day visit to your motherland —
Truly full of results.
A thousand newsmen report it,
The television news coverage — splendid.
Six million people
Have looked at you with reverence.
Who has ever seen such a grand occasion?
Your spirit —
As lofty as the rainbow spanning the sky,
Your speeches —
As magnificent as mountains and rivers:
The stubborn receive an unexpected shock;
Your children, great joy;
The kindhearted, huge encouragement.

You fought the Wolf for a long time
In your country;
You won brilliant spiritual victories
On the Lord's battlefield.
Outstanding in courage, insight, ability and virtue,
You have been gloriously given
The Triple Crown.

公父親臨光照，

鐵幕雲將散。

主榮彰顯，

教威增長，

僕僕風塵義深遠！

註：《人民日報》曾報導，聖父於 1979 年
6 月 2 日至 10 日訪問了他的祖國。

54. 欣悉
教宗若望保祿二世訪美

玉連環
蓬安勞改營
1979 年 10 月 20 日

牧靈心壯，

大洋橫渡過，

友邦探訪。

眾記者、報導爭先，

亦傳播電台，

實情真況。

矍鑠精神，

數百萬、人民瞻仰。

As Universal Father,
You went personally
To give illumination beyond the Iron Curtain
And the clouds there will vanish.
Having manifested the glory of the Lord,
Having increased the prestige of the Church,
Your difficult travels have profound significance!

Note: The *People's Daily* reported our Holy Father
had visited his motherland during June 2 to 10, 1979.

54. Upon Learning Joyfully Of The Visit Of Pope John Paul II To The USA

To the Tune of Yu Lian Huan
(Chain of Jade)
Peng'an Labor-Reform Camp
October 20, 1979

Intent and eager on your pastoral mission,

Crossing the wide ocean, Holy Father,

You pay a visit to a friendly nation.

Scores of correspondents
Hurry to report the facts,
The radio spreads the great event
As it really is.
You are seen by millions of people with reverence;
They note your vigor, your strength.

接待隆重禮，
元首且超；
震驚魔妄！

紐約哈林看望，
黑人溫暖受，
歡呼街上。
謬論駁、時弊糾匡。
竭力救蒼生，
真理頻講。
成就輝煌，
料影響、定將深廣。
咒徒然，
車輪歷史，
北京焉擋？

　　註：聖父於 1979 年 10 月 1 日至 7 日訪問了美
　　　　國，《人民日報》最近曾予報導和評論。

The reception for you is far more solemn
Than that for any head of state,
Shocking the powers of darkness!

You call on New York's Harlem;
Filled with your warmth,
The black people cheer you in the streets.
To refute fallacies,
To redress current ills,
To help people with their salvation,
You teach the truth again and again.
Your brilliant successes
Will have far-reaching effects.

Beijing curses in vain,
How can it stop the wheels of history
Running forward so strongly?

Note: The *People's Daily* recently reported and commented upon the
visit of the Holy Father to the USA during October 1-7, 1979.

55. 伽利略將獲昭雪

虞美人
蓬安勞改營
1980 年 1 月 29 日

沉冤審理今頒諭，
公父英明舉。
巨人科學可心安，
三百年前屈辱即將完！

慎前顧後慈親好，
遇事多思考。
溺中撈草北京狂，
枉費心機毀教拒真光！

註：本月《人民日報》既報導伽利略案將
　　予重審，復乘機攻擊教會。

55.   Galileo Will Be Exonerated

To the Tune of Yu Mei Ren
(The Beauty of Yu)
Peng'an Labor-Reform Camp
January 29, 1980

To deal with a gross injustice
Done to Galileo,
The Universal Father
Recently promulgated an edict.
This is a wise deed.
Galileo, a giant in science,
Set your mind at rest:
Your humiliation
Three hundred years ago
Is about to be ended!

The Church, our loving Mother,
Is very good in looking back on the past
While carefully considering the future.
She reflects again and again whatever happens.
Grasping at a straw,
Beijing goes mad
As it drowns.
It uses this event
To slander the Church,
To reject the light of truth—
A futile effort!

Note: This month the *People's Daily* reported that the case of Galileo would be
reopened. The newspaper also took this occasion to attack the Church.

56. 坐牢二十五週年

眼兒媚
蓬安勞改營
1980 年 11 月 7 日

寒冬念五抗風霜，
績效頗昭彰。
追懷往事，
遠瞻前景，
鬥志昂揚！

延長考驗何妨礙？
愈戰愈堅強。
好天讚頌，
世人拯救，
續戰豺狼！

56.   The Twenty-Fifth Anniversary Of My Imprisonment

To the Tune of Yan Er Mei
(The Eyes' Fascination)
Peng'an Labor-Reform Camp
November 7, 1980

The struggle against the wind and frost
During the last twenty-five cold winters
Has achieved successes —
Successes quite evident.

While turning my thoughts to the past,
While looking to the future in the distance,
I am full of fight!

What does it matter
If the trial is prolonged?
Through fighting
I become stronger and stronger.

For the praise of the good Heaven,
For the salvation of the world,
I will continue to combat
The jackals and the wolves!

57. 教宗若望保祿二世
訪問西德一瞥

江城子
蓬安勞改營
1980 年 11 月 16 日

岸然華髮志凌雲，
出宮門，
到萊茵，
良莠愚頑真理誨諄諄。
聖父親臨榮幸事，
歡舉國，
慶黎民。

螢屏映出父精神，
鐵窗身，
仰瞻欣，
祝願健康長壽牧羊群。
冀望餘生能往謁，
呈彙報，
領慈恩！

註：今晚我們觀看電視。聖父出訪情景，
　　令我非常興奮。

57. A Glimpse Of The Visit Of Pope John Paul II To West Germany

To the Tune of Jiang Cheng Zi
(The Town by the River)
Peng'an Labor-Reform Camp
November 16, 1980

The Holy Father, dignified and silver-haired,
With aspirations reaching the clouds,
Leaving the apostolic palace,
Comes to the Rhine
To instruct earnestly and tirelessly
In the truth
The good and bad, the ignorant and stubborn.
At his visit—
A glorious and happy event—
The whole nation is jubilant,
The people rejoicing.

His glowing looks appear vividly
On the television screen.
While bodily in jail,
I look at him with joy and reverence,
Wishing him good health and a long life
To tend the flock.
I hope to go to his presence
One day in my remaining years
To present my personal report,
To obtain his kind blessing!

Note: Tonight we watched television.
I was greatly moved by the scenes of His Holiness's visit.

58. 過南充

七律
南充
1981 年 7 月 26 日

果州一別卅年更，
路過今朝感慨盈。
順慶府中高屋聳，
嘉陵江上大橋橫。
牆邊修院思佳景，
池畔蓮花憶舊情。
主教堂樓空屹立，
神鐘難再醒生靈！

58.   **Passing Through Nanchong**

In the Poetic Style of Qilu
Nanchong
July 26, 1981

My departure from the ancient Prefecture of Guo
Has been covered over for thirty years
In my subconscious.
Now, today, passing through the city,
I am filled with sighs.
Many buildings tower aloft
In the district of the Shunqing Prefecture,
A great bridge
Crosses over the Jialing Jiang.

Near the wall of our monastery
I ponder the past beautiful scene,
By the bank of the Locust Lake
I recall my old feelings.
The tower of the cathedral
Reaches toward heaven in vain,
The Divine Bell
Awakens the people no longer!

59. 聞聶冀道神父
逝世

浣溪沙
遂寧
1981 年 8 月 17 日

「三自」自稱倡最先，
依然下獄實堪憐！
會中伐我為何緣？

先我出牢聞逝痛，
天鄉祝禱早登攀！
悠悠教難幾時完?!

59. Hearing About
The Death Of Fr. Nie Jidao

To the Tune of Huan Xi Sha
(Yarn Washed in the Stream)
Suining
August 17, 1981

You called yourself the first one
Who sponsored the "Three Autonomies."
Pitifully, you were still thrown into prison!
During study meetings
Why did you have to attack me?

You got out of jail earlier than I;
Now I am very sorrowful
Hearing of your death!
I hope and pray:
You will ascend to the Heavenly homeland very soon!
Oh, on what day will the long persecution end?!

60. 「國慶」有感

浣溪沙
遂寧
1981 年 10 月 1 日

黃葉枝頭舞興濃，
南歸好雁促西風，
寒空望盡渺無蹤！

景象蕭條迎節日，
鬧街行走鬱心胸，
討錢乞丐累相逢！

60.   Thoughts
On "National Day"

To the Tune of Huan Xi Sha
(Yarn Washed in the Stream)
Suining
October 1, 1981

Yellow leaves on branches dance joyfully,
The west wind urges the good wild goose
To start its south homing return.
Looking up at the cold sky into the far distance,
No trace of its path can be found!

A desolate scene welcomes the festival,
I walk along the busy streets
With a heavy heart,
Repeatedly coming across beggars pleading for money!

61. 黃昏漫涉涪江邊

攤破浣溪沙
（山花子）
遂寧
1981 年 10 月 13 日

月色雲間暗又寒，
隻身孤影踱江邊。
偶遇扁舟逆流溯，
志昂然！

小豆多年霜雪育，
歸來釜內豆萁煎！
信鴿西飛三月矣，
幾時還？

61. Strolling
Along The Fu Jiang Bank
At Dusk

To the Tune of Shan Hua Zi
(The Mountain Flowers)
Suining
October 13, 1981

The moonlight through the clouds
Is dim and cold;
Solitary and alone,
I pace to and fro on the edge of the river.
I meet by chance a skiff going upstream:
An inspiration to get my spirit high and unafraid!

Having been reared in frost and snow
For many years,
I, the returned little bean,
Am now cooked in the cauldron
With the beanstalk!
The carrier pigeon
Has flown westwardly for three months,
When will it return home?

62. 喜獲
郎毓秀教授回信

七律
遂寧
1981 年 11 月 21 日

歸來立命雁開航，
遠望晴空喜若狂。
旱裡逢霖欣槁樹，
雪中送炭謝愁腸。
盛情邀訪真榮幸，
大力支援實慨慷。
慈愛穹蒼常撫育，
冬梅定會吐芬芳！

62.   **Joyously Receiving A Reply From Professor Lang Yuxiu**

In the Poetic Style of Qilu
Suining
November 21, 1981

Upon your return,
You charged your "goose" to fly off;
Looking at the clear sky into the distance,
I go into rapture.
A welcome rain after a long drought,
I, a withered tree, am gratified;
Given charcoal in snowy weather,
I, weighed down with anxieties, feel grateful.

I am truly honored
By your kind invitation to visit;
You are so generous
As to give me your energetic support.
With the constant nurture
Of the loving Heaven,
I, a winter plum,
Shall surely send forth fragrance!

63. 訪呂金鰲小姐家

浪淘沙
成都
1981 年 12 月 27 日

念有六寒冬，
違晤諸忠，
三亡餘散渺無蹤。
但見**玉聰**賢姪輩，
慨對**蒼穹**！

尊府聚群雄，
議抗愚兇，
互相慰勉氣天衝。
衛**教**激情回首憶，
樂也融融！

63.   A Visit To The Family Of Miss Lu Jin'ao

To the Tune of Lang Tao Sha
(Wave-Washed Sands)
Chengdu
December 27, 1981

For twenty-six cold winters
I have been separated
From you, Oh, loyal ones!
Three of you have passed away,
The rest have dispersed,
Leaving without a trace.
Meeting only Yucong, your good nephew,
I sigh in the presence of Heaven!

Often gathering in your house,
As a group of heroes,
We discussed
How to resist the stupid and the fierce ones;
Our ideals were soaring to the sky
In mutual consolation and encouragement.
Recalling our past zeal to defend the Church,
My joy knows no bounds!

64. 聞姜齊芳修女
逝於勞改營

浣溪沙

成都

1981 年 12 月 27 日

為主昂然戰惡狼，

威脅管制又何妨！

坐牢至死永流芳！

戰友四冬齊衛教，

半年共事誼深長。

音容爽朗似春光！

64.   Hearing Of The Death Of Sr. Assumption Jiang Qifang In A Labor-Reform Camp

To the Tune of Huan Xi Sha
(Yarn Washed in the Stream)
Chengdu
December 27, 1981

With high resolve
You fought the evil and savage Wolf;
Threats and surveillance,
No matter to you!
Imprisoned until death,
You have left an aromatic name forever!

As battle companions for four winters,
We defended our Church together;
As fellow workers for half a year,
We built our profound friendship.
Your voice and countenance are
As candid as the spring light!

65. 元旦

鷓鴣天
成都
1982 年 1 月 1 日

錦水洶洶爆竹鳴，
心潮澎湃慮叢生。
大洋彼岸風光好，
回首這邊景冷清。

離境夢，
影隨形，
夜間常擾到天明。
借來天使淩雲翅，
飛越汪洋頌主名！

65.   New Year's Day

To the Tune of Zhegu Tian
(Partridges in the Sky)
Chengdu
January 1, 1982

The Jin Jiang surges forward,
The firecrackers are set off:
I feel an upsurge of
Countless anxieties within me.
On the other shore of the great ocean
There is a wonderful sight.
Looking back on this side,
I face a cold and cheerless view.

The dream of leaving the country,
Like a shadow following a person,
Has often disturbed me
Through the night until daybreak.
If I could borrow
The soaring wings of an angel,
I would fly across the boundless ocean thither
To praise the name of the Lord!

66. 自成都
返回遂寧

七絕
遂寧
1982 年 1 月 6 日

冬陽驅散霧茫茫，
風順一帆回故鄉。
若暗若明前景望，
何時慶幸渡重洋?!

66.   Return To Suining From Chengdu

In the Poetic Style of Qijue
Suining
January 6, 1982

The winter sun drives away the thick fog,
With smooth sailing
I come back to my hometown.
I gaze far afield
At my prospects,
Now vague, now distinct.
When will I rejoice to fly across
The seas and oceans?!

67. 喜讀
黃國維神父覆函

搗練子
遂寧
1982 年 1 月 23 日

看手劄，
湧歡濤，
卅七春秋離恨消。
慨餽銀錢情義重，
感恩當面望來朝！

67.   Cheerfully Reading
A Reply From
Fr. Bernard Huang Guowei

To the Tune of Dao Lian Zi
(Pounding Silk Floss)
Suining
January 23, 1982

Reading your letter,
A wave of joy emerges within me;
My parting sorrows of thirty-seven springs and falls vanish.
You generously present me a sum of money,
Showing me your deep friendship;
I am eagerly looking forward
To extending my gratitude personally
Some day in the near future!

68. 春節

如夢令
遂寧
1982 年 1 月 25 日

爆竹煙花鳴放，
黎庶街頭熙攘。
佳節氣氛真?!
何以自由難享？
神將，
神將，
解甲歸田休想！

68.   The Spring Festival

To the Tune of Ru Meng Ling
(Like a Dream)
Suining
January 25, 1982

Firecrackers and fireworks are set off and resound,
People bustle about in the streets.
Is there a real atmosphere of the Festival?!
Why is it still hard for them
To enjoy their freedom?
Divine General,
Divine General,
Do not imagine
You should be demobilized!

69. 遊廣德寺

眼兒媚
遂寧
1982 年 1 月 26 日

遊人春節喜觀光，
塔獨享馨香。
既無菩薩，
亦無和尚，
古刹淒涼！

多年廟宇遭侵佔，
憑弔我心傷！
燒香百姓，
討錢殘老，
同沐春光。

69.   Excursion To
The Guangde Temple

To the Tune of Yan Er Mei
(The Eyes' Fascination)
Suining
January 26, 1982

During the Spring Festival
Visitors delightfully come sightseeing;
Alone,
The tower enjoys the fragrance of burning incense.
There can be found
Neither Buddhas nor Buddist monks;
The ancient Buddist temple is desolate and dreary!

The temple has been occupied for many years;
Paying a visit,
My heart is broken!
The people, burning joss sticks,
The crippled and the old, begging money,
Both bathe themselves together
In the sunshine of spring.

70. 唐天壽神父回信

西江月
遂寧
1982 年 2 月 15 日

暮暮朝朝期待，
迎來今日華箋。
龍蛇字若玉金言，
謝爾恩情慰勉。

別苦離愁多載，
而今化作雲煙！
雄圖宏願滿胸間，
異國何時實現？

70.   A Reply From
Fr. Felix Tang Tianshou

To the Tune of Xi Jiang Yue
(Moon over the West River)
Suining
February 15, 1982

Having awaited long days and nights,
I now welcome your esteemed letter.
Your penmanship is as vigorous and lively,
As dragons and snakes wriggling,
Your words are as precious
As gold and jade;
I am so grateful
For your loving-kindness,
For your consolation and exhortation.

The sorrows of separation for many years now part,
Now become
As dissipating cloud or lifting mist!
My heart is full of
Abundant plans and great intentions,
When will they be realized in a foreign land?

71. 訪銀大娘

七絕
成都
1982 年 3 月 7 日

曩昔併肩戰鬼昂，
重逢今日喜洋洋。
古稀年過身猶健，
酬爾恩情望彼蒼！

71.   A Visit To Aunt Yin

In the Poetic Style of Qijue
Chengdu
March 7, 1982

In former times
We fought the devil
Side by side with high spirit.
Today meeting again,
We are beaming with joy.
You are now more than seventy years old,
You are still in good health.
For all your favors
I wish Heaven to repay you!

72. 台灣大姪女
周曉貞來函

浣溪沙
遂寧
1982 年 2 月

飛越重洋爾短箋，
沉沉愁緒化為煙。
安康欣悉爾椿萱。

美夢黃粱非幻影，
投奔瓊島好機緣。
寒寮鐵幕禱於天！

72.   A Letter From Zhou Xiaozhen, My Eldest Niece In Taiwan

To the Tune of Huan Xi Sha
(Yarn Washed in the Stream)
Suining
February 1982

Having flown across the oceans,
Your brief letter reaches me,
Turning the heavy gloom of my heart into smoke.
I rejoice to hear
Your parents are in the best of health.

My Golden Millet Dream is not illusionary;
It may be a good opportunity for me
To go to Taiwan, the Precious Island,
For shelter.
I offer my supplications to Heaven
In my small room, cold and humble,
Behind the Iron Curtain!

73. 過春節

七絕
遂寧
1983 年 2 月 13 日

新衣童著戲街頭，
煙火門聯艷競求。
良辰美景無心問，
但願真光照九州！

73.   Celebrating
The Spring Festival

In the Poetic Style of Qijue
Suining
February 13, 1983

In new clothes
The children play in the streets,
Fireworks in the air and the couplets on the gateposts
Contend in a riot of color.
I find no interest
In the beautiful scene of the bright day;
I wish only
The Light of Truth
To illuminate the land of China!

74. 過成都

七絕
成都
1984 年 10 月 10 日

黃葉陰天抵錦城，
剛留四日欲辭行。
成都飯店何高聳？
救世神鐘早失聲！

74.   Passing Through Chengdu

In the Poetic Style of Qijue
Chengdu
October 10, 1984

On a day
Of yellow leaves and overcast sky,
I came to the City of Brocade.
I have to say goodbye
After just four days here.

Why do you tower aloft,
Hotel of Chengdu?
The Divine Bell of salvation
Lost its voice long ago!

75. 抵北京

七絕
北京
1984 年 10 月 10 日

風雨淒淒別錦官，
兩時銀燕到京歡。
久聞優美名都景，
夜盡天明細察看！

75.   Arrival In Beijing

In the Poetic Style of Qijue
Beijing
October 10, 1984

Parting from Chengdu, the City of Brocade,
In wailing wind and weeping rain,
Our silver swallow has arrived
In the capital with joy
After a two-hour flight.

I have heard for a long time
Of the wonderful sights of this famous city.
I will explore them
When night is over,
When day breaks!

76. 登長城

鷓鴣天
北京
1984 年 10 月 15 日

日麗風和出鳳城，
名垣古老喜攀登。
行於城上崎嶇路，
絡繹遊人讚歎驚。

防外患，
保生靈，
流芳百世爾功名。
內憂多載今猶在，
何不為民力蕩平?!

76.   Ascending
The Great Wall

To the Tune of Zhegu Tian
(Partridges in the Sky)
Beijing
October 15, 1984

The sun is radiant and the wind gentle,
I go out of the capital
To joyfully ascend the famous ancient Wall.
Walking on the tortuous and rugged road of the Wall,
The endless stream of sightseers
Admires and marvels.

Guarding against foreign aggression,
Protecting the people,
You, Great Wall, have left
A signal merit and a good name
For a hundred generations.
Internal disturbances still exist
After many years,
Why should you not strive
To quell the tumult for the people?!

77. 遊陶然亭公園

七絕
北京
1984 年 10 月 24 日

獨倚陶園瑞象亭，
盡收眼底北京城。
遠方十架忠魂舉，
插入藍天一血旌！

77.   Roaming Taoranting (Joyous Pavilion) Park

In the Poetic Style of Qijue
Beijing
October 24, 1984

In the park,
Alone,
I lean against
The Pavilion of the Auspicious Picture,
Having almost a panoramic view
Of the city of Beijing.

In the distance
A crucifix,
Lifted up by loyal souls,
Penetrates the blue sky,
As a Banner soaked in Blood!

78. 遊北海公園
（冬宮）

漁家傲
北京
1984 年 11 月 6 日

秀美御園遊覽爽，
水波湖裡隨風漾，
塔殿亭廊雄麗壯。
天氣朗，
鎦金白塔光芒放。

禁苑芬芳休自賞，
帝王逸樂悠遊暢，
疾苦人民非所想。
全命喪，
讚歌誰為來高唱?!

78.   Roaming
Beihai (The North Sea) Park
(The Winter Palace)

To the Tune of Yu Jia Ao
(Fisherman's Pride)
Beijing
November 6, 1984

I feel happy
While sightseeing at the elegant Imperial Garden.
The waves in the lake
Ripple with the wind;
The towers, halls, pavilions and corridors
Are beautiful and magnificent.
On this sunny and fine day,
The gilded White Pagoda sheds its rays.

You, Forbidden Garden,
Should not admire your own fragrance alone;
The Emperors wallowed here
In rest, pleasure and strolling,
Without thinking of
The sufferings of the people.
The Emperors have all passed away,
Who sings loudly
A past or a future paean to them?!

79. 遊景山公園

浪淘沙
北京
1984 年 11 月 6 日

登上**萬春亭**，

俯瞰京城，

形骸輕快暢心情。

眼底**禁城**休得意，

逝矣**明清**！

北海右邊橫，

湖水晶瑩，

中南海上冷清清。

赤色君臣其毋蹈：

覆轍**崇禎**！

註：**中南海**位於**景山**右前方，北海前面和**故宮**右
　　側，係**中共**黨政最高當局的**赤色**皇宮，是禁
　　區，是絕密地。「**崇禎**」是**明朝**末代皇帝的
　　年號。1644 年 3 月 19 日，當**李自成**率領反
　　抗軍攻進**北京**時，崇禎帝於**煤山**（1655 年後
　　改稱**景山**）槐樹上懸帶自縊而死。

79. Strolling
In Jingshan Park

To the Tune of Lang Tao Sha
(Wave-Washed Sands)
Beijing
November 6, 1984

Having ascended the Ten Thousand Springs Pavilion,
I look down at the capital city
With ease in body, joy in mind.
Forbidden City, unfolding before my eyes,
You should not be pleased with yourself:
Gone away are the Ming and the Qing dynasties!

The Beihai (North Lake) stretching out on the right,
With water sparkling and crystal clear;
The Zhongnanhai seems cold and deserted.
Red monarch and Red subjects,
You must not repeat
The tragic fate of Chongzhen!

Note: The Zhongnanhai, situated at the right front side of Jingshan Park, in the front of
the Beihai and on the right of the Imperial Palace (the Forbidden City), is the Red
Imperial Palace of the supreme authorities of the Chinese Communist Party and
Government, a forbidden and a top-secret zone. Chongzhen was the title of the reign of
the last Emperor of the Ming Dynasty. He died by hanging himself on a locust-tree
in Meishan (Coal Hill), which has been called Jingshan since 1655, on March 19,
1644, when Li Zicheng, leading his insurgent troops, stormed into Beijing.

80. 參觀
「毛主席紀念堂」

七絕
北京
1984 年 11 月 7 日

蝨賊靈堂枉壯昂！
罪軀善保豈流芳？
「汝民塗炭緣何怨，
朕臥晶棺痛斷腸！」

80.   A Visit To The Chairman Mao Memorial Hall

In the Poetic Style of Qijue
Beijing
November 7, 1984

Futile magnificence —
Futile grandeur —
Such the mourning hall of the chairman,
A vermin harmful to all!
Will his sinful body,
Though well preserved,
Leave a fragrant memory?

"Why should you people complain
Of living in an abyss of misery?
Look at me,
Your Chairman, your Emperor,
I lie in a crystal sarcophagus,
But my soul is full of sorrow!"

81. 大雪

浣溪沙
北京
1984 年 11 月 18 日

冷氣寒流忽逞狂，
鳳城今日著新裝，
街頭巷尾閃銀光。

如玉乾坤堪讚賞，
朦朧煙霧已逃亡，
陽光午照暖心房。

81.   **Heavy Snow**

To the Tune of Huan Xi Sha
(Yarn Washed in the Stream)
Beijing
November 18, 1984

Currents of waves of cold air come suddenly,
Showing off their violent power.
The capital is dressed in new clothes,
Taking a new look;
The streets and the lanes glisten in silvery light.

As pure as jade,
Heaven and earth are praiseworthy;
The dim smoke and the mist flee.
Sunlight appears at midday,
Warming the heart.

82. 過上海

七絕
上海
1984 年 11 月 27 日

雨中安抵長江口，
平順過關謝上蒼。
飛出鐵籠神鳥慶，
天空海闊任翱翔！

82.   Passing Through Shanghai

In the Poetic Style of Qijue
Shanghai
November 27, 1984

In the rain
We safely arrive
At the mouth of the Chang Jiang.
Going through customs smoothly,
I acknowledge my debt to Heaven.

Flying out of the iron cage,
I, as a Divine Bird, rejoice!
Now, I am able to soar at will
In the boundless sky,
Over the unlimited sea!

83. 參觀聖安德肋修院
青少年之家

鷓鴣天
美國加州化野漠聖安德肋修院
1985 年 1 月 18 日

靜宇幽林悅眾童，
斯尋天父訴私衷。
年輕弟妹如歸至，
山谷荒涼春意濃！

魚入海，
鳥淩空，
來遊學子興沖沖。
念年績著前程美，
青少家園氣概雄！

註：今天早晨九點鐘，若望·博杰爾丁院長開
　　車，領我前往參觀了 1966 年 10 月 3 日由
　　本修院興辦於附近的「青少年之家」。我們
　　在那裡會見了貝蒂·科塔吉太太和她的女
　　兒喬伊斯·科塔吉小姐二位工作人員，以
　　及一些參加退省的年輕人。

83.   A Visit
To The Youth Retreat Center
At St. Andrew's Priory

To the Tune of Zhegu Tian
(Partridges in the Sky)
St. Andrew's Priory, Valyermo, CA, USA
January 18, 1985

The quiet buildings,
The secluded wood
Give pleasure to the children;
Here they seek the Heavenly Father,
Pouring out to Him
Their inner thoughts and feelings.
Visitors, young brothers and sisters,
Feel at home;
Spring is very much here
Over the waste hills and valley!

As fish entering the sea,
As birds soaring to the skies,
Students visit this center
With joy and interest.
The past twenty years — fruitful,
The future — bright;
This home for youth
Is endowed with a heroic spirit!

Note: At 9:00 am, Fr. Prior John Borgerding drove me to visit the nearby Youth Center, established by the monastery on October 3, 1966. There we met the staff, Mrs. Betty Cottage and her daughter, Miss Joyce Cottage, as well as some young retreatants.

84. 稿呈
羅光總主教

清平樂
聖安德肋修院
1985 年 5 月 2 日

春光明媚，
修院蒙臨蒞。
初稿面呈申敬意，
再赴名城洛市。

賴公祈禱支援，
黑牢赤膽離歡。
拙稿馨香一縷，
冀望上達蒼天！

註：1985 年 4 月 30 日，在自羅馬經美返
　　台途中，羅光總主教曾來修院訪
　　問。此闋小詞，是敬獻於送別機場
　　時。

84.   Presentation Of My Manuscript To Archbishop Stanislaus Luo Guang (Lokuang)

To the Tune of Qing Ping Yue
(The Qing Ping Song)
St. Andrew's Priory
May 2, 1985

On a radiant and enchanting spring day,
You, Archbishop,
Honored the Priory with your presence.

To present you personally
With the first draft of my manuscript,
To show my respect,
I come once more
To the celebrated city of Los Angeles.

With the support of your prayers,
With a loyal heart,
I left happily the dark prison.

May my humble manuscript,
Like fragrant incense,
Ascend to Heaven!

Note: April 30, 1985, on his way back from Rome to Taiwan via the USA,
Archbishop Stanislaus Luo Guang visited our monastery.
This poem was presented while seeing him off at the airport.

85. 題照贈
汪惠娟女士

七律
聖安德肋修院
1985 年 5 月 2 日

相識有緣民主邦，
春花競艷播芬芳。
凱歌歡樂引吭唱，
往事神奇回味香。
寶島風光多旖旎，
長城景色卻淒涼。
寰球兄妹同心禱，
聖棧終歸大陸羊！

註：汪惠娟女士當時是羅光總主教的秘
　　書，現為台灣輔仁大學哲學教授。

85.   Dedication On A Picture To Ms. Wang Huijuan (Hui-Chuan)

In the Poetic Style of Qilu
St. Andrew's Priory
May 2, 1985

I meet you here in a democratic country
By fate, by the hand of Providence,
When spring flowers contend in beauty,
Spreading their fragrance.
Joyful, my triumphant songs
I sing heartily;
Miraculous, the events of the past
I ponder over sweetly.

The scene of the Precious Island—
Gorgeous,
The sight of the Great Wall—
Miserable.
Brothers and sisters
Of the whole world,
Let us pray with a single mind:
May the sheep on the Mainland
Finally rejoin the holy Fold!

Note: Ms. Wang Huijuan was then secretary to Archbishop Stanislaus Luo Guang.
Now she is a professor of philosophy in Fu Jen University in Taiwan.

86. 訪聖家修院

七律
聖安德肋修院
1985 年 5 月 5 日

加州五月好風光，
綠樹鮮花遍地香！
懦懦無榮傾碧血，
區區有幸慕群芳。
漫長考驗言難述，
深厚神恩僕未忘。
鬧市身居心嚮主，
救人淑已返天鄉！

註：今天下午，依撒格・凱利納修士開
車領我去洛杉磯，訪問了凱琳・魏
爾赫米修女和其座落在達尼爾・墨
菲中學的聖若瑟修女會修院。

86.   A Visit To
The Holy Family Community

In the Poetic Style of Qilu
St. Andrew's Priory
May 5, 1985

May —
A wonderful sight in California,
Everywhere
The sweet scent
Of green trees and fresh flowers!
In my weakness,
I was not given the honor
Of shedding my blood;
In humility,
I now have the good fortune
Of admiring the fragrant flowers.

Words fail to describe
My prolonged trials,
But I cannot forget
The profound divine kindness.
You, Sisters, live among the busy streets
With your hearts set toward the Lord;
You will return to the heavenly homeland
Through unceasingly perfecting yourselves,
Through helping others to salvation!

Note: This afternoon Br. Isaac Kalina drove me to Los Angeles to visit Sr. Karen
Wilhelmy, C.S.J., and her convent of the Sisters of St. Joseph at Daniel Murphy
High School.

87. 贈別熱羅尼莫·
內費爾德神父

西江月
聖安德肋修院
1985 年 5 月 18 日

血雨腥風華夏，
春花秋月加州！
同狼搏鬥卅三秋，
半載同居惠受。

慈愛萬能基督，
黃粱一枕貔貅！
鴻文蒙餽念長留，
一曲陽關為奏！

87.   Seeing
Fr. Jerome Neufelder Off

To the Tune of Xi Jiang Yue
(Moon over the West River)
St. Andrew's Priory
May 18, 1985

In China
A foul wind,
A bloody rain;
But in California
The spring flowers,
The fall moon!
I struggled against the Wolf
For thirty-three autumns;
I have reaped
The kindness of your company
For half a year.

Because of
The love and omnipotence of Christ,
The wild Animal's dream is folly!
You have given me your book,
Leaving me a memento;
I wish to play some parting music
For you, my dear Father!

88. 誓發大願日有感

憶江南
聖安德肋修院
1985 年 6 月 29 日
聖伯多祿及聖保祿宗徒慶節

觀禮客，
濟濟聖堂中。
宣誓禱歌霄漢震，
忠心百鍊獻**蒼穹**！
長夜夢非空！

88.   Reflections On The Day Of My Solemn Profession

To the Tune of Yi Jiang Nan
(Remembering the South of the River)
St. Andrew's Priory
June 29, 1985
Solemnity of Sts. Peter and Paul, Apostles

Numerous guests,

Attending the ceremony,

Gather together in the chapel.

Solemn vows, prayers, chants

Shake the skies;

A time-tempered loyalty

Has been dedicated

To Heaven!

The dream throughout a long night —

By no means empty!

Br. Peter, an oblate student of Chengdu Priory, in the last semester of his senior high school; Chengdu, Sichuan, China, March 1947.

1947年3月，筆者是中國四川省成都市成都修院的一名在學修生，正讀高中最後一個學期。

Br. Peter with three fellow oblate students of Xishan Priory during his first semester of junior high school; Nanchong, Sichuan, fall 1941. (L-R) James Mao Yongchang (now in Taiwan), Fr. Felix Tang Tianshou (died in CA, April 14, 1994), Br. Peter, age 15, and He Guoliang.

1941年秋，在讀初中頭學期時，筆者與西山修院三位同窗修生合照於四川省南充縣。（左起）毛永昌（在台灣）、唐天壽神父（1994年4月14日逝於加州）、筆者（當時15歲）和何國亮。

(L-R) Fr. Wilfrid, Fr. Vincent, Fr. Prior Raphael, Fr. Emile, Fr. Hildebrand, Fr. Eleutherius and (front row) two Chinese novices at the gates of Xishan Priory; Nanchong, December 1936.

（左起）衛民德神父、丁谷鳴神父、文嘉禮院長、武津理神父、馬懿德神父、華倫士神父和（前排）兩名中國初學修士；1936年12月，攝於南充西山修院大門前。

270

Br. Peter with a priest, three Catholics and the three Communist spies, Li, Zhu and Fan, (hidden by the Underground Church in Chengdu) in the spring of 1955. (L-R): (front row) Br. Peter, Vincent Yuan Nengding, Fr. Lawrence Li Wenjing and an unidentified Catholic; (back row) Li Zhenyu, Jia Zhishan, Zhu Chaoqian and Fan Tingsen.

1955年春，筆者與一位神父、三位教友和潛伏在成都地下教會內的三名共黨間諜李、朱、范合影。（左起）：（前排）筆者、袁能鼎、李文景神父和一位記不起名字的教友；（後排）李震宇、賈止善、朱朝乾和范廷森。

Br. Peter's original Benedictine community, Xishan Priory (1929-1944), Nanchong.

此為筆者原先進入的南充西山本篤會修院(1929-1944)。

A pastel of the new building of Br. Peter's Chengdu Priory (1944-1952) by Fr. Werner Papeians de Morchoven, O.S.B.

這是白徵明神父關於筆者所屬的成都修院（1944-1952）新樓房的一幅寫生粉畫。

Br. Peter's brother, John Baptist, and his family at the Spring Festival on Mainland China, January 31, 1995.

筆者在中國大陸的哥哥周本固的全家福，攝於1995年1月31日春節。

（左起）：（前排）周仲碧、王素貞（1921.4.5- 2010.3.31）、周本固、蔣貴華、周仲珍；（後排）宋華志、宋富年、劉明、蔣進、蔣雲、周仲玉和劉世銀。
(L-R):(front row) Zhou Zhongbi, Wang Suzhen(4/5/1921-3/31/2010), Zhou Bengu, Jiang Guihua, Zhou Zhongzhen; (back row) Song Huazhi, Song Funian, Liu Ming, Jiang Jin, Jiang Yun, Zhou Zhongyu and Liu Shiyin.

James Mao Yongchang and family in Taoyuan, Taiwan, 1989, (Br. Peter's fellow oblate student and old classmate both in Xishan and Chengdu Priory, 1938-1945). (L-R): (front row) Mao Shuxuan, Chen Shen, James Mao Yongchang, Mao Shufeng: (back row) Mao Zixuan, Mao Shuhui, Mao Ziling and Mao Shuhua.

毛永昌1989年在台灣桃園的全家福（他是筆者1938年到1945年間在西山修院和成都修院的同窗修生和學友）。（左起）：（前排）毛蜀珇、陳甚、毛永昌、毛蜀鳳；（後排）毛子萱、毛蜀慧、毛子玲和毛蜀華。

Br. Peter's brother in Taiwan, Philip Zhou Zhimin (L), with his wife, Wang Shuzhao, and their two sons, Zhou Zhongkuan and Zhou Zhongguang (R); taken in November 1981.

筆者在台灣的哥哥周止民（左）和他的妻子王淑昭、他們的兩個兒子周仲寬、周仲光（右），合影於1981年11月。

Br. Peter with Archbishop Stanislaus Luo Guang (L) and Fr. Prior John Borgerding, O.S.B. (R); taken at the Priory refectory, April 30, 1985.

1985年4月30日，筆者與羅光總主教（左）和若望‧博杰爾丁院長（右）合影於修院餐廳。

Br. Peter with Archbishop Stanislaus Luo Guang's secretary, Ms. Wang Huijuan, April 30, 1985.

1985年4月30日，筆者與羅光總主教秘書汪惠娟女士合影。

Diane Richardson of Oregon, Br. Peter's continual correspondent since December 1985. (L-R) Diane, her son, Bob, her parents, Harold and Marie Abel, and her husband, Douglas; her family phsto at a picnic, July 1982.

俄勒岡州黛安‧理查森自1985年12月以來就與筆者常通書信，這是她的全家福，攝於1982年7月的一次野餐中。（左起）黛安、她的兒子鮑勃、父母哈羅德和瑪利亞‧亞伯爾、夫婿道格拉斯。

Br. Peter's (third right) pilgrimage to Subiaco, Italy, October 31, 1986, with (L-R) Abbot President Ambroise Watelet, Marie-Therese Thoreau, Br. Isaac Kalina, Agnes Thoreau, Fr. Adrian Nocent and Fr. Gaetan Loriers (the disappearing photographer).

筆者（右三）曾於1986年10月31日去義大利蘇比亞角朝聖。陪同前往者是：（左起）分會長盎博羅削・瓦特萊特大院長、瑪利亞一德肋撒・托洛、依撒格・凱利納修士、雅妮・托洛、艾德里安・諾森神父和駱愷騰神父(他是本照的拍攝者，因而未現身於此)。

Br. Peter's (third left) visit to Fr. Adolf Mignot (second left) in Brussels, Belgium, November 29, 1986, together with (L-R) Marie Alghisi, Genevieve Alghisi, Fr. Gaetan Loriers, Leopold Davreux and Primo Alghisi (the disappearing photographer).

1986年11月29日，筆者（左三）隨同（左起）瑪利亞・阿爾吉西、熱納維埃夫・阿爾吉西、駱愷騰神父、萊奧波特・達夫雷和普里莫・阿爾吉西（本照的拍攝者，因而未現身於此）拜訪了比利時布魯塞爾阿道夫・米諾神父(左二)。

Cardinal Timothy Manning with Jim and Peggy Class of San Marino, CA, Br. Peter's constant correspondents since first meeting in Rome on October 30, 1986.

弟茂德・曼寧樞機主機同加州聖馬利諾吉姆和佩吉・克拉斯伉儷的合照。他們二人是筆者自1986年10月30日相識於羅馬以來的常有信函相往還者。

At a dinner for Supervisor Michael Antonovich, Los Angeles, CA, March 10, 1988. (L-R) Br. Peter, Elaine L. Zhao (Chao), Supervisor Antonovich, and Fr. Subprior Francis Benedict.

1988年3月10日，在縣政委員彌額爾・安東諾維奇的宴會上。（左起）筆者與趙小蘭、縣政委員安東諾維奇和方濟各・本篤副院長合照。

Br. Peter during physical therapy given by physical therapist Jean DeBettignies; Santa Barbara, CA, March 16, 1989. (L-R) Susan Mary Decker, Tricia Brown and Jean.

1989年3月16日，筆者在加州聖巴巴拉市接受理療醫師吉恩・德・貝蒂尼的治療。（左起）蘇珊・瑪利亞・德克爾、特利夏・布朗和吉恩。

Br. Peter's visit to the Greenwood family in Sepulveda, CA, March 18, 1989, in the company of Jean DeBettignies and Susan Mary Decker (the disappearing photographer). (L-R) Jean, Amy, Br. Peter, her daughter, Leonita, and her husband, Leo

1989年3月18日，筆者在吉恩・德・貝蒂尼和蘇珊・瑪利亞・德克爾的陪同下，訪問了加州塞普爾維達市格林伍德家。（左起）吉恩、艾米、筆者、她的女兒良尼塔和她的夫婿良（由未入照片的蘇珊拍攝）。

Br. Peter with two of his volunteer typists, Terry Thompson (L) and Suky Lee (R); taken by the Priory lake, April 14, 1989.

1989年4月14日，筆者與他的兩位打字義工特麗‧湯普森（左）和李聖淑（右）合影於修院水池邊。

Kathy Ho, Kyoung Suie, in Korea, April 29, 1989; one of Br. Peter's close Korean friends.

許庚淑在1989年4月29日攝影於韓國。她是筆者的一位韓國好友。

Br. Peter with five close friends(L-R): (front row) Fr. Xavier Manavath (a Claretian priest from India), Betty Floate, Dolores Chavez, Br. Peter, (back row) Bill Floate and Gilbert Chavez; taken in front of the Priory chapel, July 15, 1989.

1989年7月15日，筆者與五位好友合影於修院聖堂前面（左起）：（前排）沙勿略‧馬納瓦斯神父（印度聖母聖心孝子會神父）、貝蒂‧弗洛特、多洛蕾‧賈維茲、筆者、（後排）比爾‧弗洛特和吉爾伯特‧賈維茲。

Kenneth L. and Elaine E. Lapean, Br. Peter's good friends in Carpinteria, CA.

肯尼思和伊萊‧拉皮安是筆者在加州卡平特利亞的好友。

Lori Hartill (top), one of Br. Peter's English teachers in Clackamas Community College in Oregon, along with her parents, Charlie and Irene Hartill (bottom), long-term correspondents since December 1985.

洛蕾‧哈蒂爾（上）是筆者在俄勒岡州克拉克瑪社區學院的英語教師之一，她的父母查利和艾琳‧哈蒂爾（下）還是筆者自1985年12月以來的長期通信者。

Sr. Karen Wilhelmy, C.S.J. (holding cat), Br. Peter's English teacher, and her Sisters of the Holy Family Community, Los Angeles, CA.

凱琳‧魏爾赫米修女（手抱小貓者）和她在加州洛杉磯的聖家修院同院修女們的合影，她曾是筆者的英語老師。

Br. Peter and Marianna So, a close Korean friend; taken at the right side of the Priory chapel, November 11, 1991.

1991年11月11日，筆者與韓國好友徐美仙合影於修院聖堂右側。

Br. Peter (R) enjoying a Merry Christmas with the Abrera family in Burbank, CA, December 25, 1991. (L-R) Jaime, Audrey; their children: Jainee, Joseph, Janine (front row).

1991年12月25日，筆者（右）與加州柏班克市阿伯雷拉家共享聖誕歡樂。（左起）杰姆、奧德麗；他們的子女：杰妮、若瑟、杰寧（前排）。

Br. Peter's Community, St. Andrew's Abbey at Valyermo, after the election of their first Abbot, Fr. Francis Benedict, O.S.B., May 15, 1992. (L-R): (front row) Br. Peter, Fr. Felix, Fr. Gaetan, Fr. Abbot Ambroise, Fr. Abbot Francis, Fr. Eleutherius, Fr. Werner; (back row) Br. Dominic, Br. Benedict, Fr. Luke, Fr. John Bosco, Fr. Isaac, Br. Paul, Fr. Molaise, Fr. Joshua, Fr. Philip, Fr. Gregory and Br. Marius.

筆者所屬化野漠聖安德肋大修院於1992年5月15日選出方濟各·本篤神父為首任大院長後的全院合影。（左起）：（前排）筆者、唐天壽神父、駱愷騰神父、盎博羅削大院長、方濟各大院長、華倫士神父、白徵明神父；（後排）多明我修士、本篤修士、路加神父、若望·鮑思高神父、依撒格神父、保祿修士、莫勒斯神父、若穌厄神父、斐理伯神父、額我略神父和馬里斯修士。

278

Br. Peter in the company of his editor, Cynthia Clark, presents his newly-released autobiography to Cardinal Roger Mahony at the grand ceremony of Fr. Abbot Francis' Abbatial Blessing, St. Andrew's Abbey, August 2, 1992.

1992年8月2日，於聖安德肋大修院舉行的方濟各大院長領受大院長祝福的盛典中，筆者在其書的編輯辛西婭‧克拉克的陪同下，向羅杰‧馬洪尼樞機主教獻上了自己最近出版發行的自傳。

At the end of the Abbatial Blessing Mass, Fr. Abbot Francis Benedict reads to the assembly Br. Peter's poem which welcomed the presence of Cardinal Roger Mahony to St. Andrew's Abbey, August 2, 1992.

1992年8月2日，方濟各‧本篤大院長在領受大院長祝福的彌撒即將告終時，向大會朗誦筆者所填的一闋歡迎羅杰‧馬洪尼樞機主教光臨聖安德大修院的《江城子》詞。

Br. Peter and Juliette Pare during the 35th Valyermo Fall Festival, September 28, 1991.

1991年9月28日，筆者與朱麗葉‧帕爾合影於化野漠三十五屆秋節期中。

Br. Peter (second right) with his editor, Fr. Simon J. O'Donnell (second left). and three of his close Korean friends and sponsors, Christina Kim (C) and her daughters, Jennifer (R) and Amanda (L), in the Abbey refectory after the Easter Vigil at 1:20 am, April 16, 2006.

2006年4月16日，在復活節前夕守夜禮後的一點二十分鐘，筆者（右二）與他的審稿者西滿・奧多尼爾神父（左二）和他的三位贊助者韓國好友，基督蒂娜・金（中）、她的女兒詹妮弗（右）和阿曼達（左）合影於修院餐廳。

Br. Peter visits the Prieure Saint-Andre of Clerlande, Ottignies, Belgium, November 19, 1986. Fr. Francois de Grunne (L) and Fr. Philippe Neri Verhaegen (R).

1986年11月19日，筆者在訪問比利時奧蒂尼克勒朗德修院時與耿芳績神父（左）和斐理伯・內里・韋拉讓神父（右）合影。

Br. Peter on vacation with some of his friends: (L-R) Irene Foertsch, Fr. Emery R. Tang, O.F.M., Br. Peter, Daniel V. Daly and Hugo Foertsch, at Serra Retreat, Malibu, CA, July 15, 1993.

1993年7月15日，筆者在度假期中與一些好友合影於加州馬里埔賽拉退省院。（左起）艾琳・福爾斯、鄧和平神父、筆者、達尼爾・戴利和雨果・福爾斯。

280

Br. Peter with his publisher, Jim Moeller (R),
and his editor, Cynthia Clark (L), during the
36th Valyermo Fall Festival at St. Andrew's
Abbey in front of his book booth, September
27, 1992.

1992年9月27日，在聖安德肋大修院的化野
漠36屆秋節期中，筆者與他的出版者吉姆·
莫勒（右）和他的編輯辛西婭·克拉克（左）
合影於他的書攤前面。

(L-R) Philippus H. and Flora Luciana
Herkata and their daughter, Agustina
Sicilia, from Calabasas Park, CA; Br.
Peter's close Indonesian friends since
May 16, 1988.

（左起）斐理伯和弗洛拉·露西婭
娜·赫凱塔以及他們的女兒阿古斯
蒂娜·西西莉婭。他們自1988年
5月16日以來就是筆者的印度尼西
亞好友，他們住在加州卡拉巴沙公
園市。

Br. Peter (second left) follows his host
monks leaving the choir stalls at Prince
of Peace Abbey, Oceanside, CA, at the
conclusion of Vespers, during an overnight
visit on July 13, 1993, arranged by his
good friends, Hugo and Irene Foertsch.

在好友雨果和艾琳·福爾斯的安排下，
筆者於1993年7月13日往訪了加州洋邊
市基督和平之王修院。照片顯示：他（
左二）在留宿當晚唸完暮課經後，正隨
同眾位修士離開唱經團座位。

Br. Peter with Fr. Adrien Nocent, Marie-Therese Thoreau and her daughter, Agnes Thoreau, at Subiaco, the famous shrine, outer suburbs of Rome, Italy, October 31, 1986.

1986年10月31日，筆者與艾德里安・諾桑神父、瑪利亞－德肋撒・托洛和她的女兒雅妮・托洛合影於義大利羅馬遠郊著名聖地蘇比亞角。

Edward Littlejohn with his wife, Ellen, and their two daughters on their son's wedding day; Santa Barbara, CA, May 25, 1991. (L-R) Edward, Alexandra, Christopher, Monique, Ellen and Christina.

愛德華・利特爾若翰和他的太太埃倫以及他們的兩個女兒在他們的兒子於加州聖巴巴拉市舉行婚禮的1991年5月25日；（左起）愛德華、亞歷山德拉、克里斯托弗、莫尼加、埃倫和基督蒂娜。

Br. Peter with Fr. Jean de Britto, O.S.B., in the Collegio di Sant 'Anselmo, Rome, Italy, May 6, 2001.

2001年5月6日，筆者與若望・布里托神父合影於義大利羅馬聖安瑟而莫學院。

Br. Peter visits two of his new friends, Henri and Marie Ha Duy, a married couple, in Carpentras, France, May 11-12, 2001; photo taken by Henri.

2001年5月11日到12日，筆者探訪了在法國卡爾麗特臘的新友亨利和瑪利亞·哈杜优儷倆；亨利拍了此照片。

Br. Peter visits Anne Deprez (L), her community, la Fraternite d'Eglise Liege-Chine, at Banneux in Liege, Belgium, and two of her fellow members, May 17, 2001.

2001年5月17日，筆者拜訪了安娜·德普雷（左）和她在比利時列日邦諾的"天主教列日－中國友愛會"團體以及她的兩位會友。

Br. Peter with Frederique Barloy at Lourdes, France, May 20, 2001. With her financial help and in her company, Br. Peter makes a pilgrimage to this Marian shrine. She is the French translator of his English book, *Dawn Breaks in the East*. Her translation was published in Paris in February 2001.

2001年5月20日，筆者與費敏合影於法國露德。筆者在她的資助和陪同下，朝覲了這座聖母聖地。她是筆者的英文書《東方黎明在望》的法文本譯者，她的譯著已在2001年2月於巴黎出版。

283

Br. Peter with Angie E. Winston (L) and Tom Miller (R) at his book booth on the grounds of St. Andrew's Abbey during the Valyermo Fall Festival. September 24, 2005.

2005年9月24日秋節期中，筆者與安吉‧溫斯頓（左）和湯姆‧米勒（右）合影於聖安德肋大修院場地上自己的書攤旁。

Br. Peter with his new friends, Elaine Huang Huiling from Taiwan and her fiance Michael L. Cotter, on the Abbey grounds, June 18, 1988.

1988年6月18日，筆者與來自台灣的新友黃慧玲和她的未婚夫彌頦爾‧科特合影於修院場地。

Bellie Xiao Bai, Br. Peter's good friend, taken in Chengdu, Sichuan Province, China, on November 30, 1989. She emigrated to Brazil more than ten years ago. She is a daughter of Doctor Michel Xiao Ji (died on September 17, 2006, age 96) and Pansy Lang Yuxiu, a professor and a soprano.

筆者好友蕭柏在1989年11月30日攝於中國四川省成都市，她十多年前移居巴西。她是蕭濟醫生（2006年9月17日逝世，享年96歲）和女高音歌唱家郎毓秀教授的女兒。

Philippus H. and Flora Luciana Herkata, Br. Peter's good friends and sponsors, in an audience with Pope John Paul II in the Vatican in 1996.

筆者好友和贊助者斐理伯和弗洛拉·露西婭娜·赫凱塔伉儷，於1996年在梵蒂岡晉謁教宗若望保祿二世。

On August 21, 2009, at the close of the burial of Fr. Eleutherius Winance in the Abbey cemetery, Br. Peter with his editor, Theresa Marie Moreau.

2009年8月21日，在華倫士神父葬禮將完時，筆者與審稿女士德肋撒·瑪利亞·莫洛合影於修院墓地。

Br. Peter with his two good friends and sponsors, Elaine Huang Huiling and her husband, Michael L. Cotter; taken at the right side of the Abbey chapel, May 20, 2006 by Br. Daniel Bordynski.

2006年5月20日，筆者與他的好友和贊助者黃慧玲女士和她的夫君彌額爾·科特，合影於修院聖堂右側，由達尼爾·波定斯基修士拍攝。

Br. Peter with Br. Tim Mayworm, F.S.C. (third right), Chairman of the Los Angeles Archdiocesan Council of Religious Brothers, at a "Brotherhood Recognition Dinner" held at the Holy Spirit Retreat Center, Encino, CA, October 13, 1996.

1996年10月13日，筆者與洛杉磯總教區無品修士會主席蒂姆・梅威修士（右三），在加州恩西諾聖神避靜中心舉行的"修士表揚餐會"上。

Bellie Xiao Bai, Br. Peter's good Chinese friend, with her son, Xiao Hua (L), and her friend, Martin Balcker (R) ; taken in Sao Paulo, Brazil, at the beginning of 2005.

筆者的中國好友蕭柏同她的兒子蕭華（左）和她的友人馬丁・包格（右），2005年初攝於巴西聖保羅市。

Br. Peter(C) with his new Chinese friends, Monica Yang and her group, taken on the Abbey grounds on November 10, 2006.

2006年11月10日，筆者(中)同他的中國新友，楊莫尼加和她的團體合影於修院場地。

Br. Peter (R) with his eldest nephew, Jiang Guihua, in the Shaocheng Park in Chengdu, Sichuan, China, on April 6, 2008.

2008年4月6日，筆者在中國四川省成都市，與大姪女婿蔣貴華同遊少城公園。

Br. Peter's eldest niece, Zhou Zhongzhen, in the Shaocheng Park in Chengdu, Sichuan, China, on April 6, 2008.

2008年4月6日，筆者大姪女周仲珍也在中國四川省成都市同遊少城公園。

Br. Peter with his grandniece Jiang Yun in the Shaocheng Park in Chengdu, Sichuan, China, on April 6, 2008.

2008年4月6日，筆者與姪外孫女蔣雲合影於中國四川成都市少城公園。

Br. Peter (C) with his grandnephew, Jiang Jin, Jiang Jin's wife, Liang Jie, and son, Jiang Xuqi in the Shaocheng Park in Chengdu, Sichuan, China, on April 6, 2008.

2008年4月6日，筆者(中)與姪外孫蔣進、蔣進的妻子梁潔和小孩蔣旭麒合影於中國四川成都市少城公園。

Br. Peter with his second nephew, Liu Shiyin, in Deyang City, Sichuan, China, on April 13, 2008.

2008年4月13日，筆者與二姪女婿劉世銀合影於中國四川德陽市。

Br. Peter with his second niece, Zhou Zhongyu, in Deyang City, Sichuan, China, on April 13, 2008.

2008年4月13日，筆者與二姪女周仲玉合影於中國四川德陽市。

288

On October 24, 2009, Br. Peter visits once again his fifth sister-in-law's family in Dongshan Township in Yilan County, Taiwan. (R-L): (front row) Br. Peter, his fifth sister-in-law, Wang Shuzhao; (back row) his eldest niece, Zhou Xiaozhen, his second niece, Zhou Zhonglan, and his eldest nephew, Zhou Zhongxuan.

2009年10月24日，筆者再次探望了住在台灣宜蘭縣冬山鄉的五嫂家。（右起）：（前排）筆者、五嫂王淑昭；（後排）大姪女周曉貞、二姪女周仲蘭和大姪兒周仲喧。

Br. Peter's eldest nephew, Zhou Zhongxuan, and eldest nephew's wife, Wang Lingyu, in Yilan County, Taiwan, May 4, 2008.

筆者在台灣宜蘭縣的大姪兒周仲喧和大姪媳王玲玉，攝於2008年5月4日。

On October 19, 2009, Br. Peter and his good classmate and hospitable host, Mr. James Mao Yongchang, sightsee at the Riyuetang (Sun and Moon Lake) in Nantou County, Taiwan.

2009年10月19日，筆者和同窗好友、慇懃東道毛永昌先生，同遊台灣南投縣日月潭。

On October 12, 2009, under the guidance of Fr. Matthew Zhu Lide, Br. Peter calls on Mr. Jiang Baoqing, the boss of the Yeong Wang Cultural Enterprise Company in Taipei City, Taiwan. (L-R) Br. Peter (seated in the front row). Fr. Matthew Zhu, Mr. Jiang and Miss Yang, one of his employees.

2009年10月12日，朱立德神父帶領筆者拜訪了台灣台北市永望文化事業有限公司老闆姜寶慶先生。（左起）筆者（坐於前排）、朱神父、姜先生和他一位員工楊小姐。

On October 13, 2009, with the help of Mr. John-Paul Lin Yongming, Br. Peter has an audience with the Most Reverend Archbishop John Hong Shanchuan (Hung Shan-chuan) at the cathedral in Taipei City, Taiwan. (L-R) Br. Peter, Archbishop John Hong and Mr. John-Paul Lin.

2009年10月13日，在林永明先生的幫助下，我到台灣台北市主教座堂，晉謁了最可敬的洪山川總主教。（左起）筆者、洪總主教和林先生。

On August 14, 2009, at a grand dinner in the Abbey refectory in celebration of Br. Raphael Salandra's entering his novitiate, Br. Peter (R) with him (C) and his parents, Salvatore Salandra and Barbara Montroni.

2009 年8 月14日，在慶祝辣法額爾·薩蘭德拉修士進入初學期的晚宴時，筆者（右）與他（中）和其雙親薩爾瓦托里·薩蘭德拉、巴巴拉·蒙特羅尼合影於修院餐廳。

Br. Peter with his new Chinese friend, Wang Ning, in the Abbey refectory on March 14, 2010.

2010年3月14日，筆者與中國新友王凝合影於修院餐廳。

Br. Peter (L) with Br. Cassian Di Rocco by the back windows of the Abbey refectory leading to the kitchen, in May 2010.

2010年5月，筆者（左）與卡辛·迪·洛果修士合影於修院餐廳通往廚房的後窗旁邊。

On September 25, 1993, during the 37th Valyermo Fall Festival at St. Andrew's Abbey, Br. Peter (C) with his publisher, Jim Moeller(R), and his book's graphic artist, Ken Moeller(L), in front of his book booth; taken by press photographer, Dana Peters.

1993年9月25日，在聖安德肋大修院的37屆化野漠秋節期間，筆者（中）與他的出版者吉姆·莫勒（右）和他書的製圖者肯·莫勒（左），合影於他的書攤前；由攝影記者達納·彼得斯拍攝。

On April 9, 1994, Br. Peter(L) in the Abbey cemetery with an aged visiting married couple, two old good Chinese friends of his Chengdu Benedictine monastery, Michel Xiao Ji (2nd left), a retired surgeon, and Pansy Lang Yuxiu(R), a musical professor and famous soprano.

1994年4月9日，筆者（左）與來訪的高齡伉儷，原成都本篤會修院的中國好友，退休的外科醫生蕭濟（左二）和音樂教授、著名女高音歌唱家郎毓秀（右）合影於修院墓地。

A family photo in May 1995 of Br. Peter's good Korean friends; (L-R) Paul Kim, Jennifer Kim, Amanda Kim and Christina Kim.

筆者的韓國好友在1995年5月的全家福；（左起）金明天、詹妮弗·金、阿曼達·金和金純熙。

On April 19, 1998, on the Abbey grounds, Br. Peter(R) with his visiting old good friend and brave battle companion in Chengdu, Lucia Shu Dejun (C) and her friend, Joan Lustbader(L).

1998年4月19日，筆者（右）與來訪的昔日好友和驍勇的成都戰友舒德君（中）以及她的友好瓊·拉斯特巴德（左），合影於修院場地。

On January 28, 2012, Br. Peter's good Korean friends, Miss Amanda Sophie Kim and Mr. Scott Ethan Calvert, at their wedding dinner in Redondo Beach, CA.

2012年1月28日，筆者的韓國好友阿曼達・索菲・金小姐和斯科特・埃撒・卡爾維特先生，在他們加州雷東多比奇婚宴上的恩愛照。

On May 27, 2012, Br. Peter with his new good friend, Ms. Jennifer Lee, on the Abbey grounds.

2012年5月27日，筆者與新好友李賢洙女士，合影於修院場地。

A lovely photo after their wedding on August 4, 2012, of Michaela Ludwick and Maurice Russell, Br. Peter's good friends and important aides to his annual workshop in the Abbey retreat house.

筆者好友陸美珮和莫里斯・拉塞爾於2012年8月4日婚後的甜蜜照片。他們是筆者在修院退省客房的年度講座的重要助手。

On September 10, 2012, Br. Peter with four visitors from Hong Kong on the Abbey grounds; (R-L) Elena Kho Wang, Catherine Woo Lee, Fr. John Lam, Br. Peter and Lucy Wong.

2012年9月10日，筆者與來自香港的四位訪客合影於修院場地：（右起）王許秀蓮、胡儀芝、林健漢神父、筆者和黃慕蘭。

On December 22, 2012, Br. Peter with six new friends on the Abbey grounds; (R-L) Jerry Koh, Jacqueline Koh, Tina Halim, Sr. Teresa Fang (from Xi'an), Br. Peter, Sr. Clare Zhang (from Hebei) and David Woo (from Korea).

2012年12月22日，筆者與六位新友合影於修院場地：（右起）葛維舟、葛燕鴻、林瓊玎、方小贊修女（來自西安）、筆者、張佳琴修女（來自河北）和吳達味（來自韓國）。

On August 21, 2013, Br. Peter (C) on the Abbey grounds with a married couple visitors, Devin Craig (R) and Brittney Craig (L).

2013年8月21日，筆者（中）與一對伉儷客人，德文‧克雷格（右）和布里特尼‧克雷格（左），合影於修院場地。

On August 29, 2013, Br. Peter with three fellow monks on the Abbey grounds: (R-L) Fr. Francis Benedict, Br. Peter, Br. Angelus Echeverry and Br. Dominic Guillen.

2013年8月29日，筆者與三位院友合影於修院場地：（右起）方濟各‧本篤神父、筆者、安吉拉斯‧厄徹維利修士和多明我‧吉倫修士。

On August 29, 2013 Br. Peter with five employees of the Abbey on the monastery grounds: (R-L) Carolyn Jordan, Randi Mailes, who has helped Br. Peter many times with her emails to receive or to send all the proofread pages of his four books, her husband, Ted Mailes, Neri Valladares, Br. Peter and Maria Moore.

2013年8月29日，筆者與本院五位員工合影於修院場地：（右起）卡羅琳‧喬丹、蘭迪‧梅勒斯（她曾以其電子信箱多次協助筆者，收發他四本書的校正件）、她的丈夫特德‧梅勒斯、內里‧瓦拉達雷斯、筆者和瑪利亞‧穆爾。

On August 29, 2013, Br. Peter with five fellow monks on the Abbey grounds: (R-L) Br. Alfonso Daniel, Fr. Matthew Rios, Fr. Isaac Kalina, Br. John Mark Matthew, Fr. Stephen Coffey and Br. Peter.

2013年8月29日，筆者於修院場地與五位院友合影：（右起）亞方索‧丹尼爾修士、瑪竇‧里奧斯神父、依撒格‧凱利納神父、若望‧馬爾谷‧瑪竇修士、斯蒂文‧科菲神父和筆者。

295

On September, 2. 2013, Br. Peter with the Abbot and eight fellow monks on the Abbey grounds: (R-L) Br. John Mark Matthew, Fr. Subprior Patrick Sheridan, Br. Joseph Iarrobino, Br. Peter, Br. Benedict Dull, Fr. Martin de Porres Yalas, Fr. Philip Edwards, Fr. Abbot Damien Toilolo, Fr. Prior Joseph Brennan and Fr. Carlos Lopez.

2013年9月2日，筆者於修院場地與大院長和八位院友合影：（右起）若望‧馬爾谷‧瑪竇修士、帕特里克‧謝里登副院長、若瑟‧雅洛比諾修士、筆者、本篤‧達爾修士、瑪爾定‧耶拉斯神父、斐理伯‧愛德華茲神父、大院長戴米恩‧托依洛洛、若瑟‧布倫南院長和卡洛斯‧洛佩神父。

On September 2, 2013, Br. Peter with Miss Terry Qin Lijun, his good friend from Taiwan, on the Abbey grounds.

2013年9月2日，筆者與來自台灣的好友秦麗君小姐，合影於修院場地。

On September 21, 2013, Br. Peter with two good friends on the monastery grounds: (L-R) Mona Alerte, Connie Guc and Br. Peter.

2013年9月21日，筆者與兩位好友合影於修院場地：（左起）莫娜‧亞勒爾特、倪美玲和筆者。

296

November 28, 1984, after having victoriously walked out the prison, passed through the Iron Curtain and honorably returned to the original monastery, reestablished at Valyermo in the USA, I was seated beside Fr. Prior John Borgerding at the following midday great banquet of the whole community.

1984年11月28日，在勝利地跨出監獄，穿越鐵幕，並且還榮幸地返回重建於美國化野漠的原修院後，筆者於次日中午的全修院盛大的歡迎宴會上，就坐於若望‧博杰爾丁院長身旁。

In the morning, October 31, 1986, Fr. Adrian Nocent, O.S.B., drove and led us, five visitors from afar, from The Collegio Di Sant'Anselmo in Rome, to a pilgrimage to Subiaco. We were attending Mass in front of the altar set up in the grotto of St. Benedict's hermitage and beside his Statne.

1986年10月31日清晨，艾德里安‧諾森神父由羅馬聖安瑟而莫學院，開車帶領我們五名遠客往朝蘇比亞角，並在設置於聖本篤隱居的巖穴內和他的雕像旁的祭臺前望了彌撒。

89. 化野漠聖堂
新穎的宗教舞蹈

攤破浣溪沙
（山花子）
聖安德肋修院
1985 年 8 月 24 日

莊重輕盈美舞姿，
聖經意味細尋思。
伴樂歌聲關不住，
夜空飛！

堂內燈光星月映，
終場齊舞眾何怡！
七十妹兄同譜寫——
頌**神**詩！

註：像以往十二年一樣，為結束一週來的夏季
　　宗教舞蹈講座，卡爾拉・德索拉女士，於
　　今晚夜課經後八時半至九時半，在聖堂內
　　指揮了一場宗教舞蹈。三十位舞蹈者，表
　　演了諸如主顯節的光輝和加納婚筵上的奇
　　蹟之類的一些福音經書上的動人情景。

89.   A New Sacred Dance In Valyermo Chapel

To the Tune of Shan Hua Zi
(The Mountain Flowers)
St. Andrew's Priory
August 24, 1985

The dancers' gestures —
Solemn, lithe, graceful;
The significance of the Biblical passages —
Meditated and expressed.
The musical accompaniment, the songs
Unwilling to be enclosed,
Fly up to the night sky!

The lights of the chapel reflect
The shining of the stars and the moon.
How joyful are we all,
Arising, dancing together
To conclude the performance!
Seventy sisters and brothers
Compose in unison
A hymn of praise to God!

Note: As in the past 12 years, to conclude the one-week summer workshop on sacred dance, Ms. Carla DeSola directed a sacred dance in the chapel after Vigils from 8:30 to 9:30 pm. The thirty dancers performed some moving scenes from the Gospels, such as the radiance of the Epiphany and the miracle during the wedding at Cana.

90. 望羅杰・彌額爾・馬洪尼 總主教的大禮彌撒

漁家傲
聖安德肋修院
1985 年 9 月 7 日

銀髮樞機辭職務，
接班壯志姿英武。
聖母名城歌又舞。
修士女，
兩千往賀宏堂聚。

期望答詞金玉語，
讚歌祈禱聞**天父**。
美景秋光新樂譜。
天國路，
群羊隨牧同奔赴。

註：1985 年 9 月 4 日，羅杰・彌額爾・馬洪尼
鈞座，以四十九歲之年，繼七十五高齡的
弟茂德・曼寧樞機鈞座任洛杉磯第四任總
主教。今天他邀請了總教區內諸修會團體
的修士、修女前來聖維碧安娜主教座堂，
參與大禮彌撒，分享其樂。

90. Attendance At The Pontifical Mass Of Archbishop Roger Michael Mahony

To the Tune of Yu Jia Ao
(Fisherman's Pride)
St. Andrew's Priory
September 7, 1985

The silver-haired Cardinal
Resigned his good office;
He who comes after him
Has great aspirations, heroic bearing.
The famous city of Our Lady is filled
With singing and dancing.
Religious Brothers and Sisters,
Two thousand,
Have gathered at the grand Cathedral
To honor him.

Both petitions and responses —
Words of gold and jade.
Chants and prayers ascend
To the ears of our Heavenly Father.
The scene, shining in the autumn sun,
Scores a new music.
On the road leading to the Kingdom of Heaven
The sheep will follow their Shepherd in unison.

Note: On September 4, 1985, His Excellency Roger Michael Mahony, age 49,
succeeded His Eminence Cardinal Timothy Manning, aged 75, as the Fourth
Archbishop of Los Angeles. Today he invited the religious of all foundations in
the Archdiocese to come to the Cathedral of St. Vibiana for the Pontifical Mass
and to share his joy.

91. 化野漠廿九屆秋節

漁家傲
聖安德肋修院
1985 年 9 月 29 日

沙漠荒山經改造，
藍天綠地秋光好。
慶祝良辰遊客到。
多熱鬧，
清池碧樹齊歡笑。

聖祭獻呈天昊昊，
餘音雅樂樑縈繞，
息唱停鳴枝上鳥。
秋月皎，
舉頭欣賞**嫦娥**貌！

註：今天適逢農曆八月十五日，也是傳
統的中國中秋節。在這節日期間，
人們喜歡吃「月餅」，望「滿月」。

91.   The 29th Fall Festival
At Valyermo

To the Tune of Yu Jia Ao
(Fisherman's Pride)
St. Andrew's Priory
September 29, 1985

Desert and barren hills transformed;
The beauty of autumn is around us:
Sky blue,
Earth green.
Visitors come to celebrate the bright day,
So lively and exciting.
The clear lake
And green trees
Look happy and smiling.

The Holy Sacrifice is offered to Heaven,
Agreeable music of hymns lingers in the air;
Even the birds stop singing in the branches.
The autumn moon—
Clear and bright,
I raise my head to enjoy
The appearance of its celestial spirit, Chang E!

Note: Today is also the traditional Chinese Mid-Autumn Festival.It falls on the 15th
day of the 8th lunar month. During the Festival people enjoy eating the "moon
cake" and watching the "full moon".

92. 祝賀黃國維神父
棄俗修道四十五週年

西江月
俄勒岡州俄勒岡市
1985 年 10 月 3 日

信奉真神將冠，
無何看破紅塵。
離家背井樂園奔，
壯志盈懷興奮。

治學修身勤勉，
牧靈授業歡欣。
未來燦爛定如昀，
祝願高歌猛進！

註：黃神父在皈依兩年後，離開香港，
　　前往四川省南充縣，進入了本篤會
　　西山修院。1945 年，他奉派來美國
　　攻讀神學。1963 年至 1981 年間，他
　　任教於俄勒岡州波特蘭大學。

92.   Congratulations Upon The 45th Anniversary Of Fr. Bernard Huang Guowei's Leaving The Secular For The Monastic Life

To the Tune of Xi Jiang Yue
(Moon over the West River)
Oregon City, Oregon
October 3, 1985

You began to believe in the true God
At the age of nineteen;
You saw through the vanities of the mortal world
Shortly afterward.
You left your family and native place
For the monastery, a paradise,
With lofty ideals,
With an ardent heart.

You were diligent
In studying,
In cultivating moral character;
You have enjoyed the work
Of parochial ministry and teaching.
Your future will be
As brilliant as the sunshine.
My wishes to you —
Advancing along your way vigorously,
Singing joyful songs!

Note: Two years after his conversion, Fr. Bernard left Hong Kong for the Benedictine
Xishan Monastery in Nanchong County, Sichuan Province.
In 1945 he was sent to the USA to study theology. From 1963 to 1981
he taught at the University of Portland, Oregon.

93. 初訪
聖瑪爾定大修院

浪淘沙
華盛頓州萊西聖瑪爾定大修院
1985 年 10 月 13 日

忽雨忽晴空，
雨遇長虹，
飛車俄頃抵仙宮。
幽雅樓房何處匿？
蔥翠林中。

寂夜望蒼穹，
恬適心胸，
追求主愛樂融融。
堂內讚歌傳四野，
和日清風。

93.   The First Visit
To St. Martin's Abbey

To the Tune of Lang Tao Sha
(Wave-Washed Sands)
St. Martin's Abbey, Lacey, Washington
October 13, 1985

In the sky,
Raining one moment, sunny the next,
Seeing the long rainbow twice,
Speeding as if flying,
Our car soon reached a fairyland.
Its tranquil and elegant buildings,
Where do they hide themselves?
In the green woods.

Staring up at the heavens
In the quiet night,
With peaceful and comforted hearts,
The monks delight in seeking the love of the Lord.
The chants of praise spread
From the chapel to the surrounding country,
Like the warm sunshine,
Like the lovely breeze.

94. 感恩節歌

西江月
俄勒岡市克拉克瑪社區學院
1985 年 10 月 15 日

負笈**俄城**榮幸，

「**感恩歌**」曲清新。

樂音輕快味津津，

學唱心情振奮。

爾等相親敬主，

豐收慶祝歡欣。

年年愈謝主深恩，

必愈興隆國運！

註：今日在第二節課中，「**英語為第二語言**」班
裡的一位老師洛蕾·哈蒂爾小姐，教我們
這些新來的外國學生唱了一首「**感恩節
歌**」。歌詞全文如下：

火雞冰箱裡，餡餅廚架上，
炸麵食品室：我不禁神往！
我如進廚房，定會聽人講：
「明天**感恩節**，屆時即可享！」

94.   The Thanksgiving Song

To the Tune of Xi Jiang Yue
(Moon over the West River)
Clackamas Community College, Oregon City
October 15, 1985

I feel honored
To carry my schoolbag to Oregon City.
The *Thanksgiving Song*
Has a pure and fresh melody.
The song, lively and interesting,
Lifts my spirits
As I learn to sing.

You, American people,
Are so dear to each other,
So worshipful of the Lord
As to be able to celebrate
Your bumper harvest with jubilation.
The more grateful you are to Him
For His vast bounties year after year,
The more prosperous your country will be!

Note: Today, during the second class, Miss Lori Hartill, one of our teachers in the
English as a Second Language (ESL) program, taught a *Thanksgiving Song* to us,
her new foreign students. The text of its words reads as follows:

There's a turkey in the ice box,
There are pies upon the shelf,
There are donuts in the pantry.
But I cannot help myself!
If I step into the kitchen,
I will hear somebody say,
"You just wait until tomorrow.
It will be Thanksgiving Day!"

95. 三訪聖雅各伯堂
趙朝繼本堂神父

七絕
俄勒岡州莫拉拉
1985 年 11 月 3 日

公在異鄉長牧羊，
涼秋造訪似春陽。
滿腔慨歎呈文稿；
故國何時見主光？

95.   Three Visits To
Fr. Joseph Zhao,
Pastor Of St. James Church

In the Poetic Style of Qijue
Molalla, Oregon
November 3, 1985

You have tended the divine sheep
In this strange land for a long time.
On my visits to you
I have felt a spring light,
Though it is the cool fall.
I present my manuscripts to you
With a full heart.
Our dear Motherland,
When will she see the light of the Lord?

96. 重訪
聖瑪爾定大修院

西江月
萊西聖瑪爾定大修院
1985 年 11 月 9 日
都爾·聖瑪爾定主教節前二日

節日歡欣分享，
疾馳北上征程。
識途老馬一身輕，
愉快重遊心境。

景色風光綺麗，
禱聲友愛虔誠。
惠鄰益世主榮增，
望育於斯賢聖！

96.   Another Visit
To St. Martin's Abbey

To the Tune of Xi Jiang Yue
(Moon over the West River)
St. Martin's Abbey, Lacey
November 9, 1985
Two days before the Feast of St. Martin of Tours, Bishop

To share the joy of your feast day,
We speed fast on the road north.
As an old horse knowing the way,
I feel relaxed.
In a cheerful frame of mind,
I visit you once more.

The scenery and sights of your Abbey —
Gorgeous,
Your prayers and fraternity —
Sincere.
To benefit your neighbors,
To profit the world,
To give added glory to the Lord,
May saints be fostered here!

97. 訪西雅圖
吉朝芳蒙席和中國教友

七絕
華盛頓州西雅圖
1985 年 11 月 10 日

萊西朝別沐秋陽，

百里飛馳到北方。

貞女山堂思聖母，

同胞喜識在他鄉。

97.   A Visit To Msgr. John Ji And Chinese Catholics In Seattle

In the Poetic Style of Qijue
Seattle, Washington
November 10, 1985

Bidding farewell to Lacey in the morning,
We enjoy the autumn sun;
We travel rapidly north
For a hundred miles.
In the Mount Virgin Church
Thinking of Our Lady,
I am full of joy
In meeting my compatriots
In an alien land.

98. 波特蘭市

五絕
俄勒岡州波特蘭
1985 年 11 月 10 日

落日留霞蔚，
華都萬盞燈。
光輝相映妙，
凝望壯懷興。

註：自西雅圖返俄勒岡市途中，正日落黃昏，
　　遙望此美麗城市，得即景詩一首。

98.   **Portland**

In the Poetic Style of Wujue
Portland, Oregon,
November 10, 1985

While the setting sun
Is leaving its glow behind,
In the beautiful city
Ten thousand lamps are shining.
The radiance from heaven and earth
Reflects one to another.
Gazing at this wonderful scene,
Great aspirations rise in my heart.

Note: An extempore verse while looking at the beautiful
city in the distance at dusk on the way back from Seattle
to Oregon City.

99. 喜雪

浪淘沙
俄勒岡市
1985 年 11 月 22 日

夢斷鬧鐘喧，
起望窗前，
驚奇白絮滿坤乾。
純潔光輝銀世界，
豈已今天？

「瑞雪兆豐年」：
農諺真詮，
中原自古已流傳。
願此自由之國度：
物茂民歡！

99.   A Welcome Snowfall

To the Tune of Lang Tao Sha
(Wave-Washed Sands)
Oregon City
November 22, 1985

My dream is shattered
At the sound of the alarm clock.
I get up and look outside the window,
I am surprised to see heaven and earth
Full of white cotton wadding.
A pure and brilliant silver world,
Has it already come today?

"A timely snow promises a good harvest."
This farmer's proverb is true,
And is handed down
Through each generation in China.
My wish for this country of freedom—
May the crops flourish,
And may the people enjoy happiness!

100. 來美一年書懷

浣溪沙
克拉克瑪社區學院
1985 年 11 月 27 日

歷史長河僅瞬間，

戰**龍赤縣**卅三年！

凱歌再唱滿心歡。

師長同窗來四面。

一堂聚首盡開顏。

思源飲水謝**蒼天**！

註：明天是**感恩節**，今日中午，本班
　　師生於課堂聚餐慶祝。

100.　Some Feelings Since Arrival In The United States One Year Ago

To the Tune of Huan Xi Sha
(Yarn Washed in the Stream)
Clackamas Community College
November 27, 1985

But a drop
In the great river of history—
My thirty-three years
In the fight against the Dragon in China!
Full of joy,
I sing a song of victory once more.

Teachers and classmates from all quarters,
We gather here together,
Rejoicing and laughing.
While drinking water,
Thinking of its source,
I express my gratitude to Heaven!

Note: Tomorrow will be Thanksgiving Day. Earlier today, the teachers and students
of our class had a dinner in the classroom at noon to celebrate.

101. 天使山大修院
難忘的訪問

卜算子
俄勒岡州聖本篤天使山大修院
1985 年 11 月 28 日

名仰半年前，
腦際時縈繞。
院照凝神注視歡，
急欲乘風到。

勝地現身臨，
喜看奇風貌。
已育諸賢百載中，
來聖知多少？

註：我們聖安德肋修院的若蘇厄・李修
　　士，給我寄來了這些照片，他當時
　　正在天使山大修院攻讀神學。

101.   Unforgettable Visit To Mt. Angel Abbey

To the Tune of Pu Suan Zi
(The Fortune Teller)
Mt. Angel Abbey, St. Benedict, Oregon
November 28, 1985

I admired the name of your Abbey
Half a year ago,
From time to time
It lingered in my mind.
I looked with pleasure
At pictures of the Abbey,
I was eager
To ride the wind to it.

Now I am at this beautiful place;
I rejoice in its wonderful sights.
For a century
You have nurtured many virtues,
How many future saints will you have?

Note: Br. Joshua Lee of St. Andrew's Priory, who was studying theology at
Mt. Angel Abbey, sent me these pictures.

102. 詠雪

江南春
天使山大修院
1985 年 11 月 30 日

雲淡淡，
世茫茫，
銀花飛四面；
修院放霞光。
乾坤如玉多奇偉！
萬類同歌天地王！

註：早餐畢，大雪降；
　　雪不期而遇，爰填詞以讚。

102. **Ode To Snow**

To the Tune of Jiang Nan Chun
(Spring in the South of the River)
Mt. Angel Abbey
November 30, 1985

The clouds—pale,

The world—blurred.

Silver flowers are flying on all sides,

The monastery shines like rays of sunlight.

What a wonderful sight:

This universe like jade!

All manner of beings sing in unison

The praises of the King of heaven and earth!

Note: It began to snow heavily after breakfast.
The unexpected snow inspired me to compose a poem in its praise.

103. 告別
天使山大修院

減字木蘭花
天使山大修院
1985 年 12 月 3 日

周圍俯視，
鶴立雞群修院峙。
遠眺窗前，
夜有千燈畫雪山。

兩尊雕像，
挺屹園中光彩放。
惜別悠悠，
雕像凝眸望再遊。

註：**聖心雕像**和**天使雕像**，
　　分立於修院聖堂兩側。

103.   Saying Goodbye
To Mt. Angel Abbey

To the Tune of Jian Zi Mulan Hua
(The Magnolia)
Mt. Angel Abbey
December 3, 1985

Surveying all from its height,
The Abbey stands erect
Like a crane among chickens.
Through its windows I see in the distance
At night, a thousand lamps,
In the day, snowcapped mountains.

Two statues
Standing upright,
Shine brilliantly in the garden.
I feel distressed to depart,
I long for a second visit to contemplate them.

Note: The Sacred Heart Statue and the Angel Statue are on
either side of the Abbey Church.

104. 三訪
聖瑪爾定大修院

生查子
萊西聖瑪爾定大修院
1985 年 12 月 7 日

影留初訪時，
雕像**貞娘**處。
無玷節恭迎，
今且衷情訴。

慈祥**聖母**求，
請禱**懷中主**：
雨露與陽光，
常賜斯園圃！

註：10 月 13 日，尼爾・羅特副院長曾為
　　拍照二張於**法蒂瑪聖母雕像**旁。聖母
　　始胎無原罪慶節，今年是在 12 月 7
　　日星期六。

104.   The Third Visit To St. Martin's Abbey

To the Tune of Sheng Zha Zi
(Fresh Berries)
St. Martin's Abbey, Lacey
December 7, 1985

On my first visit,
For a sounenir, I was photographed
Beside the statue of the Virgin Mother.
Welcoming the Solemnity
Of her Immaculate Conception,
Today I pour out my heart to her.

I beseech you, loving Holy Mother,
To pray to the Lord in your arms
To bestow rain, dew and sunlight
On this garden always!

Note: Fr. Subprior Neal G. Roth, O.S.B., took two pictures of me beside the Statue of Our Lady of Fatima on October 13. This year the Solemnity of the Immaculate Conception of Our Lady falls on December 7, Saturday.

105. 祝賀
洛雷塔・瑪都莉奇博士
獻身於主廿五週年

憶秦娥
俄勒岡市
1985 年 12 月 8 日

胸超脫，
妙齡十九心情熱。
心情熱，
耶穌愛慕，
獻貞愉悅！

建成新會遵規則，
唸經教學甜年月。
甜年月，
追求**天國**，
卓然風格！

105. Congratulating Dr. Loretta Matulich On The 25th Anniversary Of Her Dedication To The Lord

To the Tune of Yi Qin E
(Remembering the Beauty of Qin)
Oregon City
December 8, 1985

Aiming high,
At the young age of nineteen,
You, Loretta, had an ardent heart.
With an ardent heart
You loved Jesus,
Dedicating your virginity to Him with joy!

Having founded a new religious community,
You created and followed its rule.
Devoted to praying and teaching,
Your months and years are sweet.
In sweet months and years
You seek the Kingdom of Heaven
In a unique way!

106. 離別
克拉克瑪社區學院

漁家傲
俄勒岡市
1985 年 12 月 13 日

西北寒潮來逞暴，
狂飆赤縣長呼嘯。
卻道疾風知勁草！
誰曾料：
機緣竟獲聆師教?!

俄勒岡城天氣好，
校園雨潤陽光照，
座座樓房青樹繞。
洵懊惱：
驪歌聞唱枝頭鳥！

106.   Farewell To Clackamas Community College

To the Tune of Yu Jia Ao
(Fisherman's Pride)
Oregon City
December 13, 1985

Since from the northwest
The cold wave came and wreaked havoc,
The storm has roared over China
Through the years.
Yet, the force of the wind
Reveals the strength of the grass!
Who could have ever foreseen —
I would have the opportunity of hearing
The lectures of the teachers here?

The weather is agreeable in Oregon City;
The campus is moistened by rain,
Shining in the sun.
Green trees surround every building.
Really sad
To hear the birds
Sing a parting song from the branches!

107. 致謝告辭
黃國維神父和
洛雷塔 · 瑪都莉奇博士

蝶戀花
俄勒岡市
1985 年 12 月 14 日

得獲自由曾倚靠，
喜渡汪洋昔日籠中鳥。
情意何深成譯稿！
謝忱臨別言難表。

千里迢迢完稿道，
馬不停蹄矢志朝前跑。
付梓之期唯主曉
屆時鴻雁傳音耗！

註：過去通過黃神父和洛雷塔，我自化野漢本
修院獲得了離開**赤色中國**的必要幫助。今年
10 月 2 日，他們又邀請我來俄勒岡市學習
英文，並助我將文稿譯成英文。他們兩位
同為**天主之僕團體**的創立人。洛雷塔是克拉
克瑪社區學院的英文教師。

107.   Saying Thanks And Goodbye To Fr. Bernard Huang Guowei And Dr. Loretta Matulich

To the Tune of Die Lian Hua
(Butterflies Courting Flowers)
Oregon City
December 14, 1985

By means of your support,
I have gained my freedom;
With great joy
The former caged bird crossed the ocean.
How good and gracious of you
To translate my manuscript!
As we part
I am unable
To express my feelings of gratitude.

Only after a thousand-mile journey
Will the manuscript be completed;
I am resolved to make this journey
Without interruption,
Like a running horse unwilling to halt.
Only the Lord knows
The time of publication;
At the appointed time
The swan will bring you the news!

Note: Through Fr. Bernard and Loretta, I obtained the help from my monastery at
Valyermo necessary to leave Red China. On October 2, they invited me to come to
Oregon City to study English and with their assistance, to get my manuscript
translated into English. They were the founders of the Community of the Servant of God.
Loretta is an English teacher in Clackamas Community College.

108. 和葉素貞修女

七絕
聖安德肋修院
1986 年 9 月 18 日

主愛高歌來美歡，

榮臨盛會識英賢。

獻身事主扶鄰里，

燦爛光輝十六年！

註：北美華人聖職聯會，上月在加州阿罕布拉
市加爾默羅女修院的退省院召開了第六屆
年會。葉修女當時是加州小凡城耶穌聖心
女修院的中國修女，現刻則為該會台灣台
北分院院長。她的原詩如次：

賀周修士
戰勝共產黨迫害

七絕
1986 年 9 月 12 日

奮戰妖魔三十年，

詩文字字扣心弦。

忠貞激勵中腸熱，

為主人靈力救焉！

108.   An Answer To Sr. Grace Ye Suzhen's Poem

In the Poetic Style of Qijue
St. Andrew's Priory
September 18, 1986

Singing aloud the love of the Lord,
I was glad to come to the United States.
I felt honored
To attend the great Convention,
To meet you, an exemplary woman.

You have dedicated your life
To serve God,
To help your neighbor.
Your last sixteen years
Have been brilliant!

Note: The Sixth Annual Convention of the Chinese Clergy and Religious Association
in North America was held last month at the retreat house of the
Carmelite Sisters in Alhambra, CA. Sr. Grace was then a
Chinese Sister of the Sacred Heart Convent in Solvang, CA, and is now the superior of
Taipei Mission, Taiwan. Her poem reads as follows:

Congratulations Upon Br. Peter Zhou's Victory Over Communist Persecution

In the Poetic Style of Qijue
September 12, 1986

You courageously fought the Devil for thirty years.
Every word of your poems and articles
Tugs at my heart-strings.
Your loyalty stirs my emotions;
I strive ever more energetically to win souls for the Lord!

109. 首途羅馬——
從洛杉磯到紐約

西江月
紐約
1986 年 10 月 15 日

聖母名都又到，
前年美夢重溫。
昔來樂土滿歡欣，
今赴**聖城**興奮。

瑰麗國邦橫越，
輝煌秋景如春。
姿容甫整「**自由神**」，
新貌難瞻遺恨！

註：比利時瑪利亞－德肋撒・托洛太太
和安納－瑪利亞・洛雷小姐的資
助，使駱愷騰神父和我有了可能前
往羅馬，晉謁教宗若望保祿二世。
昨日下午我們離開修院，宿於鄰近
洛杉磯國際機場的貝蒂・吉尼特太
太家。

109.   Starting A Trip To Rome –
From Los Angeles To New York

To the Tune of Xi Jiang Yue
(Moon over the West River)
New York
October 15, 1986

Once again
Getting to the celebrated city of Our Lady,
I relive my wonderful dream
Of the year before last.
At that time I greatly rejoiced
To come to this land of happiness,
And now I am excited
At departing for the Holy City.

Crossing this grand, beautiful country,
I see the scenery of autumn
As splendid as that of spring.
The Statue of Liberty
Has just been refurbished;
A pity –
I am unable to witness its new look!

Note: The financial help of Mrs. Marie-Therese Thoreau and Miss Anne-Marie
Loriers of Belgium made it possible for Fr. Gaetan Loriers and me to go to Rome to visit
Pope John Paul II. Yesterday afternoon we left the Priory. We stayed overnight
at the home of Mrs. Betty Guignet close to Los Angeles International Airport.

110. 倫敦

七絕
倫敦
1986 年 10 月 16 日

泰晤飛臨見曙光，

莎翁伯達饗芬芳。

大英帝國成陳跡，

悲嘆京華威已亡！

註：威廉・莎士比亞（1564-1616）是英國詩人
　　和劇作家，可敬者聖伯達（673-735）是英
　　國神學家、歷史學家和教會聖師。

110.   **London**

In the Poetic Style of Qijue
London
October 16, 1986

The early rays of the sun shine
As we fly to the Thames River.
Shakespeare and Bede
Offer us their fragrance.
Since the Great British Empire
Is a thing of the past,
The capital sighs —
Her power withered away!

Note: William Shakespeare (1564-1616),
English poet and dramatist;
St. Bede the Venerable (673-735),
English theologian and historian, and Doctor of the Church.

111. 抵布魯塞爾

浪淘沙
比利時布魯塞爾
1986 年 10 月 16 日

初渡太平洋，

欣喜如狂，

而今又越大西洋。

慈愛寵恩深且厚，

再謝穹蒼。

迎接動衷腸，

五友情長；

西風拂面送清涼。

盥畢鳳城秋雨裡，

益燦容光。

註：今晨 8 點 20 分，托洛太太、洛雷小
　　姐、達夫雷老先生和巴普斯夫婦，
　　曾來首都機場相迎。

111.   **Arriving In Brussels**

To the Tune of Lang Tao Sha
(Wave-Washed Sands)
Brussels, Belgium
October 16, 1986

When I flew across the Pacific Ocean,

I was wild with joy;

Today, I have crossed another ocean — the Atlantic.

For His loving-kindness,

For His abundant blessings

I am grateful to Heaven once more.

Greeting us on arrival,

Five friends touch us

With their consideration,

With their affection.

The west breeze strokes our faces,

Refreshing us.

The capital has been washed by autumn rain,

Shining more brightly.

Note: At 8:20 this morning, we were greeted at the capital airport by Mrs. Marie-Therese Thoreau, Miss Anne-Marie Loriers, Mr. Leopold Davreux and Mr. and Mrs. Louis Baps.

112. 會晤
進修傳教人員

七絕
布魯日
1986 年 10 月 19 日

聚會精英自四方，
熱情壯志滿胸膛。
略陳經歷期同勉：
力照人前世界光！

註：今晚八時半，雷蒙德・洛莎神父帶
　　領駱愷騰神父和我到修院一間客
　　廳，會晤了來自非洲和中南美洲的
　　十四位神父和修女。

112.   A Meeting With Missionaries In Advanced Studies

In the Poetic Style of Qijue
Bruges
October 19, 1986

Exemplary souls from all quarters,
You have gathered here,
You are filled with zeal and high ideals.
I speak briefly of my experiences,
Hoping to encourage both you and myself.
Let us, as lights of the world,
Strive to shine before men!

Note: At 8:30 this evening Fr. Raymond Rosa led Fr. Gaetan Loriers and me
to one of the halls of Saint Andrew's Abbey to meet a group of 14 priests and sisters
from Africa, and Central and Latin America.

113. 初訪熱旺克爾肯聖安德肋大修院

七律
布魯日
1986 年 10 月 18-20 日

幾度夢魂遊母院，

今知終熟昔黃粱！

林中樓宇容顏秀，

世外桃源景色香。

遺物**陸公**瞻仰喜，

芳蹤賢哲步隨昂。

秋風瑟瑟**長城**凜，

子院何時返故鄉？

註：陸徵祥神父，1871 年生於中國上海。
　　從清朝末葉至 1927 年，他先後出任
　　過公使、國務總理和外交總長。1927
　　年 7 月，他進入了這座大修院；1949
　　年 1 月 15 日，他以七十有九的高齡
　　逝世。在去世前三年，他曾被教宗庇
　　護十二世任命為根特聖伯多祿修院
　　名譽大院長。

113.   The First Visit To
The Sint-Andriesabdij, Zevenkerken

In the Poetic Style of Qilu
Bruges
October 18-20, 1986

Several times I dreamed of
Visiting here the motherhouse;
Now I come to know
That the fulfillment of those dreams
Is true at long last!
The buildings of the Abbey—
Beautiful amidst the woods,
The scenery of the haven of peace—
Sweet and captivating.

I look with reverence and joy
At the things left behind
By Fr. Peter Celestine Lu;
I will courageously follow
In the footsteps
Of that virtuous and wise monk.
The Great Wall is still cold
In the rustling autumn wind,
When will the daughter Priory
Go back to her native place?

Note: Fr. Peter Celestine Lu Zhengxiang, O.S.B., born in Shanghai, China, in 1871,
served as envoy, Prime Minister of the State Council and Minister of Foreign Affairs
from the last years of the Qing Dynasty until 1927. He entered this Abbey in
July1927. He died on January 15, 1949, at the age of 79. Three years before his death,
he was appointed the Titular Abbot of Saint-Pierre-de-Gand by Pope Pius XII.

114. 贈依撒伯爾

七絕
布魯日
1986 年 10 月 20 日

沃土良疇繞爾家，
盛情厚誼勝朝霞。
金風細雨無寒意，
慈主虔求育厥花！

註：迪德瓦爾太太請我於午飯前，
為其十歲女兒賦詩一首。

114.   A Poem For Isabelle

In the Poetic Style of Qijue
Bruges
October 20, 1986

Fertile soil and good farmland
Surround your house.
Your warm hospitality pleases us more
Than the rosy clouds of dawn.
Indoors there is no chill
In spite of autumn wind and fine rain.
We earnestly pray the loving Lord on high
To nurture you, His flower, here below!

Note: Mrs. d'Ydewalle asked me to compose a poem before lunch
for her daughter of ten.

115. 初訪克勒朗德
聖安德肋修院

浣溪沙
奧蒂尼
1986 年 10 月 21 日

曲逕通幽至客廳，
千言難盡內心情。
窗前有雨卻無聲！

斬棘披荊逾十載，
桃源世外乃成形。
引來尋主好心靈！

115.   The First Visit To The Prieure Saint-Andre De Clerlande

To the Tune of Huan Xi Sha
(Yarn Washed in the Stream)
Ottignies
October 21, 1986

A winding path through a secluded spot
Leads me to your parlor.
In a thousand words
I would not be able
To express my inner feelings.
Though it is raining outside the windows,
There is no sound inside!

You have worked hard
For over ten years
To make a haven of peace.
It has taken shape,
And has attracted good souls
To seek the Lord!

116. 訪馬爾蘇
聖本篤大修院和分會長
盘博羅削‧瓦特萊特大院長

清平樂
德內市馬爾蘇
1986 年 10 月 22 日

途中風雨，
院內溫而煦。
宏宇華堂猶穩固，
儘歷百年寒暑。

筆耕兩夏園丁，
鬥爭紀要恭呈！
風雨雞鳴故國，
何年何月天晴？

116.   A Visit To The Abbaye Saint-Benoit De Maredsous And Abbot President Ambroise Watelet, O.S.B.

To the Tune of Qing Ping Yue
(The Qing Ping Song)
Maredsous, Denee
October 22, 1986

Wind and rain on the way,
Mild and warm in the Abbey.
The great buildings and the magnificent church —
Still firm,
Despite the cold and heat
Of a hundred years.

As a gardener,
I have ploughed with the pen
For two summers;
Now to you,
Father Abbot Ambroise,
Reverently I present
The product — the record of my struggle!
In my mother country
The wind blows,
The rain falls,
The cocks crow.
In what year,
In what month
Will the weather clear?

117. 獻給瑪利亞——
德肋撒・托洛太太

江南春
列日附近的昂布爾
1986 年 10 月 23 日

房雅靜，
草芳青。
塵居心向上，
身健志崢嶸。
耶穌爾愛於言行，
天朗風和辭典型！

117.   A Poem Dedicated To Mrs. Marie-Therese Thoreau

To the Tune of Jiang Nan Chun
(Spring in the South of the River)
Embourg near Liege
October 23, 1986

Your house, tasteful and quiet,
Is surrounded with green, fragrant grass.
You live in this mortal world
With a heart lifted up to the Heavens;
You are hale and hearty, aiming high.
You love Jesus with words, with actions;
In the clear sky,
In the gentle wind
We bid farewell to you,
An example for us!

118. 離布魯塞爾
赴羅馬

減字木蘭花
布魯塞爾
1986 年 10 月 25 日

四人載運，
晨霧破開車挺進。
奔向何方？
羅馬城中梵蒂岡。

稿言志氣，
恃主窖中堅未碎！
切盼殊榮：
著作親身聖父呈。

註：今晨八時半，瑪利亞—德肋撒‧托
洛太太、她的女兒和我們大家的司
機雅妮小姐、駱愷騰神父和我，啟
程前往羅馬。

118.   Leaving Brussels For Rome

To the Tune of Jian Zi Mulan Hua
(The Magnolia)
Brussels
October 25, 1986

Carrying four of us,
The rushing car ploughs
Through the morning fog.
To what place is it hurrying?
The Vatican
In the city of Rome.

My manuscript describes
A will relying firmly on God
Not to be crushed in bitter circumstances!
I am eagerly awaiting
The unusual honor of offering personally
The writings to the Holy Father.

Note: At 8:30 am, Mrs. Marie-Therese Thoreau, Miss Agnes, her daughter
and our driver, Fr. Gaetan Loriers and I started on our journey to Rome.

119. 過盧森堡
大公國

如夢令
盧森堡
1986 年 10 月 25 日

公國蔥蘢興旺，
愉快安寧爽朗。
入境甫飛車，
頓覺心情舒暢。
舒暢，
舒暢，
轉瞬驪歌須唱！

119.   Passing Through
The Grand Duchy
Of Luxemburg

To the Tune of Ru Meng Ling
(Like a Dream)
Luxemburg
October 25, 1986

The Duchy —

Green and luxuriant,

Happy, quiet and clear.

The car rushing into the country,

I feel cheerful.

Cheerful,

Cheerful,

The farewell song

Should be sung,

In the twinkling of an eye!

120. 入法國

西江月
法國
1986 年 10 月 25 日

車入自由疆土，
途逢風雨陰晴。
朝雲晦暗晚霞明，
世界變遷無定！

碧落驚雷頻震，
依然水秀山清。
黎民勤穎志如鵬，
祝願永生馳騁！

120.   **Entering France**

To the Tune of Xi Jiang Yue
(Moon over the West River)
France
October 25, 1986

The car enters a land of freedom;
We are en route —
The weather now windy, now rainy,
Now overcast, now sunny.
The morning clouds — gloomy,
The sunset glow — clear:
The world — changeable and uncertain!

Despite terrifying thunder repeatedly in the sky,
The waters remain clear,
The hills green.
The French people — industrious, talented
With ideals high like the eagle;
May they ever run on the way of everlasting life!

121. 奧特孔布
本篤會修院一宿

菩薩蠻
法國薩瓦省辛德雷
1986 年 10 月 26 日

里昂昨抵天將暮，
陌生旅客初迷路。
修士匿何山？
難尋於夜間！

歸途晨囑訪，
院長深情饗。
臨別四圍看，
湖光映眼前。

121.   An Overnight Stay At The Benedictine Abbey Of Hautecombe

To the Tune of Pusa Man
(Strange Goddess)
Chindrieux, Savoie, France
October 26, 1986

It was getting dark
When we arrived in Lyons last evening.
At first, we strangers lost our way.
In what mountain
Did the monks hide themselves?
To find them at dusk —
Difficult!

This morning Fr. Abbot asked us
To pay another visit on our way back;
He showed his sincere friendship.
At the time of departure
We take a last look around;
The light reflected on the lake
Shines before our eyes.

122. 阿爾卑斯山

減字木蘭花
阿爾卑斯山
1986 年 10 月 26 日

盤旋而上，
車迫山巔奇景望：
白雪茫茫，
秋水藍湖映日光。

風光壯麗，
阿爾巍巍堪敬畏。
遊客難逢——
路滑秋深刺骨風。

122.   The Alps

To the Tune of Jian Zi Mulan Hua
(The Magnolia)
The Alps
October 26, 1986

Winding up the road,
Our car approaches
The top of the mountain.
We look out over a wonderful scene,
White snow — endless,
Blue lake — antumn waters:
Mirroring the sunshine.

The view is spectacular,
We are awed
By the grandeur of the Alps.
We meet few other tourists —
The road is slippery,
It is late fall,
Cold wind pierces to the bone.

123. 米蘭

七絕
義大利米蘭
1986 年 10 月 26 日

古邑名城心嚮往，

華燈初上見容光。

言傳身教望先哲，

接踵而歸迷路羊！

註：我們於晚間六時半到達這座城市。
　　聖盎博羅削（339-397）是米蘭主教、
　　教會聖師、作家和作曲家。他促成
　　了聖奧斯定的回頭歸正。

123. **Milan**

In the Poetic Style of Qijue
Milan, Italy
October 26, 1986

I have yearned in my heart for you,
Ancient and famous city!
This evening
I see your face
Through your brightened streets with light and color.
We hope
The past sage will continue to teach the people
By personal example as well as verbal instruction
So that
The stray sheep may return in great number!

Note: We arrived in this city at 6:30 pm. Saint Ambrose (339-397)
was Bishop of Milan, Doctor of the Church, author and composer,
and contributed to the conversion of St. Augustine.

124. 夜宿本篤會
維波爾東女修院

蝶戀花
米蘭
1986 年 10 月 27 日

暮靄沉沉來昨晚，
破曉醒來困倦如雲散。
日上三竿秋色絢，
征程重上車如箭。

八百多年嘗冷暖，
面皺增多修院仍康健。
上主光輝猶體現，
堂中古畫生機顯！

註：在清早的全院彌撒中，駐院專職神
　　父饗我以雅座；臨別時，大院長復
　　贈我們院刊，人手一冊。

124. Stayover
At The Benedictine Convent,
L'Abbazia Di Viboldone

To the Tune of Die Lian Hua
(Butterflies Courting Flowers)
Milan
October 27, 1986

Late last evening
In the heavy mists
We arrived at the convent.
This morning when I woke at dawn,
My fatigue had vanished
As passing clouds.
The day is advancing,
The autumn scenery is bright;
As we continue our journey,
Our car again flies like an arrow.

Having suffered cold and heat
For over eight hundred years,
The Abbey is still in good health,
Despite increasing wrinkles.
Continuing to reflect
The radiance of the Lord,
Ancient paintings in the church
Speak to the soul!

Note: The chaplain of the convent gave me an exceptional seat at the morning
conventual Mass. At our departure the Abbess presented each of
us with a copy of their abbatial brochure.

125. 羅馬吟

七律
羅馬
1986 年 10 月 27 日

名都歷史早聽聞，
梵蒂岡宮常有春。
先烈芳蹤猶勵眾，
奧皇帝國已成塵！
教堂隨處藏珍品，
公父全心救世人。
美夢當年今實現，
聖城來到此殘身！

註：我們於今晚五時半抵達羅馬。奧古
斯都・屋大維（公元前 63 —公元 14）
是羅馬帝國（公元前 30 —公元 476）
首任皇帝。

125.   A Song Of Rome

In the Poetic Style of Qilu
Rome
October 27, 1986

I learned long ago
The history of this celebrated city.
A constant spring blossoms
In the Vatican palaces.
The records of the martyrs here
Still encourage us,
While the empire of Augustus
Has turned to dust!

There are treasures
In all the churches,
The Universal Father seeks
The salvation of all men, heart and soul.
I live my former dream,
A mere pipe dream in those years;
Handicapped in body,
I am appearing in the Holy City!

Note: We arrived in Rome at 5:30 this evening. Augustus Octavian (63 B.C. - 14 A.D.)
was the first Emperor of the Roman Empire (30 B.C. - 476 A.D.).

126. 親瞻教宗
若望保祿二世神采
於其星期三接見群眾時

減字木蘭花
梵蒂岡
1986 年 10 月 29 日

廣場宏偉，
眾聖華雕常守衛。
燦爛秋光，
六萬教徒聚一堂。

語言七種，
善牧誨羊嘗使用。
慶獲良緣，
神采親瞻擁抱歡！

註：因著阿里維爾・拉凱神父的幫助，我獲
准於上午九時進入聖伯多祿廣場，就坐
前排。當教宗在兩個鐘頭的接見群眾告
終而走近我們時，我由分會領導人盎博
羅削・瓦特萊特大院長介紹給了他。

126. Personally Gazing On The Graceful Face Of Pope John Paul II During His Wednesday General Audience

To the Tune of Jian Zi Mulan Hua
(The Magnolia)
Vatican
October 29, 1986

The Square —
Great and magnificent,
Splendid statues of the saints —
Its constant guardians.
The sunlit scene of autumn — brilliant,
Sixty thousand faithful
Gather here today.

The good Shepherd
Instructs his flock,
Speaking seven different languages.
Having been given
This wonderful opportunity,
I am happy
To gaze on his glowing face
And to be embraced by him!

Note: With the help of Fr. Olivier Raquez, O.S.B., I was admitted to
Saint Peter's Square at 9:00 am and sat in the front row. I was
introduced by Fr. Abbot President Ambroise Watelet, O.S.B., to the Holy Father
as he approached us at the conclusion of the two-hour general audience.

127. 個別觀見
教宗若望保祿二世

定風波
梵蒂岡
1986 年 10 月 30 日

日出東方放彩光，
聖宮進謁喜洋洋。
樓上小堂洵壯麗，
聖祭，
虔誠莊重獻**穹蒼**。

傾聽留神看譯稿，
擁抱，
再回接見父慈祥。
和煦秋陽窗上映，
情景，
永生永世亦難忘！

註：由於昨天盎博羅削·瓦特萊特大院
　　長曾為求得宗座宮廷總管瑪爾定主
　　教的許可，我前往望了教宗若望保
　　祿二世於今晨七點半鐘，在其私人
　　小堂所舉行的彌撒。彌撒後，當我
　　們這批約四十名與祭者在觀見室晉
　　謁時，我向教宗呈交了《東方黎明在
　　望》的英文譯稿和賦於獄中有關他的
　　四首詩詞。

127.   A Private Audience
With His Holiness John Paul II

To the Tune of Ding Feng Bo
(Calming Storm)
Vatican
October 30, 1986

The sun is rising from the east
With splendor;
Full of joy,
I enter the apostolic palace.
In the chapel upstairs,
Truly magnificent,
The Holy Sacrifice is offered
To Heaven devoutly, solemnly.

Listening attentively,
Glancing at my manuscript,
The Holy Father embraces me;
He is kind to grant another audience.
The warm autumn sun
Is mirrored on the windows:
The scene —
Unforgettable for ever and ever!

Note: With the permission obtained yesterday through Fr. Abbot Ambroise Watelet, O.S.B., from Bishop Martin, Prefect of the apostolic palace, I attended the Mass celebrated by Pope John Paul II in his private chapel this morning at 7:30. After the Mass when we, about forty attendants, had an audience with him in the audience room, I presented to him a copy of the English translation of my manuscript, *Dawn Breaks In The East*, and four of my poems about His Holiness composed in prison.

128. 詠聖伯多祿大殿

四言詩
梵蒂岡
1986 年 10 月 30 日

殿堂壯麗，
舉世無雙；
心嚮神往，
萬民萬邦。

歷史悠久，
源遠流長；
高聳城中，
飽經風霜。

故殿毀矣，
何可悲傷？
今廈雄偉，
與日爭光！

華雕彩畫，
滿目琳瑯；
四百年來，
常放光芒。

128.   Ode To St. Peter's Basilica

In the Poetic Style of Siyan Shi
Vatican
October 30, 1986

In dimension, magnificence and splendor,
The Basilica is unrivaled.
In their hearts and minds
All people and nations yearn to see it.

It has a long story,
Like a great river
With a distant source,
With an endless course.
After many weather-beaten years,
It still towers over the city.

If the original Basilica is gone,
Why should we grieve?
The present edifice,
Much more magnificent,
Matches the sun in splendor!

The beautiful statues,
Paintings rich in color —
All a feast for the eyes;
For four hundred years
They have been shedding
Their brilliant rays.

栩栩如生，
救世君王；
聖賢英姿，
颯爽堂堂。

基督遺體，
痛抱貞娘：
米開《母愛》，
萬世頌揚！

大理石鋪，
地面煌煌；
壁柱天使，
展翅欲翔。

聖伯多祿，
就義慨慷；
墓上祭壇，
肅穆端莊。

重大慶節，
歌詠鏗鏘，
聖父舉祭，
樂極群羊。

The face
Of the King, the Savior of the world —
Still lifelike;
The heroic bearing
Of the saints and sages —
Bright, brave and grand.

The Body of Christ
The Virgin Mother embraces sorrowfully:
The Pieta by Michelangelo
Is praised generation after generation!

The marble floor —
Resplendent and brilliant;
The angels on the walls and columns
Spread their wings
As if they would fly.

St. Peter
Died a martyr's death generously;
The altar above his tomb —
Dignified and solemn.

On certain great solemnities,
When amidst sonorous chants
The Holy Father celebrates Mass,
The attending sheep are full of jubilation.

歷代**教宗**，
安息此堂；
堂多祭壇，
常禱**彼蒼**。

遊人來自，
四面八方；
終年不斷，
朝聖觀光。

伯鐸芳表，
雄壯斯堂：
勵眾奮戰，
人生疆場。

淑己救人，
吾儕其昂！
載歌載舞，
勇赴天鄉！

註：米開朗基羅・布奧納羅蒂（1475
　　-1564）是義大利畫家、雕刻家、建
　　築師和詩人。

Popes through the ages
Rest peacefully here in the Basilica.
Before its many altars
Prayer is offered to Heaven without ceasing.

Tourists come
From all the corners of the world,
Without interruption,
All the year round
On pilgrimage
Or for sightseeing.

The example of St.Peter
And this grand and magnificent Basilica
Have encouraged millions of people
Courageously to fight in the battlefield of life.

In perfecting ourselves,
In saving others,
With high spirits,
Singing and dancing,
Let us heroically hasten to the Heavenly homeland!

Note: Michelangelo Buonarroti (1475 - 1564),
Italian painter, sculptor, architect and poet.

129. 聖伯多祿廣場讚

采桑子
梵蒂岡
1986 年 10 月 30 日

柱廊頂部群雕立，
氣宇軒昂。
碑峙中央，
兩座噴泉萬道光。

週三接見歡聲震，
牧誨群羊。
語重心長，
聆教羊兒旋梓昂！

129.   Praise To St. Peter's Square

To the Tune of Cai Sang Zi
(Picking Mulberries)
Vatican
October 30, 1986

The statues,
Crowning the colonnade,
Have an impressive presence.
At the center an obelisk towers;
Two fountains spurt water,
Shedding ten thousand rays of light.

Each Wednesday
Giving a general audience
Amid resounding cheers,
The Shepherd instructs his sheep.
With the memory of his words and his affection,
They go back inspired to their native places!

130. 頌聖雅妮堂
地下墓穴

浣溪沙
羅馬
1986 年 10 月 30 日

曲徑縱橫通四方，
塋逾千載史輝煌。
垣中猶有骨忠良。

胸際焚燒神愛火，
期望斯火放霞光，
提攜萬眾上天堂！

130.   In Praise
Of The Catacombs
Of Saint Agnes' Church

To the Tune of Huan Xi Sha
(Yarn Washed in the Stream)
Rome
October 30, 1986

With crisscrossing paths
Winding in all the directions,
The catacombs have a glorious history
Of over a thousand years.
In the walls
Bones of faithful Christians
Are still preserved.

The fire of divine love
Is kindled in my heart.
Let that fire send forth brilliant rays!
Let it carry all men to the Heavenly Paradise!

131. 喜獲
與教宗合影照片

長相思
羅馬
1986 年 10 月 30 日

先廣場，
後客堂，
接見神州打虎郎。
恩情公父長！

初七張，
再九張，
溫暖囚心似太陽。
促奔天上鄉！

註：昨日午後六時和今天下午四時，「幸
福照相館」和「梵蒂岡城《羅馬觀察家
報》攝影服務社」，分別派員送來了，
與教宗若望保祿二世在兩次接見時
的十六張合影照片。

131.   Happily Receiving The Pictures Taken With His Holiness

To the Tune of Chang Xiang Si
(Enduring Love)
Rome
October 30, 1986

First at the Square,
Then in a parlor,
The Universal Father grants
An audience to one of his children
Who has beaten the Tiger in China.
His kindness — profound!

The first seven pictures
And the second nine,
As the sun,
They give warmth to the heart of a prisoner,
Urging him to march on
Toward his Heavenly home!

Note: At 6:00 pm yesterday and 4:00 pm today, the Foto Felici and the Servizio Fotografico de 'L' Osservatore Romano' della Citta del Vaticano sent sixteen pictures of me with Pope John Paul II taken during the two audiences.

132. 蘇比亞角朝聖

滿庭芳
羅馬
1986 年 10 月 31 日

旭日清新，
車行百里，
蒞臨聖地名山。
迴旋公路，
引往洞中天。
幽谷青峰峭壁，
秋光下、嫵媚嬋娟。
迎遠客，
胸懷舒展，
斯院是桃源！

歸天，
千載越，
良師本篤，
典範猶鮮。
在其隱修巖，
置祭臺焉。

132.   A Pilgrimage To Subiaco

To the Tune of Man Ting Fang
(Fully Fragrant Court)
Rome
October 31, 1986

In the fresh morning sun
We drive some forty miles;
We arrive at the sacred shrine—
A well-known mountain.
The spiraling highway
Leads us to the grotto—
A place of unique beauty.
Under the sunshine of autumn
The deep secluded valley,
Green peaks and precipices—
Lovely and charming.
Welcoming visitors from afar,
Opening their hearts,
St. Scholastica's Monastery
Is a haven of peace!

Having gone to Heaven
Over a thousand years ago,
Benedict, our good master,
Left his example—
His example still lives in our days.
In the grotto of his hermitage
An altar was set up.

雕像旁彌撒望，

情意遠、禱主誠虔。

當年景，

窟中重現，

激勵眾成賢！

註：今晨，艾德里安‧諾森神父帶領分會長盎
　　博羅削‧瓦特萊特大院長、駱神父、托洛
　　太太、雅妮、依撒格‧凱利納修士和我，
　　前往蘇比亞角和聖女斯哥拉斯諦加大修院
　　朝聖。

To attend Mass near his statue
Was of a profound significance to me;
We devoutly offered our prayers to God.
The scenes of long ago
Come alive again in the grotto,
Encouraging us to become virtuous!

Note: This morning Fr. Adrian Nocent, O.S.B., took Abbot
President Ambroise Watelet, Fr. Gaetan, Mrs. Thoreau, Agnes,
Br. Isaac Kalina and me on a pilgrimage to Subiaco and
St. Scholastica's Abbey.

133. 告別
聖安瑟而莫學院

浣溪沙
羅馬
1986 年 11 月 1 日

歷史悠悠享盛名，
梵宮鄰近育賢英。
八方廣廈聚師生。

修士禱聲堂內震，
塵囂逕上達**天庭**。
別時耳際似猶鳴。

註：在羅馬逗留的五天裡，駱神父和我
宿於作為本篤會總會長常年駐地的
聖安瑟而莫學院，托洛太太和其女
兒則住在附近的一座女修院。昨日
中午，曾應馬爾谷·謝里登院長之
邀，進食其桌，會見全院；飯後，
復談己經歷。

133.   Farewell To
The Collegio Di Sant'Anselmo

To the Tune of Huan Xi Sha
(Yarn Washed in the Stream)
Rome
November 1, 1986

Having a long history,
The college enjoys a great reputation.
Close to the Vatican Palaces,
It has been fostering souls,
Virtuous and learned.
In its large buildings
Gather professors and students
From all quarters.

Resounding in the chapel,
The prayers of the monks are carried
Through the earthly uproar
Up into the Heavenly court.
They still ring in my ears
At this parting moment.

Note: During our five-day stay in Rome, Fr. Gaetan and I lodged at the Collegio di
Sant' Anselmo, the permanent residence of the Primate of the Benedictine
Confederation, while Mrs. Thoreau and her daughter put up at a convent nearby.
Yesterday at noon we were invited by Fr. Prior Mark Sheridan to take lunch at
his table and to meet the whole community. After lunch he invited me to give
a talk on my experiences.

134. 辭別羅馬

卜算子
羅馬
1986 年 11 月 1 日

梵蒂振精神，
科洛興哀思。
百態千姿湧噴泉，
堂殿雄奇麗。

半百逝年華，
宿願終償喜！
惜別依依永世城，
何日重相會？

註：梵蒂指梵蒂岡。科洛指科洛西姆，
　　是羅馬一座古老的大鬥獸場的名
　　字，在最初三世紀的羅馬教難中，
　　曾有眾多的基督徒殉道於此。

134. Saying Goodbye To Rome

To the Tune of Pu Suan Zi
(The Fortune Teller)
Rome
November 1, 1986

The Vatican Palace lifts one's spirit,
The Colosseum evokes sad memories.
The fountains —
Gushing in many patterns,
The churches and basilicas —
Grand, wonderful and unique.

Fifty years in my life have passed;
To my great joy,
A long-cherished wish has finally been fulfilled!
Oh, Eternal City,
Lingering on memories of you,
I bid farewell!
On what day
Will we see each other again?

Note: The Colosseum is the name of an ancient large amphitheater
in Rome. There many Christians were martyred during the
first three centuries of Roman persecution.

135. 過佛羅倫薩

七絕
義大利佛羅倫薩
1986 年 11 月 1 日

壯麗名都經午後，
風光觀賞入城中。
聖堂一座宏奇偉，
力引世人登主宮！

135. **Passing Through Florence**

In the Poetic Style of Qijue
Florence, Italy
November 1, 1986

Passing through the beautiful, famous city
In the afternoon,
We enter the central section
To enjoy its wonderful sights.
There is a church,
Great, marvelous, magnificent,
Striving to lead people
To ascend to the Palace of the Lord!

136. 再見，義大利！

西江月
義大利
1986 年 11 月 2 日

史越兩千餘載，
名傳四海五洲。
由茲聖教播寰球，
愷奧亦多成就。

文化光輝燦爛，
烝民勤智雄遒。
猶期更上一層樓：
榮主身修世救！

註：「愷」指羅馬獨裁官葉斯·儒略·凱
撒（公元前 100-44）；「奧」指羅馬
首任皇帝奧古斯都·葉斯·屋大維
（公元前 63-公元 14）。

136.   **Goodbye, Italy!**

To the Tune of Xi Jiang Yue
(Moon over the West River)
Italy
November 2, 1986

Your history has continued
For over two thousand years.
Your fame has spread
To all the seas and continents.
Holy Church has gone out
From here to the whole world.
Caesar and Augustus have also
Their measures of greatness.

Your culture —
Splendid and magnificent,
Your people —
Industrious, talented, brave and vigorous.
We still wish you
To scale new heights,
To give glory to the Lord
Through perfecting yourself,
Through saving the world!

Note: Caesar - Roman Dictator Gaius Julius Caesar (100-44 B.C.);
Augustus - first Roman Emperor Gaius Octavian (63 B.C. -14 A.D.).

137. 阿爾卑斯山隧道

七絕
阿爾卑斯山
1986 年 11 月 2 日

上月登山望雪景，
天鄉嚮往喜心神。
漫長隧道今歸越，
希冀靈魂脫此身！

137. The Tunnel Through The Alps

In the Poetic Style of Qijue
The Alps,
November 2, 1986

Last month,
When I climbed the mountains,
When I gazed upon the snow scene,
My heart and spirit rejoiced
Yearning for the Heavenly homeland.

Now,
On the way back,
Passing through the long tunnel,
I wish the separation of my soul
From this body!

138. 里昂

七絕
法國里昂
1986 年 11 月 2 日

妖嬈斯邑今重越，
貞母大堂凌九天。
聖父來巡青史映，
去年景憶樂陶然。

138. Lyons

In the Poetic Style of Qijue
Lyons, France,
November 2, 1986

I pass once more
Through this lovely and enchanting city.
The Church of the Virgin Mother
Reaches to the heavens.

The visit of the Holy Father last year
Will ever shine in the annals of Lyons;
The thought of it
Brings joy to my mind.

139. 會見漢斯若瑟·
蒂本先生

憶王孫
布魯塞爾
1986 年 11 月 7 日

比京來晤出牢身，
經歷艱辛豈勵人？
萍水還逢爾友欣。
問**張君**：
「真諦人生曾否聞？」

註：蒂本先生來自德意志聯邦共和國，
張瑋娜女士是他的中國朋友和譯
員。

139.   An Interview With Mr. Hansjosef They-Ben

To the Tune of Yi Wang Sun
(Thinking of Wang Sun)
Brussels
November 7, 1986

You come to the Belgian capital
To see a man released from prison.
Will his story of those hard years
Inspire others?
I meet also unexpectedly your friend with joy.
I wish to ask her, Ms. Zhang:
"Have you ever heard of
The true meaning of life?"

Note: Mr. They-Ben is from the Federal Republic of Germany,
Ms. Zhang Weina is his Chinese friend and interpreter.

140. 在雅妮·
托洛小姐家午餐

采桑子
昂杜蒙-孔日
1986 年 11 月 9 日

天空晴朗秋陽照，
出訪良緣。
東道鄉間，
景色田園展眼前。

牧場池水芳菲樹，
媲美爭姘。
極目山巒，
手舉金樽謝昊天！

140.   Luncheon At The Home Of Miss Agnes Thoreau

To the Tune of Cai Sang Zi
(Picking Mulberries)
Gomze, Andoumont
November 9, 1986

The sky clears,
The autumn sun shines:
A good occasion for a visit.
My hostess lives in the country,
A rural scene unfolds before my eyes.

Pastures, pool, flowers, grass and trees
Contend in beauty.
Seeing a chain of mountains in the distance,
We raise our glasses
In thanksgiving to Heaven!

141. 再訪熱旺克爾肯聖安德肋大修院

西江月
布魯日
1986 年 11 月 16 日

歲近千秋尊院，
重生八十年前。
聖堂高聳入雲端，
獨特堂皇璀璨。

遠佈**福音**諸位，
嘗沾恩澤**中原**。
垂青賞識昔南冠，
千里騏焉不勉?!

註：初訪時，大院長保祿·斯坦達爾
　　特宿我於貴賓專用房間。

141.   The Second Visit
To The Sint-Andriesabdij,
Zevenkerken

To the Tune of Xi Jiang Yue
(Moon over the West River)
Bruges
November 16, 1986

Your Abbey is almost a thousand years old;
It was reborn at the turn of this century.
Your church soars high in the clouds,
Unique, magnificent, splendid.

You have carried the Gospel to distant places;
China has ever enjoyed your generosity.
You show special appreciation for a former prisoner.
As a fleet steed in the stable,
How can he possibly not be inspired
To continue galloping?

Note: During my first visit Abbot Paul Standaert put me up
in a room reserved for honored guests.

142. 訪魯汶-拉-尼夫
聖女日多達女修院

七絕
奧蒂尼
1986 年 11 月 17 日

為主鬥爭非枉然，
殘陽斜照訪秋寒。
平生素昧同修會，
數語寥寥見寸丹！

註：下午三時半，剛一抵達克肋朗
　　德聖安德肋修院，亞爾伯特・
　　達夫雷神父就驅車帶領駱神
　　父和我，往訪附近兩座聖堂和
　　三座女修院。

143.   A Visit To
The Prieure Conventueel
De Rixensart

In the Poetic Style of Qijue
Ottignies
November 17, 1986

In the haze at dusk
Your convent — peaceful.
In the chapel
Your voices joined in chant and prayer — sonorous.
We were all exhilarated
By the pleasant meeting,
By the lively conversation.
The bright moon hanging
In the sky,
We say goodbye to you,
Loyal Sisters!

144. 訪奧蒂尼嘉布遣第三修女會聖伯多祿診所

七絕
奧蒂尼
1986 年 11 月 17 日

嚮晚驅車多適意，
青青樹繞院堂昂。
嫦娥引路來尊處，
留下音容餘韻香！

144.   A Visit To
The Soeurs Tertiaires Capucines
Of Clinique St. Pierre
At Ottignies

In the Poetic Style of Qijue
Ottignies
November 17, 1986

What a joy to drive out
As evening falls!
Surrounded by green trees,
The convents and churches—
Magnificent.
Chang E, the celestial spirit of the moon,
Leads us to your residence.
Your voices, your faces stay with me—
A sweet aftertaste!

145. 訪博蘇
聖母升天女修院

江南春
奧蒂尼
1986 年 11 月 18 日

遊貴國，
喜登門。
承情談往事，
覽照悅諸君。
知袁垂暮蒙關照
誠意仁鄰芳範遵！

註：熱爾梅娜‧布雷‧袁太太，在 1948
　　年暑假期中曾是我的法文老師。
　　1952 年 2 月 10 日，她未能為其中國
　　籍丈夫袁能鼎先生求得許可，隨同
　　離開中國成都前來比利時。從那時
　　直到去世，她經常處於孤單寂寞中。

145.   A Visit
To The Prieure Simple
De L'Assomption At Bossut

To the Tune of Jiang Nan Chun
(Spring in the South of the River)
Ottignies
November 18, 1986

A visitor to your country,
I am very happy to visit you.
In response to your kindness,
I describe my past.
You are all pleased
To look at my pictures with the Pope.
Learning of your caring
For Mrs. Yuan in her old age,
I vow to follow your example
In loving my neighbor in all sincerity!

Note: Mrs. Germaine Braye Yuan was my French teacher during the summer
vacation of 1948. On February 10, 1952, she failed to obtain permission for her
Chinese husband, Mr. Vincent Yuan Nengding, to leave Chengdu, China,
for Belgium with her. From then until her death, she was always alone.

146. 再訪克勒朗德聖安德肋修院

攤破浣溪沙
（山花子）
奧蒂尼
1986 年 11 月 18 日

葉落枝枯秋已深，
幽幽修院臥叢林。
樂土人間遊上月，
喜重臨。

溫暖客廳賓主聚，
語宣神愛盡吾心。
將別晚經齊誦唸，
主追尋！

146.   The Second Visit To The Prieure Saint-Andre De Clerlande

To the Tune of Shan Hua Zi
(The Mountain Flowers)
Ottignies
November 18, 1986

Fallen leaves and bare branches
Show that it is late autumn.
The monastery is deep and quiet,
Nestled in the woods.
Last month I visited this earthly paradise,
I am joyful to come once more.

Guests and hosts
Gather in the warm parlor;
I do my utmost
To bear witness to divine love.
Before parting we say Compline together,
Seeking the Lord!

147. 赴安納——
瑪利亞・洛雷小姐
孔夫子酒家的午宴

玉蝴蝶
布魯塞爾
1986 年 11 月 21 日

深秋細雨綿綿，
安納意馨暄。
餚饌酒家鮮，
驅除內外寒！

淹留將兩月，
關照實周全。
東道誼難諼，
禱呈**基督**前！

147.   Present At Miss Anne-Marie Loriers' Lunch At The Confucius Restaurant

To the Tune of Yu Hudie
(The Jade Butterfly)
Brussels
November 21, 1986

The light rain of late autumn
Goes on and on.
Anne-Marie,
Your affection — sweet and warm.
The food at the restaurant is delicious,
Driving out
The cold within me and without!

I will be staying at your house
For two months;
You have taken good care of me.
My dear hostess,
Your friendship is unforgettable;
On your behalf
I offer my prayers in the presence of Christ!

148. 赴魯汶天主教大學 克洛德・蘇坦教授家宴

憶王孫
布魯塞爾
1986 年 11 月 21 日

重洋遠涉識仁人，
取義無榮猶恨存。
繫獄春秋何足論！
謝佳醇，
更謝關懷華夏民！

148.   Dinner At The House Of Claude Soetens, A Professor At The Catholic University Of Louvain

To the Tune of Yi Wang Sun
(Thinking of Wang Sun)
Brussels
November 21, 1986

Across the seas and oceans,
I meet you, one with noble qualities.
I still feel regret
For not having been privileged
To give up my life for the just cause.
My years of imprisonment—
Not worthy of mention!
I appreciate your good wine,
I am grateful particularly
For your concern for the people of China!

149. 再訪瑪利亞——
德肋撒・托洛太太

踏莎行
昂布爾
1986 年 11 月 25 日

秋雨征途，
熱情東道，
晨醒不覺東方曉。
重逢**巴牧**午餐時，
雅妮晚宴繁星照。

主日彌撒，
讚歌樑繞；
兒孫來晤添歡笑。
夜談經歷大廳中，
喜將**主愛**來傳報。

149.   Another Visit To Mrs. Marie-Therese Thoreau

To the Tune of Ta Suo Xing
(Walking across the Meadow)
Embourg
November 25, 1986

Autumn rain on the way,
Warmth from you, our hostess.
Waking up in the morning,
I am unaware of
The dawn already breaking in the East.
At lunch we meet again your pastor,
Fr. Maximilien Balthazar.
Countless stars are shining,
When Agnes entertains us at dinner.

During the Sunday Mass,
The Gregorian chant lingers in the air.
Your children and grandchildren come
To see us,
Bringing us more joy and laughter.
In a big hall on Sunday evening
I speak of my experiences;
I am overjoyed
To spread the love of the Lord.

150. 贈瑪爾大‧
本凱爾──勒孔特太太

憶江南
昂布爾
1986 年 11 月 25 日

何足怪？
坎坷在人間。
涕泣谷中多困苦，
冥思凡智亦難詮，
信者自瞭然！

謙、樸、善，
敬主爾誠虔。
無怨無尤兒女育，
謹承天命白頭歡。
芳範眾遵焉！

註：勒孔特太太家住斯普里蒙，昨天下午曾
　　來向我索取親筆簽名。自托洛太太處獲
　　悉：由於全心依靠上主，這位女士成功
　　地經受住了，在有關其四個子女的問題
　　上罕見而長期的困難。

150.   A Poem For
Mrs. Martha Benker-Lecomte

To the Tune of Yi Jiang Nan
(Remembering the South of the River)
Embourg
November 25, 1986

Why should we be surprised
At the misfortunes
Existing in the world of man?
Many are the hardships of human life
In this valley of tears.
Even with long hours of thought,
The worldly wise
May find explanation difficult;
The believer certainly understands!

Humble, honest, good,
You, Martha,
Have worshiped the Lord devotedly;
You have uncomplainingly made every effort
To bring up your children well.
You have well done the will of Heaven,
Now you are happy in your old age.
All of us can follow your example!

Note: Yesterday afternoon Mrs. Lecomte of Sprimont asked me to give her my
autograph. I learned from Mrs. Thoreau that totally trusting in the Lord,
this lady has undergone successfully unusual and protracted difficulties with
her four children.

151. 赴普里莫·
阿爾吉西伉儷家宴

畫堂春
布魯塞爾
1986 年 11 月 26 日

鳳城入夜景輝煌，
五光十色街房。
雅居鬧市亦安詳，
餚美醇香。

三世同堂今晚，
愛鄰敬主忠良。
五孩繞膝國之樑，
前景無疆！

註：這三代人是指：普里莫和熱納維埃
夫伉儷；他們的雙親達夫雷老先生
和老太太，他們的兩位叔父，亞爾
伯特·達夫雷神父和路加·達夫雷
先生；以及他們的五個子女，瑪利
亞、伯納黛特、維奧蘭、貝朗熱爾
和戈蒂埃。

151.   Dinner At The House Of Mr. And Mrs. Primo Alghisi

To the Tune of Hua Tang Chun
(Spring in the Hall of Paintings)
Brussels
November 26, 1986

At nightfall
The capital is a magnificent sight;
The buildings and the streets —
Bright with many colors.
Though in the busy part of town,
Your house is quiet;
The dishes are tasty,
The wine fragrant.

This evening in your family
There are three generations —
Grandparents, parents and children.
Through loving your neighbor,
Through worshiping the Lord,
You show yourselves
To be honest and faithful.
Your five children around you
Will be pillars of the state.
May they have boundless prospects!

Note: The three generations — Primo and Genevieve; their parents, Leopold and Marie-Therese Davreux, their two uncles, Fr. Albert and Mr. Luc Davreux; and their five children, Marie, Bernadette, Violaine, Berengere and Gauthier.

152. 去國兩週年有懷

眼兒媚
布魯塞爾
1986 年 11 月 27 日

幾多往事湧心頭？

淚眼望神州！

今猶欣幸：

挺身抗暴，

繫獄蒙羞！

儘朝母院和羅馬，

壯志待全酬！

成書榮主，

登壇獻祭，

將在何秋？

152.   Reflections On The Second Anniversary Of Departing From The Motherland

To the Tune of Yan Er Mei
(The Eyes' Fascination)
Brussels
November 27, 1986

How many memories of the past
Well up in my mind?
I contemplate China, the Divine Land,
With tearful eyes!
I still rejoice
To have stood up against the violent repression,
To have been imprisoned and humiliated!

Though I have been a pilgrim
At our mother Abbey and in Rome,
My aspirations
Still await complete realization!
The completion of my book
To glorify the Lord,
Stepping onto the altar
To offer the Sacrifice,
In which autumn will this be?

153. 邦諾朝聖

浪淘沙
布魯塞爾
1986 年 11 月 27 日

煦日照晨空，
聖母憐窮，
往朝致敬興沖沖。
聖地風光多壯麗，
「**活水**」淙淙。

助眾進**天宮**
母顯慈容，
恩如泉湧五三冬。
肅穆小堂心曲訴，
樂也融融！

註：吉蘭・法維神父，高齡七秩有六，
今天帶領駱神父和我往謁比利時聖
地。從 1933 年 1 月 15 日到 3 月 2
日，作為「**窮人之母**」的聖母，曾在
列日附近斯普里蒙的邦諾村，八次
顯現給十一歲的貧窮女孩瑪利埃
特・貝科。

153.   A Pilgrimage To Banneux

To the Tune of Lang Tao Sha
(Wave-Washed Sands)
Brussels
November 27, 1986

The mild sun
Is shining in the morning sky,
We are bursting with enthusiasm
To go on a pilgrimage
To pay our respects
To the Blessed Virgin,
Who has compassion for the poor.
The scene of the shrine
Is of great beauty,
The "Living Water" gurgles.

To help people
To enter the Heavenly Palace,
Our loving Mother graciously appeared.
Her kindness as a spring
Has welled up abundantly for pilgrims
For the last fifty-three winters.
I pour out my heart
In the solemn chapel,
My happiness knows no bounds!

Note: Today Fr. Ghislain Favaits, S.C.J., age 76, took Fr. Gaetan and me
to visit the Belgian sacred place. Our Lady, "The Virgin of the Poor", appeared
eight times, from January 15 to March 2, 1933, to Mariette Beco,
a poor girl of eleven, at the village of Banneux, Sprimont, Liege.

154. 三訪克勒朗德
聖安德肋修院

人月圓
布魯塞爾
1986 年 11 月 28 日

良辰主保同君慶，
日暮出京城。
當初一院，
如今三院，
佳節齊迎。

客廳聚會，
詩歌蕩漾，
一片歡騰！
晚經誦畢，
原途而返，
時近三更。

註：聖安德肋宗徒是比利時布魯日聖安德肋大修
院，和其兩座分別在比利時奧蒂尼克肋朗德與
美國加州化野漢的同名子院的共同主保。

154.   The Third Visit
To The Prieure Saint-Andre
De Clerlande

To the Tune of Ren Yue Yuan
(The Family Reunion and the Full Moon)
Brussels
November 28, 1986

To celebrate with you
The feast day of our common patron,
We leave the capital at sunset.
Originally in one abbey,
Now in three different monasteries,
The happy feast
Is simultaneously celebrated.

During the gathering
The parlor is alive with rejoicing
As poems and songs
Follow one another
Rising and falling like waves!
After Compline,
We go back the same way,
It is nearing midnight.

Note: Saint Andrew, Apostle, is the common patron of the Sint-Andriesabdij,
Zevenkerken, Bruges, Belgium, and its two daughter priories,
the Prieure Saint-Andre de Clerlande, Ottignies, Belgium, and
St. Andrew's Priory at Valyermo, California, USA.

155. 訪阿道夫·
米諾神父

七絕
布魯塞爾
1986 年 11 月 29 日

誰言「七十古來稀」？
八四耆儒健步飛！
雅士常迎觀賞客，
古堂府側放光輝。

註：今晨十時，瑪利亞·阿爾吉西小姐帶領
　　她的外祖父、她的雙親、駱神父和我，
　　去拜訪了米諾神父，並參觀了那座建於
　　十三世紀的珍貴小聖堂。

155.   A Visit
To The Reverend
Fr. Adolf Mignot

In the Poetic Style of Qijue
Brussels
November 29, 1986

Who should say:
"Since ancient times
Very few people
Have reached the age of seventy?"
You, Father,
A venerable scholar of eighty-four,
Walk fast and vigorously
As if on wings!

You, a fine gentleman,
Often welcome visitors
To view and admire the ancient chapel
Next to your house,
Still shedding its brilliant rays.

Note: This morning at ten o'clock, Miss Marie Alghisi took
her grandfather, her parents, Fr. Gaetan and me to visit
Fr. Mignot and the precious chapel built in the
13th century.

156. 贈巴普斯伉儷

憶江南
布魯塞爾
1986 年 11 月 30 日

榮與晤，
月半宿尊房。
蒙領觀光京夜景，
華居今宴敘家常。
情誼至輝光！

156. A Poem For Mr. And Mrs. Louis Baps

To the Tune of Yi Jiang Nan
(Remembering the South of the River)
Brussels
November 30, 1986

I felt honored to meet you.
I stayed in your house
For one and a half months.
You took me
To view the night scene of the capital;
Today you invite me
To lunch in your home
To chat freely.
Your friendship shines out!

157. 喜晤德爾維爾‧
西塞特太太

歸自謠
布魯塞爾
1986 年 12 月 4 日

情意美，
一唱雄雞君即起，
驅車越境來相會。

兩張彩照酬深誼。
多欣喜，
結交遠客承天意！

註：今天中午，托洛太太領著西塞特太
太，從昂布爾前來布魯塞爾相晤。
她的老同學住在靠近比利時邊界的
法國境內。

157.   A Joyful Meeting With Mrs. Derville Cisette

To the Tune of Gui Zi Yao
(Return from afar)
Brussels
December 4, 1986

So kind, so gracious,
You, Derville,
Up at cockcrow!
Driving across the border,
You came here
To make a personal call.

I offer you two color photos
In thanksgiving for your deep affection.
What a joy
To do the Divine Will
In making the acquaintance of a guest from afar!

Note: This noon, Mrs. Thoreau brought Mrs. Cisette from Embourg to Brussels
to pay me a visit. Her old schoolmate lives in France, on the border of Belgium.

158. 再訪伯大尼
本篤會女修院

七律
布魯塞爾
1986 年 12 月 8 日

三十三年戰赤狼，
終歌勝利渡重洋。
無榮為主捐軀體，
有幸來歐訪貴邦。
文稿敬呈酬盛意，
歷程略敘頌穹蒼。
闃然尊院冬陽暖，
隨姊齊奔天上鄉！

158.   The Second Visit To The Benedictine Convent, The Conventueel Priorij O.L.V. Van Betanie

In the Poetic Style of Qilu
Brussels
December 8, 1986

I fought with the Red Wolf
For thirty-three years.
Finally singing the song of victory,
I crossed the seas and oceans.
Though not given the glory
Of laying down my life for the Lord,
I am granted the honor
Of coming to Europe,
Of visiting your country.
I have presented my manuscripts respectfully
In gratitude for your hospitality,
I have spoken of my experiences briefly
In praise of Heaven.
The winter sun is warm
In your quiet convent;
Following and accompanying you, my Sisters,
I run toward our Heavenly homeland!

159. 敬獻給達夫雷老先生和老太太

天仙子
布魯塞爾
1986 年 12 月 11 日

相識有榮秋雨冷，
敬老尊賢頻探省。
京都**聖母大堂**邊，
餐廳靜，
兩宴請，
饌美窗明餐桌淨。

辦證官廳嘗帶領，
彌撒經書題字勁。
辭行在即願恭呈：
承**天命**，
欣晚景，
愛**主**仁鄰臻聖境！

159.   Dedicated To
Mr. And Mrs. Leopold Davreux

To the Tune of Tian Xian Zi
(Celestial Maidens)
Brussels
December 11, 1986

During the chill autumn rain
To meet you, Leopold and Marie-Therese, — a great honor.
Several times
I have called on you,
A venerable and aged couple,
To pay my respects.
Nearby the Church of Our Lady in the capital,
At a quiet restaurant
Twice invited,
I found the food delicious,
The windows bright and the tables clean.

You took me to the government office
To obtain an official certificate;
Your autograph on the missal given to me
Is strong.
As the moment of parting nears,
I present you respectfully
My best wishes:
By doing well the Will of Heaven,
You will be happy
In your remaining years;
In loving the Lord,
In showing kindness to your neighbor,
You will reach
The realm of the saints!

160. 告別比利時諸友

傷春怨
布魯塞爾
1986 年 12 月 13 日

景色非依舊，
試問**灞橋**知否？
念友聚今晨，
欲折居然無柳！

降伊**延安獸**，
晤爾諸英秀。
麗日暖身心，
舉首望、求天祐！

註：灞橋是灞水上的一座橋，位於中國
　　陝西省西安市東面。漢唐人送客至
　　此，折柳贈別。延安是陝北一座城
　　市，從 1937 年至 1947 年，為毛澤
　　東控制下的中共中央機關所在地。

160.   Goodbye
To All Friends In Belgium

To the Tune of Shang Chun Yuan
(Sorrow in Seeing Spring Leaving)
Brussels
December 13, 1986

Do you know, Ba Qiao,
That the scene does not remain as before?
Twenty of my friends
Have gathered here this morning,
But,
They find no willow branches to break!

I subdued the Beast of Yan'an,
Now I meet you, exemplary people.
The radiant sun
Warms my body, my heart;
Raising my head to look up,
I implore Heaven to bless you all!

Note: Ba Qiao, a bridge over the Ba Shui, is situated on the east side of the city of
Xi'an, Shaanxi Province, China. People in the Han and Tang dynasties used to walk
their friends to the bridge and see them off, breaking and giving willow branches as a
parting gift. Yan'an, a city in northern Shaanxi, was the seat of the Chinese Communist
central organization under the control of Mao Zedong from 1937 to 1947.

161. 別矣，比利時！

臨江仙
比利時
1986 年 12 月 13 日

黎庶勤勞公教國，
工農科技蒸蒸。
人稠氣壯美京城。
貞娘容屢顯；
邦諾客常迎。

瓦、**佛**語殊何互怨？
相親互讓停爭，
同心治理國繁榮！
赤囚兼月客，
難述別離情！

161.   Farewell, Belgium!

To the Tune of Lin Jiang Xian
(Immortal by the River)
Belgium
December 13, 1986

A Catholic nation, You, Belgium,
Have an industrious people.
Your industry and agriculture,
Your science and technology
Are flourishing.
With a large population,
Your capital — imposing, beautiful.
Endowed with several apparitions
Of our Virgin Mother,
Banneux continues to welcome pilgrims.

The Walloons and Flemish,
Why should you complain of each other,
Though you speak different languages?
You must be mutually dear and tolerant,
You must end your quarrel.
If you govern your kingdom
With one heart,
Surely, it will prosper the more!
Once a Communist prisoner,
I have been your guest for two months;
My feelings at parting — inexpressible!

162. 自歐歸來

夜遊宮
聖安德肋修院
1986 年 12 月 14 日

兩月匆匆逝矣，
遠遊事、永難忘記。
舊識新交喜相會；
慶尤當，
教宗前，
呈戰紀。

主祐安還里，
待酬志、未來遙寄。
領品從長得計議；
趁時書，
敘征程，
宣道義！

註：駱愷騰神父和我，於昨晚返抵洛杉磯。今
　　天，多明我・吉倫修士和比爾・雷姆斯老
　　先生驅車來貝蒂・吉尼特太太家接歸。我
　　們乃於傍晚六點十分回到了化野漢。

162.   **Return From Europe**

To the Tune of Ye You Gong
(Tour to See the Palace at Night)
St. Andrew's Priory
December 14, 1986

Two months have passed quickly,
But the long trip
Will never be forgotten.
I am happy to have met some old friends
And to have made some new ones.
What was worth celebrating in particular —
The presentation to His Holiness
Of the record of my past struggle.

Relying on the blessings of the Lord,
I have come back safely
To my monastic home.
My goals, still unrealized,
Are entrusted to the distant future.
My proposed priestly ordination
Must be thought out further and discussed;
I shall seize the present favorable time
To write,
To narrate the course of my struggle
And to give voice
To the cause of truth and justice!

Note: Yesterday evening Fr. Gaetan Loriers and I returned to Los Angeles.
Today Br. Dominic Guillen and Mr. Bill Rhames came to Mrs. Betty Guignet's
house to pick us up and we were back in Valyermo at 6:10 pm.

163. 與黛安‧理查森太太和其家魚雁往還

浪淘沙
聖安德肋修院
1987 年 12 月 15 日

見母病中呻，
孝女心焚。
初聞僕事意歡欣。
撫慰萱堂愚稿誦，
贈款酬恩。

初稿亂紛紛，
竟益仁人，
宛如柳蔭爽精神。
尺素相通蒙策勵，
志欲凌雲！

註：黛安同她的母親瑪麗‧亞伯爾、夫婿道格
拉斯和兒子鮑勃，住在俄勒岡州密爾沃
基。在讀過 1985 年 11 月 28 日感恩節俄勒
岡市的《**俄勒岡人報**》刊載的關於我的一
篇文章後，她於當年十二月給我來信，要
求一份有關我經歷的粗糙稿件。

163.   Correspondence With Mrs. Diane L. Richardson And Her Family

To the Tune of Lang Tao Sha
(Wave-Washed Sands)
St. Andrew's Priory
December 15, 1987

Seeing your mother in illness, moaning,
A loving daughter, you, Diane,
Burn with anxiety.
You are joyful
Upon learning my story.
You try to console your mother
By reading my manuscript to her;
You give a donation in thanksgiving.

My first draft, though tangled,
Benefits those of good will,
Refreshing the spirit,
As the shade of willow.
My correspondence with you encourages me,
My aspirations soar to the skies!

Note: Diane lives in Milwaukie, Oregon, together with her mother,
Mrs. Marie Abel, her husband, Douglas, and their son, Bob. After reading
the article about me in *The Oregonian*, the newspaper of Oregon City, Oregon,
on Thanksgiving Day, November 28, 1985, she wrote to me in that December
asking for a copy of the rough draft about my story.

164. 爲縣政委員彌額爾·
安東諾維奇的宴會祝禱

臨江仙
聖安德肋修院
1988 年 3 月 10 日

宴會輝煌千客聚，
有榮祝禱皇天。
席間就座小蘭邊。
重逢君友慶，
合影念留歡。

秋節兩回尊駕到，
承蒙青眼相看。
八年從政績昭然。
吉人天助祐，
政委定蟬聯！

註：今晚七時半，方濟各·本篤副院長和我，
出席了縣政委員安東諾維奇在洛杉磯
瑪利奧特旅店舉辦的宴會。他在 11 月 8
日的複選中獲勝。1986 年 9 月 28 日下
午秋節期間，他曾帶領其友趙小蘭女士
初次來修院訪問。趙女士是華裔美國公
民，當時任美國交通部航運署副署長，
十六年後則是勞工部長。

164.   Invocation At The Dinner For Supervisor Michael D. Antonovich

To the Tune of Lin Jiang Xian
(Immortal by the River)
St. Andrew's Priory
March 10, 1988

At your grand dinner party, Mike,
In the presence of a thousand guests,
I am granted the privilege
Of giving the Invocation.
During the banquet
I am seated next to Ms. Elaine Zhao.
I am happy
At meeting your friend once more,
At having our group photo taken
As a memento.

You honored us
By your two visits to our Fall Festival,
By your goodwill toward us.
Your achievements
During your eight years in office
Are evident to all.
Heaven is blessing the good,
You, our supervisor,
Will surely win re-election!

Note: This evening at 7:30, Fr. Subprior Francis Benedict and I attended
Supervisor Antonovich's dinner at the Marriott Hotel in Los Angeles.
He won the November 8th runoff. During the Fall Festival, in the afternoon of September 28,
1986, he took his friend, Ms. Elaine L. Zhao, to pay his
first visit to the Priory. Elaine, an American citizen of Chinese origin, was
then the Deputy Administrator of the Maritime Administration in the
US Department of Transportation. Sixteen years later, she was the Secretary of Labor.

165. 贈特麗‧湯普森小姐

玉蝴蝶
聖安德肋修院
1988 年 7 月 9 日

欣聞豪興冬寒，
謀面豈非緣？
打字爾心專，
爭鳴任夏蟬！

勤而心手巧，
詩積百來篇。
餘稿腹中眠，
幾時酣夢完？

註：1988 年 1 月 16 日上午八時半，
　　加州拉哈布拉市特麗，懷著看一
　　看我的詩詞的願望，偕同謝麗‧
　　米漢小姐來訪，並表示了樂意為
　　我的詩詞打字。

165.   To Miss Terry Thompson

To the Tune of Yu Hudie
(The Jade Butterfly)
St. Andrew's Priory
July 9, 1988

On a cold winter day
I was delighted
To learn of your interest.
Was it not fate that we should meet?
You have been absorbed
In typing for me,
No matter how shrill the singing
Of the summer cicadas!

Because of
Your industrious and deft work,
About a hundred of my poems
have been restored one by one.
The remaining poems
Still sleep in my mind.
When will their sweet dreams be over?

Note: Hoping to see some of my poems, Terry of La Habra, CA, called on me
along with Miss Sherry Mehan at 8:30 am on January 16, 1988.
She expressed her willingness to type the poems for me.

166. 獻給艾米‧
格林伍德太太

攤破浣溪沙
（山花子）
聖安德肋修院
1988 年 7 月 24 日

電視新聞動寸心，
披肝瀝膽急光臨。
信德復甦多載後，
喜而吟！

枉顧頻繁常饋贈，
結為兄弟誼蘭金！
小史如琴歌**主愛**，
遇知音！

註：1988 年 5 月 10 日下午五點半，艾米
　　在第二頻道看到了，洛杉磯哥倫比
　　亞廣播公司電視新聞部關於我的配
　　上了新鏡頭的，曾在 1987 年 8 月 9
　　日初次播出過的重播節目。她那時
　　同夫婿良和他們的女兒良尼塔，住
　　在加州塞普爾維達市。

166.   Dedicated
To Mrs. Amy Greenwood

To the Tune of Shan Hua Zi
(The Mountain Flowers)
St. Andrew's Priory
July 24, 1988

A television news item
Touched your heart,
You were eager to come here
To express your innermost thoughts and feelings.
After an interruption of years,
Your faith is quickened.
With joy you resume the sacred hymn!

You have honored me
By your frequent visits,
By your many gifts.
You take me
Into your family as a brother;
Your affection is as precious as gold,
As fragrant as orchids!
As a piano concerto,
The telling of my little story becomes
A melody of the Lord's love;
I meet with you, a lover of music!

Note: On May 10, 1988, at 5:30 pm, Amy watched on Channel 2 a
KCBS television re-broadcast on me, with the new footage of the program
that appeared for the first time on August 9, 1987. She then lived with
her husband, Leo, and their daughter, Leonita, in Sepulveda, CA.

167. 祝韓國友人
李聖淑小姐
生日快樂！

浪淘沙
聖安德肋修院
1988 年 7 月 27 日

兩載識紅顏，
慷慨支援，
頻頻抄稿不嫌煩。
厚意深情銘肺腑，
何以銜環？

重聚上週歡，
榮晤慈萱，
誕辰恨未在當天！
此日去年曾面賀，
今獻詩篇！

167.   Happy Birthday To Miss Suky Lee, A Korean Friend!

To the Tune of Lang Tao Sha
(Wave-Washed Sands)
St. Andrew's Priory
July 27, 1988

It is two years
Since I met you, Suky!
You have generously helped me
With repeated, troublesome and untiring typing
Of my manuscripts.
Your deep kindness is engraved on my heart.
How should I repay you?

Last week
I was glad to see you again,
I was honored to meet your mother;
A pity—
Your birthday was not that day!
Last year on this day
I congratulated you on your birthday
Face to face,
Today I offer you a poem!

168. 洛蕾‧哈蒂爾小姐 的生日賀卡

人月圓
聖安德肋修院
1988 年 8 月 20 日

花間蝶舞生辰卡，
凝視憶疇芳。
啟蒙潤色，
來鴻謄稿：
恩德難忘！

椿萱樂識，
時通魚雁，
受益叨光。
好天祝福，
良師孝女，
前景輝煌！

168. A Birthday Card From Miss Lori Hartill

To the Tune of Ren Yue Yuan
(The Family Reunion and the Full Moon)
St. Andrew's Priory
August 20, 1988

On your birthday card, Lori,
Butterflies dance among the flowers;
Gazing at them,
Fragrant memories return.
Your teachings,
Your revisions of my papers,
Your letters and typing:
All your favors — unforgettable!

I gladly met your father and mother;
From frequent correspondence with them
I have greatly benefited.
With the blessings of a loving Heaven,
A good teacher and dutiful daughter,
You will have a bright future!

169. 賀黃慧玲小姐 與彌額爾·科特先生 結爲連理

攤破浣溪沙
（山花子）
聖安德肋修院
1988 年 9 月 17 日

大陸台灣各一方，
何曾夢想識他鄉？
視我如親衷曲吐，
正春光。

嘗做雙雙修道夢，
而今比翼共翱翔！
相敬親鄰崇上主：
祝鴛鴦！

註：黃小姐和科特先生，今日在洛杉磯聖巴西
　　略天主教堂舉行婚禮。8 月 29 日，我曾收
　　到過他們的請柬。我與來自台灣的黃女士
　　相識於 6 月 18 日，正是她領著科特先生和
　　比利時韓德力神父來此訪問之時。

169.   Congratulations To Miss Elaine Huang Huiling On Her Marriage With Mr. Michael Cotter

To the Tune of Shan Hua Zi
(The Mountain Flowers)
St. Andrew's Priory
September 17, 1988

While living on the Mainland and in Taiwan
Far apart from each other,
Did we ever imagine in our dreams
Our meeting in a foreign land?
Embracing me like a family member,
You, Elaine, opened your heart to me;
It is spring light.

At one time, you and your dear husband,
Both cherished a dream to live the monastic life.
Now you and he are one in marriage,
As a pair of birds
Flying wing to wing!
Respecting each other,
Loving your neighbor,
Adoring the Lord:
Here are my best wishes to you, Oh, loving couple!

Note: Today Elaine and Michael celebrate their wedding ceremony at Saint Basil's Catholic Church in Los Angeles. On August 29 I received their invitation. I met Elaine, a Chinese lady from Taiwan, on June 18 when she brought Michael and Fr. Jerome J. Heyndrickx CICM of Belgium here to visit me.

170. 阿古斯蒂娜・西西莉婭・赫凱塔小姐 爲呈詩集於敎宗

玉蝴蝶
聖安德肋修院
1989 年 2 月 3 日

君飛羅馬施恩，
詩集帶隨身。
納稿敎宗仁，
思量盛事欣。

同根生赤縣，
親故令萱椿。
詩意匪無垠，
友情常在春！

註：阿古斯蒂娜與其父母劉宗興先生和弗洛拉・露西婭娜・赫凱塔太太，住在加州卡拉巴沙公園市。他們是海外華裔，是來自印度尼西亞的移民。我於 1988 年 5 月 16 日與他們相識。本年 1 月 11 日，阿古斯蒂娜曾在聖伯多祿廣場，向聖父若望保祿二世呈獻了我的一冊詩稿。今天，我自宗座駐美大使館收到了由敎宗辦公室發來的謝函。謝函的全文如下：「親愛的周修士，1989 年 1 月 18 日。遵照聖父的指示，我致函向你表達，他對你在 1989 年 1 月 11 日的接見中所獻詩集的謝意。他希望你知道，他是多麼地讚賞你的沉思和熱忱。聖父定為你祈禱，他誠懇地賜予你宗座祝福，並為你祈求基督的恩寵和平安。你在基督內的忠誠的，顧問　塞皮蒙席。」

170.   Presentation Of The Collection Of My Poems To The Pope By Miss Agustina Sicilia Herkata

To the Tune of Yu Hudie
(The Jade Butterfly)
St. Andrew's Priory
February 3, 1989

You, Agustina, flew to Rome,

Bestowing a favor upon me;

You took my collection of poems with you.

Accepting the manuscript,

The Pope was gracious;

The thought of that grand occasion fills me with joy.

Also from China by origin,

Your parents, Philippus and Flora, are my kith and kin.

A poem has its limits,

Its flavor may not last;

But your friendship like spring

Will be with me always!

Note: Agustina and her parents, Philippus H. and Flora Luciana Herkata, live in Calabasas Park, CA. They are overseas Chinese and immigrants from Indonesia. I met them on May 16, 1988. This January 11, in St. Peter's Square, Agustina presented a copy of my poems to the Holy Father John Paul II. Today I received a letter of thanks from his office through the Apostolic Nunciature in the USA.
The letter reads as follows:
Dear Brother Peter, January 18, 1989.   I am writing
at the direction of the Holy Father to express his thanks for the collection of poems which
you offered for his acceptance at the audience of January11, 1989. He wishes
you to know how appreciative he is of your thoughtfulness and devoted sentiments.
His Holiness assures you of his prayers and cordially imparts to you his Apostolic
Blessing, invoking upon you the grace and peace of Christ.
Sincerely yours in Christ, Monsignor C. Sepe, Assessor.

171. 贈吉恩・德・
貝蒂尼小姐

卜算子
聖安德肋修院
1989 年 3 月 18 日

退省結新交，
愚照令驚異。
互饋詩詞示友情，
瞭解隨增矣。

拙稿促刊行，
援助從無已。
療我殘肢爾慨慷，
愛主心如熾。

註：吉恩是加州聖巴巴拉市理療醫師，
　　1987 年 7 月 1 日，她贈我一首頌友
　　誼的詩。那詩的譯文如次：

　　　在我們的一生中，
　　　有許多朋友忽來忽往。
　　　每位朋友都以其獨特的方式
　　　把我們的心弦來彈動撥盪。

171.   A Poem For
Miss Jean DeBettignies

To the Tune of Pu Suan Zi
(The Fortune Teller)
St. Andrew's Priory
March 18, 1989

I met you the first time during your retreat here;
You were struck by a picture of me.
We exchanged poems,
Expressing our friendship;
Our mutual understanding grows.

Urging my manuscript to publication,
You offer me your constant support.
You generously gave me physical therapy
For my crippled hand,
Loving the Lord with a burning heart.

Note: Jean is a physical therapist in Santa Barbara, CA.
On July 1, 1987, she sent me her poem praising friendship.
The poem reads as follows:

Many friends come and go
In our lives.
Each of them touches our hearts
In their own special way.

諸友和我們一起走過很多道路，
但陪同穿越心靈的蹊徑者卻僅僅是些許少量。
這些朋友是特殊別致，
是不同凡響；

他們是這樣的友人，
和我們共同面對，共同分享
我們日常生活中的
磨難考驗和歡欣舒暢；

他們是這樣的友人，
對我們喜愛體諒，
好讓我們
把愛人的門戶來開放；

他們是這樣的友人，
站在我們身旁，
助我們探查、追求
人生的價值和意向；

他們是這樣的友人，
向我們展開支援的臂膀，
使我們深入認識和理解
上主對我們的愛情、旨意和厚望。

脆弱的人性會令我們驚奇萬狀：
我們對他們的友愛為何只是在深化增長!?
我們怎未被生活中變化著的浪潮所淹沒!?
何以千里之遙亦未使我們相互間的情誼凋謝頹喪!?

我們反躬內省便發現：
他們與我們的交往已深入到我們的六腑五臟，
他們就靠近我們靈魂的中心區，
而我們的靈魂也就與**天主**相親相傍！

Our friends travel many roads with us,
But few travel with us
Through the road of our soul.
These friends are the special ones:

They are the ones
Who are with us
During the joys and trials
Of our everyday life;

They are the ones
Who love and accept us
So that we allow ourselves
To open the door to human love;

They are the ones
Who stand beside us
When we search
For the meaning of creation;

They are the ones
Who support us
In our deeper realizations
Of our Lord's love and will for us.

In our human frailty
We wonder:
Why our love for them only deepens!?
How we seem to survive
The tidal waves of changes in our lives!?
Why the miles don't fade our friendship!?

We look inside and find that
They have traveled with us
Deep in our hearts,
They live near the center of our soul,
Next to God!

172. 借問金「主教」，
節操今安在？

五言詩
聖安德肋修院
1990 年 3 月 3 日

鼎鼎公大名，
頻繁見報章；
新聞報導閱，
心痛似劍傷。

卅七年前事，
腦海今蕩漾；
院長志雄壯，
且欽且讚賞。

哲學欲攻讀，
託人為說項；
看證允復問：
「願否戰風浪？」

172.   "Bishop" Aloysius Jin Luxian, Where Is Your Integrity Now?

In the Poetic Style of Wuyan Shi
St. Andrew's Priory
March 3, 1990

Frequently, Fr. Aloysius Jin,
Your great name has appeared in the press.
Reading the news reports,
My heart was grieved
As if pierced by a sword.

Memories of events thirty-seven years ago
Flashed across my mind.
Your high aspirations,
The aspirations of a rector,
Aroused my feelings of respect,
My feelings of admiration.

To pursue my studies in philosophy,
I asked someone to intercede for me.
Having seen my certificate,
You granted admission
But with a question:
"Are you ready to fight with the winds and waves"?

惠賜入學函，
恩德永難忘；
詎料**共黨**阻，
願成夢黃粱！

受業機緣失，
慨嘆滿胸膛。
擬訪次年初，
未遂欲斷腸。

誤囑共諜謁，
代呈拙文章；
「**信函**」和「**天堂**」，
哀哉雙雙亡！

鄒鐺公入獄，
衛教緣堅強。
適值兩月後，
僕亦進牢房。

六十年代迎，
春日閱報章；
知判十八載，
相較己稍長。

You sent me graciously
The letter of admission,
Your kindness will never be forgotten.
I little expected
The Communists standing in the way,
Hopes within reach became pipe dreams!

Deprived of the opportunity
Of studying under you,
I was filled with sadness and regret.
Intending to visit you
Early in the following year,
I was heartbroken on failing to do so.

I mistakenly asked a Communist agent
To visit you,
To present you with my writings.
The *"Letter"* and the *"Paradise,"*
Alas, both of them were lost!

You were put in chains,
Thrown into prison,
Because
You had firmly defended the Church.
Just two months later,
I was also imprisoned.

Ringing in the 1960s,
I read in the newspaper one spring day
Of your sentence — eighteen years.
Mine was a little more than yours.

忽忽十七夏，
尊駕卸囚裝；
愚則八秋後，
釋禁正驕陽。

辱銬批鬥會，
獄內飯家常；
抵抗絕非易，
幾囚節無傷？

鈞座前半生，
業績實昭彰；
爾後則神秘，
謎樣公容光！

下獄不旋踵，
據說變立場；
或想「**立功勞**」，
為虎乃作倀！

出牢初十載，
養晦而韜光。
華北何公幹？
之後怎還鄉？

Seventeen summers have passed quickly
Since you put away your prison garb.
Eight autumns later,
I was released
Under the blazing summer sun.

Insults and cuffings,
Criticism and struggle meetings
Were routine in prison;
Resistance was by no means easy.
How many prisoners kept their integrity?

The first half of your life
Was really a life of successes.
What followed is mysterious;
Your face, your appearance —
Now enigmatic!

Shortly after your incarceration,
Allegedly,
You began to change your position.
Probably
"To perform meritorious services,"
You held a candle for the devil!

During the first ten years
After your release from jail,
You hid your light under a basket.
What did you do
While staying in north China?
Why should you then return
To your native place?

首腦佘山院，
「主教」徐匯堂；
職位愈擢陞，
為共愈捧場！

銜命頻出國，
遊說舌如簧；
兩面三刀弄，
欲騙好心腸！

當初拒妥協，
勇氣堪稱揚；
向共今屈膝，
主榮受損傷！

「究有何前途」？
古稀瓦上霜！
吠堯何桀犬？
返照徒回光！

節操宜珍惜，
故我莫拋荒！
晚年享平安，
懸崖勒馬韁！

You were appointed
Head of the Sheshan Seminary,
Then "bishop" of Xuhui Cathedral.
The higher your position,
The more you flattered
The Communist Party!

Going abroad frequently
According to orders received,
You drummed up support
With a glib tongue.
Engaging in double-faced tactics,
You tried to deceive the good-hearted!

At the outset
You refused to compromise,
Your courage was worthy of praise.
Now,
Bending your knees to the Communists,
You will betray your seeking
To diminish the glory of the Lord!

"What of your future?"
Already aged seventy,
You will be soon gone,
Like the frost on the roof!
Why should you, tyrant Jie's dog,
Yap at the sage-King Yao?
Like the setting sun,
You spread your last rays in vain!

You should treasure your integrity;
You should not turn your back
On your former self.
To be at peace
In the evening of your life,
Rein yourself in
At the brink of the precipice!

毋再離聖座，
毋再害忠良！
披掛重敗將，
急速返沙場！

賢良故國苦，
一日九迴腸。
赤狼何怙惡？
怎生爾下場？

哀懇萬能主，
降獸救亡羊，
以福華夏民，
以頌爾榮光！

註：在金魯賢神父被中共任命為「上海主教」的兩
　　週年紀念日，我重寫了這首曾經在台灣公教月
　　刊《鐸聲》1985 年 4 月號刊出過的詩。1954
　　年 1 月，我曾託原為共黨秘密間諜的朱朝乾，
　　將《告全國神職人員和教友書》與《從天堂到煉
　　獄》兩份文稿，呈交給當時的徐匯神哲學院院
　　長金神父。

Do not continue to stray
From the Holy See;
No longer do harm to
Those who are loyal.
Buckle on your armor again,
O you defeated general,
Hasten to return to the battlefield!

The good and the virtuous suffer
In our Motherland,
They are bowed down with sorrow.
Why Red wolf, do you pursue evil?
What will be your last end?

We beseech You,
All-powerful Lord,
To subdue the Beast,
To save the lost sheep
For the benefit of the Chinese people,
For the praise of Your glory!

Note: On the second anniversary of the appointment of Fr. Aloysius Jin by the
Chinese Communists as "Bishop of Shanghai", I rewrote the poem published in
the April 1985 issue of *Vox Cleri*, a Catholic monthly in Taiwan. In January 1954,
I entrusted to Peter Zhu Chaoqian, a hidden Communist spy, my two manuscripts,
A Letter to the Clergy and Laity of the Church in China and ***From Paradise to
Purgatory***, to be presented to him, then Rector of the Xuhui Seminary.

173. 贈達味・
基廷先生

五絕
聖安德肋修院
1990 年 10 月 5 日

佳節如斯逝，
恩情似畫留。
望君蒙主祐！
迎返盼來秋！

註：為深謝達味幫助修院籌備了最近的
七個秋節，若望・博杰爾丁院長於
今天特贈以由若望・奧古斯特・斯
旺森描繪的展示基督受洗的巨幅畫
卷《江河》和由眾修士簽名的謝卡。

173.   A Poem
For Mr. Dave Keating

In the Poetic Style of Wujue
St. Andrew's Priory
October 5, 1990

Like a flowing river,
The joyous Festival has gone.
As this painting keeps
The flowing river before your eyes,
So your generosity
Remains ever in our hearts.
May the Lord bless you!
May we welcome your return next Fall!

Note: In appreciation of Dave's help with the preparations for our last seven
Fall Festivals, today Fr. Prior John Borgerding presented him with a large painting
by John August Swanson, *The River*, showing the baptized Christ,
and with a card of thanks signed by the monks.

174. 祝賀
拉皮安伉儷金婚

西江月
聖安德肋修院
1990 年 10 月 7 日

閃閃金婚卡片，
字花容照爭妍。
風霜雨露駐朱顏，
偕老駕鴦世典！

戎馬生涯夫倥，
育孩重任妻肩。
週年今慶志彌堅：
同赴天鄉盛宴！

註：8 月 16 日，收到了肯尼思和伊萊恩
　　的卡片和請柬。拉皮安少校先生曾
　　在美國空軍服役了三十年，於 1972
　　年退伍。

174.   Congratulations On The Golden Wedding Anniversary Of Mr. And Mrs. Kenneth LaPean

To the Tune of Xi Jiang Yue
(Moon over the West River)
St. Andrew's Priory
October 7, 1990

In your glittering golden wedding card
The letters, flowers
And picture of yourselves
Vie with each other in beauty.
Wind, frost, rain and dew
Have made you hale,
Giving to the world an example —
An affectionate couple
To the end of your lives!

Ken,
You were busy with an army life,
While Elaine,
You carried the heavy responsibilities
For bringing up your children.
Today celebrating your anniversary,
You further strengthen your commitment
To march on together
Toward the grand banquet
Of your Heavenly homeland!

Note: On August 16, I received a card and an invitation of Ken and Elaine. Mr. Major LaPean served in the United States Air Force for thirty years and retired in 1972.

175. 獲台灣
毛永昌先生書信又驚又喜

眼兒媚
聖安德肋修院
1990 年 10 月 23 日

西風萬里送征鴻，
驚喜滿心胸！
華箋珍貴，
珠璣字字，
誼盛情隆。

卅年音絕多凶夢：
赤禍豈相逢？
同窗七載，
故人無恙，
頌謝蒼穹！

註：毛先生自 1938 年 8 月到 1945 年 1 月，是
我們西山和成都修院的在學修生。去年十
二月的一個清晨，台灣電視公司曾播出
過，有關 1989 年 9 月 23 日化野漢卅三屆
秋節期間採訪白徵明神父和我的記錄片。
毛先生觀看了這項節目，深有感觸；他查
出了我的住址，寄來了這封信函。他於 1979
年 5 月以中校軍階自部隊退役，育有六位
女公子。

175.   Happy Astonishment At Receiving A Letter From Mr. James Mao Yongchang Of Taiwan

To the Tune of Yan Er Mei
(The Eyes' Fascination)
St. Andrew's Priory
October 23, 1990

From ten thousand miles afar
The west wind brings me
Your migratory swan — your letter:
A great surprise and a boundless joy!
It is precious to me;
Each word is a gem,
Expressing
Your profound sentiments of friendship.

During the last forty years
Hearing nothing from you,
I have often dreamt an ominous dream:
Have you met the Red disaster?
My dear classmate of seven years,
My close friend of long standing,
For your good health
I give praise and thanks
To Heaven!

Note: Mr. Mao was an oblate student of our Priory at Xishan, then at Chengdu, from
August 1938 to January 1945. One morning of last December, Taiwan Television
Enterprise broadcast the documentary of an interview with Fr. Werner Papeians and
me during the 33rd Valyermo Fall Festival on September 23, 1989.
He watched this television program. He was so deeply touched as to find out my
address and send me this letter. He retired as a lieutenant colonel
from the army in May 1979 and has six daughters.

176. 神遊佛蒙特州
本篤會韋斯頓修院

江城子
聖安德肋修院
1990 年 12 月 29 日

動聽勵志麥斯言，
意飄然，
彩雲間。
東北飛馳，
奇景展眉前。
玉宇瓊樓林海裡，
迎遠客，
饗清泉。

「衛星」無「箭」上天難，
訴拳拳，
望支援。
東道允求，
願遂賦歸歡。
星入太空神曲播，
寰宇響，
頌蒼天。

註：早飯後，羅伯特·麥克格溫內斯教授告訴了我，有
　　關韋斯頓修院的一些情況。這使我很受鼓舞，使我
　　為出版文稿而在適當時刻前往求助滿懷希望。

176.   A Trip In Spirit
To The Benedictine
Weston Priory In Vermont

To the Tune of Jiang Cheng Zi
(The Town by the River)
St. Andrew's Priory
December 29, 1990

The words of Robert McGuinness
Captured my attention,
Giving hope to my heart.
My thoughts float in the air,
In the rosy clouds.
Swiftly I travel northeastward,
Before my eyes a wonderful scene unfolds.
Magnificent buildings in a sea of forest
Welcome me, a guest from afar,
Giving me sweet spring water to drink.

My "satellite" will scarcely be launched without a "rocket."
I make my sincere appeal,
Looking for the support of my hosts.
It is granted;
With my wish fulfilled,
I come back full of joy.
The satellite has been lifted into outer space;
A heavenly music resounds,
Ringing out over the earth,
Singing God's praises.

Note: After breakfast, Professor Robert J. McGuinness gave me some information
on Weston Priory. I was greatly encouraged and filled with hope of seeking
an opportune moment to ask its help in the publication of my manuscripts.

177. 賀中流砥柱
龔品梅主教晉陞樞機

七言詩
聖安德肋修院
1991 年 6 月 7 日

教會繁榮**上海市**，
賢哲輩出壯如虹。
本世紀中第二夏，
鈞座出生於**浦東**。

四十年代正闌珊，
神州碧落欲全紅；
形勢岌岌人心惶，
尊鐸受命危難中。

聖母玫瑰十月七，
主教權杖領從容。
奉調回**滬**作領導，
駐節**蘇州**未一冬。

教區獻於**佘山母**，
玫瑰經聲達天宮；

177.   Congratulating Bishop Ignatius Gong Pinmei, The Firm Rock In Midstream, On His Elevation To The Cardinalate

In the Poetic Style of Qiyan Shi
St. Andrew's Priory
June 7, 1991

The Church in Shanghai prospered;
Adorned with many virtues and much wisdom,
She was as magnificent as a rainbow.
In the second summer of this century,
Your Eminence was born at Pudong.

When the forties were coming to an end,
The sky of the Divine Land would turn completely to Red.
The situation was precarious,
The public feeling anxious;
Then a priest,
You were entrusted with a mission
At that critical and difficult moment.

October 7,
On the Feast of Our Lady of the Rosary,
You received the episcopal staff calmly.
You were transferred back to Shanghai
To take the leadership,
Before you had completed a full year at Suzhou.

You dedicated the diocese
To Our Lady of Sheshan;
The Rosary Prayer throughout the diocese
Ascended to the Heavenly Palace.
Braving the wind and the waves,

乘風破浪漁船駛，
闋闋凱歌震太空！

赫赫戰功頭五載，
激怒反神共黨熊。
威脅勸誘全不理，
勇進牢房主教忠！

無期徒刑被判處，
鬥辱挨銬復遭逢；
經年累月凜冽受，
並未凋謝山頂松！

告別鐵窗八日前，
暗寄弟妹信一封：
為忠於主願永囚，
浩然正氣九霄衝！

八十年代第六夏，
黔驢共黨技已窮；
繫鈴人將鈴來解，
釋放出獄八四翁！

You drove forward the "fishing boat";
The songs of your triumph
One after another shook the sky!

Your achievements in the spiritual battle
During the first five years were great,
Enraging the Communist Bear,
By nature opposed to God.
Having ignored its threats,
Having spurned its inducements,
You entered jail heroically
As a loyal bishop!

You were sentenced to life imprisonment,
You encountered criticisms and insults,
Beatings and cuffs.
Suffering the piercing cold
Year after year,
A pine on the top of a mountain,
You did not wither and fall!

On the eighth day
Before bidding farewell to prison,
You sent a letter
Secretly to your brother and sister:
To witness your allegiance to the Lord,
You preferred to be incarcerated forever.
Your noble spirit soared to the highest heavens!

In the sixth summer of the eighties,
Like the proverbial donkey
In ancient Guizhou Province,
The Communists exhausted their tricks.
To end the trouble
They themselves had started,
They released you,
A venerable bishop of eighty-four,
From jail!

兩載有半遭監管，
繼續鍛鍊熔爐中；
國際呼聲再生效；
十年假釋提前終。

兩週之後語記者：
「**愛國教會**」不苟同，
信德為保無所惜，
準備明日返牢籠！

親人志士續援助，
旋即離**申**來美東；
治病靜養於醫院，
示眾亮節與高風。

邀訪**羅馬**春日暖，
親切接見蒙**教宗**；
權杖再獲年儘邁，
忠貞昭著眾喁喁！

During two and a half years
Under public surveillance,
You continued to be tempered
In the furnace.
Once more with an international outcry,
Your remission from the ten-year probation
Was anticipated.

Two weeks later,
You spoke to journalists:
You would never accept
The "Patriotic church";
You would not spare yourself
In defending the Faith;
You would be prepared
To return to prison tomorrow!

With the continuous help from relatives,
From sympathetic crusaders for justice,
You left Shanghai soon after
For eastern America.
Getting medical treatment,
Resting in a hospital,
You have been giving to all
The example of your noble character and sterling integrity.

Invited to visit Rome
In the warm spring days,
You were cordially received by the Pope.
Despite your age,
The episcopal staff
Was once more bestowed on you;
Your loyalty, so evident,
Was admired by all!

教徒種子烈士血，
叛逆絕無濟世功；
寧為玉碎不瓦全，
甘背十架有始終！

天國戰士長奮鬥，
克服障礙萬千重；
燦爛桂冠卒奪得，
立地頂天為世宗！

鹽以鹹味能醃物，
臺上燈光照愚兒；
虎口餘生來異域，
洞悉天意豈凡庸？

芸芸羊兒遭屠戮，
濟濟鮮花凋寒冬；
橫行大陸卅二載，
害教禍國赤狼兒！

The blood of martyrs —
The seed of Christians,
The unfaithful — surely of no avail
To the salvation of the world:
You preferred to be
A shattered piece of jade
Rather than an unbroken tile,
You willingly carried your cross
From beginning to end!

A champion of the Heavenly Kingdom,
Waging a protracted and valiant struggle,
You overcame myriads of obstacles.
Finally,
You have won a splendid laurel wreath,
Becoming a model
Of the lofty and indomitable spirit!

Salt can bring its flavor to others,
The lamp on a stand can shed light
To the ignorant and the wicked.
Saved from the tiger's mouth,
You have come to a foreign land.
Do the earth-bound know
The Will of Heaven for you?

Many sheep have been slaughtered!
Many flowers have faded and fallen
In the cold winter!
Playing the tyrant on the Mainland
For forty-two years,
Bringing disaster to the Church,
To the country,
The Red Wolf is ruthless!

寬大仁慈縱無限，
正義威嚴亦蒼穹；
際茲惡貫或未盈，
改弦易轍宜匆匆！

他日皈依吾儕慶，
聖堂歡燭火熊熊；
苦盡甘來歌聖樂，
中原黎庶樂融融！

卅八年前僕境窘，
欲往徐匯神哲攻；
加辣修女為求情，
懼收劣馬未通融。

院長證明既獲悉，
詢以願否戰霜風。
警局作梗程未啟，
遺恨綿綿留五中！

Even if infinitely lenient and merciful,
God is also just and majestic.
While the measure of his iniquity
May be not yet full,
The Wolf should hurry to change course!

Some day when he does,
We will celebrate the conversion,
The candles in the churches
Will show their joy in flames.
Welcoming happiness after suffering,
Singing sacred music,
The Chinese people will be jubilant!

In an awkward situation
Thirty-eight years ago,
I intended to go to the Xuhui Seminary
To study philosophy and theology.
Sr. Marie-Claire interceded for me;
You didn't make an exception in my favor,
Afraid of receiving an inferior horse.

Informed of the certificate
From Fr. Prior Raphael Vinciarelli,
You asked whether I was ready
To brave the frost and the wind.
Because of obstruction
By the local police,
I could not start on my journey:
An eternal regret
Still remains in my heart!

聞繫縲紲憂且喜，
無何有幸步芳蹤；
長夜漫漫狴犴暗，
如公恃主意雍容。

念六年後囹圄出，
慶未屈節而卑躬。
鏖戰三秋來北美，
多諳高躅樂由衷。

英雄事蹟報刊載，
擊節捧讀為動容；
天涯海角廣傳佈，
有如麗日與和風。

前春五月迎尊駕，
洛市華堂喜色濃；
庫君嘗告呈稿事，
往謁失時恨無窮！

Learning of your imprisonment,
I was anxious,
But elated by your courage.
Shortly afterwards
I was granted the honor
Of walking in your footsteps.
During the long night of the dark prison,
Relying on the Lord as you did,
I was able to endure peacefully.

Walking out of jail
Twenty-six years later,
I was overjoyed not to have bowed,
Nor forfeited my integrity.
When coming to north America
After a further hard struggle of three autumns,
I rejoiced from the depth of my heart
To know more of your story.

Reading with great admiration in the press
Of your heroism,
My heart was deeply touched.
The news has been spread far and wide
To the ends of the earth,
Like a bright sun,
Like a gentle breeze.

Welcoming your visit in May,
The spring before last,
The Chinese church in Los Angeles
Was filled with great joy.
Mr. Joop Koopman informed me
Of offering you my manuscripts.
I regretted letting slip forever the opportunity
Of an audience with Your Eminence!

賀陞樞機庭滿客，
車如流水馬如龍！
遙獻此詩慶盛事，
為主作證典型從！

註：1985 年 7 月 13 日，我未經縝密思考和必
　　要查證，就根據《洛杉磯時報》7 月 7 日的
　　報導，冒失地賦了一首詩，指責龔品梅鈞
　　座向共黨認罪悔過。看過那首刊於 1985 年
　　9 月 1 日的《鐸聲》249 期上的長詩後，朱
　　恩榮神父自台灣發來了批判信函。我開始
　　認識到了這事件的真實情況。為答覆朱神
　　父，我隨即在上述公教月刊 251 期上發表
　　了認錯道歉的公開信。六年後的今天，我
　　改寫了那首詩，並寄給了龔樞機基金會，
　　以向剛在 5 月 29 日被教宗擢陞為樞機的堅
　　貞不屈的上海主教再次負荊請罪。浦東位
　　於上海市區黃浦江東岸。佘山為中國教會
　　聖地，在上海西南約 25 英里處。

Now,
With your elevation to the cardinalate,
Your residence
Must be thronged with heavy traffic.
Presenting you from afar
With this poem
In commemoration of this grand occasion,
I will strive to follow your example
In bearing witness to the Lord!

Note: Without careful consideration and due verification, on July 13, 1985, I rashly composed a
poem based on the report in the *Los Angeles Times* on July 7th, criticizing
His Excellency Msgr. Ignatius Gong Pinmei, S.J., for "admitting his crime and showing
repentance to the Communists." After reading that lengthy poem published in
number 249 of *Vox Cleri*, September 1, 1985, Fr. Simon Zhu (Chu), S.J., wrote me from Taiwan a
critical letter. I began to realize the facts of the case. Then in the number 251 of the above-
mentioned Catholic monthly, I published an open letter in answer to Fr. Simon's,
acknowledging my fault and expressing my deep regret. Today, six years later, I have
rewritten that poem and sent a copy to the Cardinal Kung Foundation so as to once more
offer a humble apology to the loyal and unyielding Bishop of Shanghai, just promoted to
be a cardinal by the Pope on May 29. Pudong is a section of the city of Shanghai, situated
on the eastern bank of the Huangpu Jiang. Sheshan is a sacred shrine of the Church in
China, some 25 miles southwest of Shanghai.

178. 賈維茲夫婦
驅車送我購書

歸自謠
聖安德肋修院
1991 年 7 月 2 日

賢伉儷，
今早領吾奔洛市，
遍尋卷帙於書肆。

歸途尊府炎陽避。
思天意，
晚風送返忘疲憊。

註：吉爾伯特和多洛蕾住在加州聖蓋博
　　市。有子斯蒂文，女兒迪恩，媳埃
　　莉莎。自 1990 年 10 月以來，他們
　　就一直在洛杉磯總教區終身執事培
　　訓班接受培養和訓練。

178.   On Mr. And Mrs. Gilbert Chavez Driving Me To Shop For Books

To the Tune of Gui Zi Yao
(Return from afar)
St. Andrew's Priory
July 2, 1991

You,
Gilbert and Dolores,
A good couple,
Took me this morning
To the city of Los Angeles
To look for books at various bookstores.

On the way back,
You made your house my shelter
From the heat of the sun.
In pondering the Will of Heaven,
I forgot my tiredness,
When you brought me home
In the evening breeze.

Note: Gilbert and Dolores live in San Gabriel, CA. They have a son,
Stephen, a daughter, Deanne, and a daughter-in-law, Elisa. Since October 1990
they have been accepted into the permanent diaconate formation program
in the Los Angeles Archdiocese.

179. 在菲津賓友人
阿伯雷拉伉儷家
度聖誕節

人月圓
聖安德肋修院
1991 年 12 月 25 日

去冬無幸登門謁，
拙著正琢磨。
書將付梓，
蒙邀今訪，
聖誕同歌。

燈盈**誕**樹，
馬槽貴府，
耿耿星河。
稿呈東道，
春光七載，
慶未蹉跎！

註：杰姆和奧德麗於十多年前來到加州柏班克
市。現有子女三人：杰妮、若瑟和杰寧。

179.   A Christmas At The House Of Mr. And Mrs. Jaime J. Abrera, Friends From The Philippines

To the Tune of Ren Yue Yuan
(The Family Reunion and the Full Moon)
St. Andrew's Priory
December 25, 1991

Last winter
Engaged in improving my writing,
I missed the privilege
Of visiting you.
Now,
The publication of the book is at hand;
At your invitation,
I pay a visit
To sing of the Holy Birth with you.

Sheltered
By the Christmas tree shining with lights,
The manger in your house is as bright
As the Milky Way.
To you, Jaime and Audrey, my dear hosts,
I offer my manuscript,
Rejoicing at not having wasted
These last seven radiant springs!

Note: Jaime and Audrey came to Burbank, CA, over ten years ago.
They have three children: Jainee, Joseph, and Janine.

180. 祝韓國友人涂美仙小姐前途美好！

憶江南
聖安德肋修院
1992 年 3 月 19 日

殘障母，
孝事四寒冬。
東去桃源將日內，
獻身於主樂融融。
前景壯如虹！

註：徐小姐已獲准進入印第安納州一座
　　聖衣修院。其母瑪利亞於 1990 年 9
　　月 7 日過世，享壽六十有三歲。

180.   A Bright Future
To Miss Marianna So,
A Friend From South Korea!

To the Tune of Yi Jiang Nan
(Remembering the South of the River)
St. Andrew's Priory
March 19, 1992

Upon your crippled mother, Maria,
You have waited
With filial piety
For four cold winters.

In a few days
You will be leaving
For a Haven of Peace in the east;
Your happiness knows no limits
As you dedicate yourself to the Lord.
The promise of your future,
Marianna,
Is as glorious as the rainbow!

Note: Marianna has gained admission to a Carmelite monastery in Indiana.
Her mother died on September 7, 1990, at age 63.

181. 羅杰·馬洪尼樞機主教鈞座，熱烈歡迎您光臨化野漠！

江城子
聖安德肋大修院
1992 年 8 月 2 日

歷程修院始**西山**。

受饑寒，

徙**蓉垣**。

赤禍遭逢被迫轄區遷。

卅六年來交友眾，

相互助，

享平安。

易名修院復當前。

選能賢，

撰新篇。

尊駕迎來恭聽訓詞歡。

祝福支持新院長，

深感激，

頌**皇天**！

181. A Warm Welcome To Valyermo, Your Eminence Cardinal Roger Mahony!

To the Tune of Jiang Cheng Zi
(The Town by the River)
St. Andrew's Abbey
August 2, 1992

The Monastery's historical journey
Began long ago at Xishan.
Living in hunger and cold,
We moved to the city of Chengdu.
Suffering from the Red disaster,
Forced to migrate,
We settled here —
Under your jurisdiction.
Over these thirty-six years
Many friends we have made,
Helping each other,
Enjoying peace.

Our priory now becomes Abbey.
A worthy leader elected,
We begin to write
This new page.
Welcoming Your Eminence,
Hearing your instructions,
Today we feel happy.
For your Blessing,
For your support of our new Abbot,
We are deeply grateful
And sing the praises of Heaven!

註：1929 年，比利時布魯日本篤會聖安德肋大
修院，於中國四川省南充縣西山創建了子
院。這座修院於 1952 年 3 月關閉，旋於
1956 年在加利福尼亞州重建；1992 年 4 月
16 日，經本篤會領報分會分會長盎博羅
削‧瓦特萊特大院長批准所作票決，進而
成為大修院。1992 年 5 月 15 日，方濟各‧
本篤神父當選為首任大院長，並於今天領
受馬洪尼樞機主教的隆重祝福。

182. 祝薩姆‧雷伯老先生 八十大壽

浣溪沙
聖安德肋大修院
1992 年 9 月 24 日

助爾解衣晚飯時，
三年情誼始於茲！
神奇天意有誰知？

加國出生猶太裔，
胸懷開朗壽期頤！
同登天國僕尤希！

Note: In 1929, the Benedictine Abbey of Saint-Andre in Bruges, Belgium,
founded a daughter priory at Xishan in Nanchong County, Sichuan Province, China.
The Priory closed in March 1952 and resettled here in California in 1956. It
became an Abbey on April 16, 1992, when Abbot Ambroise Watelet, President
of the Benedictine Congregation of the Annunciation, approved its voted decision.
On May 15, 1992, it elected Fr. Francis Benedict its first Abbot, who receives
this day the Solemn Blessing from Cardinal Mahony.

182.   Congratulating
Mr. Sam Raber
On His Eightieth Birthday

To the Tune of Huan Xi Sha
(Yarn Washed in the Stream)
St. Andrew's Abbey
September 24, 1992

During dinner
I helped you take off your coat.
With this, Sam, began our friendship,
That has continued
During the last three years!
Who would have known
The miraculous Will of Heaven?

Born in Canada,
You are a Jew by origin.
A man of broad mind,
You will be a centenarian!
My particular wish for both of us —
Ascending to the Heavenly Kingdom
Together!

183. 歡慶化野漠
三十六屆秋節

浪淘沙
聖安德肋大修院
1992 年 9 月 26 日

臺上舞霞裳，
處處華裝，
同兄八度慶秋光。
白髮任憑添幾許，
志壯身強！

風拂樂音揚，
鳥語花香，
新詞歌頌主慈祥。
祝姐胸盈佳節樂，
爽快安康！

183.   A Joyful Celebration –
The 36th Fall Festival
At Valyermo

To the Tune of Lang Tao Sha
(Wave-Washed Sands)
St. Andrew's Abbey
September 26, 1992

Graceful dancing on stage,
Beautiful costumes everywhere;
The eighth time with you, my dear brothers,
I celebrate the fall scenery.
No matter how many more white hairs
Appear on my head,
I feel aspiring and strong!

Musical sounds waft on the breeze,
Birds sing,
Flowers scent the fragrant air;
A new poem chants
The praises of the Lord's mercy.
May the joy of the Festival
Refresh your hearts, my dear sisters,
And give you the best of health!

184. 朱麗葉·
帕爾太太的禮品

人月圓
聖安德肋大修院
1992 年 9 月 26 日

壽高體弱乘輪椅，
秋節又光臨。
笑容可掬，
念珠再遺，
禮厚情深！

念珠勤製，
多年遍餽，
降眾甘霖！
拳拳孝敬，
知君早獲，
聖母歡心！

184. Gifts
From Mrs. Juliette Pare

To the Tune of Ren Yue Yuan
(The Family Reunion and the Full Moon)
St. Andrew's Abbey
September 26, 1992

Advanced in age,
Frail,
In a wheelchair,
You, Juliette,
Visit our Fall Festival
Once more.
Radiant with smiles,
Again you present Rosaries to me.
Your gift — generous,
Your affection — deep!

Diligently you produce Rosaries;
Over the years
You have distributed them far and wide,
Dropping a timely rain upon many!
By this sincere filial piety,
Assuredly,
You have won long ago
Our Lady's favor!

185. 與愛德華·
利特爾若翰先生同禱於
《貞母抱聖嬰》小像前

眼兒媚
聖安德肋大修院
1992 年 11 月 7 日

重逢**聖市**起春風，
審稿近三冬。
僕書問世，
爾心舒暢，
來唔融融。

手摩聖像同祈禱，
祝願獻**蒼穹**。
主榮增益，
續揮禿筆，
蒙勵心雄！

註：愛德華在經歷三月重病後，於 1993 年 9 月 26 日
身故，享壽七十有六歲。適值其去世前十二天，
我收到了他的末次改件，而他的最後審改也使即
將出版的詩集的重訂工作得以大功告成。惟望上
主為自 1989 年秋直至其最後時日對我所施恩德
而給以賞報，錫以永安；復望主賜安慰於其妻埃
倫，其女亞歷山德拉和基督蒂娜，其兒克里斯托
弗，其媳蒙妮克，其婿克里斯托弗！

185.   Praying Along With Mr. Edward Littlejohn Before A Little Statue Of The Virgin And Child

To the Tune of Yan Er Mei
(The Eyes' Fascination)
St. Andrew's Abbey
November 7, 1992

I met you again, Edward,
In your city of Santa Barbara
When the spring breezes began to blow.
You have edited my manuscripts
For some three winters.
With the publication of my book,
With a happy heart
You came here for a joyous reunion.

Touching the sacred statue
With our hands,
We pray together,
Offering our petitions to Heaven.
To give added glory to the Lord,
I shall continue
Wielding my poor writing brush:
Your encouragement raises my spirits!

Note: Having been seriously ill for three months, Edward died on
September 26, 1993, at the age of 76. Just twelve days before his death, I
received from him the last pages he had edited for me.
His final examination made complete the whole review of
the forthcoming poetry. May the Lord reward him for his kindness shown
to me from September 1989 up to his last days, and grant eternal rest to him
and consolation to his wife, Ellen, their daughters, Alexandra and Christina,
their son, Christopher, daughter-in-law, Monique, and son-in-law, Christopher!

186. 全修院
聖誕聚會
在瑪利亞・卡文太太家

踏莎行
聖安德肋大修院
1992 年 12 月 18 日

聖誕將臨，
邀奔貴府，
弟兄闔院同歡聚。
夫君謝世儘懷哀，
熱情接待仍如故！

作我鄰居，
念餘寒暑，
常來服務常相助。
親如手足共甘辛，
祝君晚景平安度！

186.   A Christmas Party
For The Monastic Community
At Mrs. Mary Carvin's House

To the Tune of Ta Suo Xing
(Walking across the Meadow)
St. Andrew's Abbey
December 18, 1992

Christmas is at hand.
Invited to your house, Mary,
All the Brothers of the Abbey
Gather joyously.
Despite your grief
At the death of your husband, Everett,
You gave us a reception
As warm as before!

Our neighbor
For over twenty seasons of cold and heat alternating,
You have visited us often
To do voluntary service,
To extend your help.
You are as dear to us
As a blood sister,
As a sharer of our weal and woe;
We wish you peace
In your remaining years!

187. 懷念克洛德‧
杜克雷–達味先生

傷春怨
聖安德肋大修院
1992 年 12 月 31 日

噩耗晴空響，
始悉心驚神愴。
細想展愁眉—
爾在登天程上！

禮珍多花樣，
睹物思形象。
異日為重逢，
決續鬥、同風浪！

187.   In Memory Of Mr. Claude Ducreux-Davy

To the Tune of Shang Chun Yuan
(Sorrow in Seeing Spring Leaving)
St. Andrew's Abbey
December 31, 1992

The sad news of your death
Thundered in the blue sky;
At first I was shocked and distressed
Upon learning of it.
On reflection,
My distress passed—
My knitted brows became smooth again—
You are on the way to Heaven!

Your gifts to me
Were precious and many;
Looking at them,
I recall your face.
To see you again one day,
I will continue battling
With the winds and the waves!

188. 再晤韓國友人
許庚淑小姐

人月圓
聖安德肋大修院
1993 年 1 月 3 日

去春別後今重晤，
敘舊道新歡。
尊門唯爾，
真光接受，
志氣昂然！

貴邦半壁，
宛如敝國，
陰暗淒寒。
土崩赤政，
身翻黎庶，
何日何年？

188.   Another Meeting With Miss Kathy Ho, Kyoung Suie, A Friend From South Korea

To the Tune of Ren Yue Yuan
(The Family Reunion and the Full Moon)
St. Andrew's Abbey
January 3, 1993

After our separation last spring,
We meet again today,
Delighting in talks
About the old days and the new days.
The only one in your family,
Having embraced the Light of truth,
You are filled
With high spirits and a firm faith!

Half of your country,
Like mine,
Has been gloomy, dreary and cold.
The collapse of the Red tyranny,
The emancipation of the people,
On what day?
In what year?

189. 在洛杉磯市
都爾・聖瑪爾定堂區之家
談己經歷

踏莎行
聖安德肋大修院
1993 年 2 月 7 日

遵約歌、柯，
烏雲無阻，
驅車來接名城赴。
街燈遍照抵堂區，
一時有半鬥爭敘。

豪雨傾盆，
廳堂和煦
盡心主愛來傳佈。
瀟瀟返院禱耶穌：
「夜深東道安還府！」

189.   A Personal Presentation At St. Martin Of Tours Parish Center In Los Angeles

To the Tune of Ta Suo Xing
(Walking across the Meadow)
St. Andrew's Abbey
February 7, 1993

By appointment,
Despite black clouds,
Gretchen Glick and Fr. Donie Keohane
Came to pick me up to the famous city.
We drove to their parish
Through streets shining with lights;
I gave a presentation of my struggle
Lasting one and a half hours.

Under torrential rains,
In the warm hall,
With all my heart
I strove to proclaim
The love of the Lord.
Later back at the Abbey,
Listening to the heavy downpour,
I prayed to Jesus:
"In the depth of night,
May my hosts return home safely!"

190. 同瑪爾大·吳丁頓·胡珀太太採購聖誕禮品

玉蝴蝶
聖安德肋大修院
1993 年 3 月 22 日

過焉**基督**生辰，
金諾爾遵循。
處處喜迎春，
商場領僕奔。

頭回珍貴禮，
依舊室中存。
恩上再加恩，
禱中常憶君！

190.   A Christmas Present Shopping Trip With Mrs. Martha Woodington Hooper

To the Tune of Yu Hudie
(The Jade Butterfly)
St. Andrew's Abbey
March 22, 1993

The Birthday of Christ
Has already gone;
You kept your promise of a festive present.
Joy is everywhere
As we welcome spring;
Today you took me shopping.

Your first precious gift
Is still preserved in my room
Just as it has always been.
For your grace added to grace
I always remember you
In my prayers!

191. 在福爾斯伉儷家
度假一週

玉蝴蝶
聖安德肋大修院
1993 年 7 月 18 日

和平修士如仙，
方宅脫塵寰。
狄耐樂園妍，
幽深植物園。

邀遊斯勝地，
供假使偷閒；
東道饗甘泉！
酬勞望好天！

191.   A Week Vacation
At The House Of
Mr. And Mrs. Hugo Foertsch

To the Tune of Yu Hudie
(The Jade Butterfly)
St. Andrew's Abbey
July 18, 1993

The monks in Prince of Peace Abbey
Look like celestial beings,
The Franciscan Serra Retreat
Stands aloof from the world.
Disneyland—
Fascinating,
The Rancho Santa Ana Botanic Garden—
Deep and serene.

Inviting me to visit these famous scenic spots,
Providing a vacation for me to snatch a rest,
You, Hugo and Irene, my dear hosts,
Have offered me
Sweet spring water!
May the good Heaven reward you
On my behalf!

192. 自瑪莉安納‧帕普女士喜獲詩稿頭批打字件

生查子
聖安德肋大修院
1993 年 7 月 29 日

洛城瑪定堂，
初晤春將到。
向爾近陳情，
蒙助承關照。

重逢一月前，
贈號呼**蜂鳥**！
蜂鳥不停歌，
為爾常祈禱！

192.   Glad To Receive From Ms. Marianne C. Papp The First Typed Pages Of My Manuscript Of Poetry

To the Tune of Sheng Zha Zi
(Fresh Berries)
St. Andrew's Abbey
July 29, 1993

At St. Martin of Tours Church
In Los Angeles
I had my first meeting
With you, Marianne,
As spring was approaching.
Recently,
To my appeal
You have responded
With your help,
With your concern.

I saw you again one month ago;
You gave me a name,
Calling me "Hummingbird!"
The Hummingbird sings
Without ceasing,
And
I will continne to pray for you always!

193. 祝賀姪外孫女蔣雲與陳文東結爲鸞儔

四言詩
聖安德肋大修院
1995 年 12 月 8 日

情投意合，
雙飛比翼！
求真從善，
其爲爾志！

193.   Congratulating You, Jiang Yun, My Dear Grandniece, On Your Marriage With Chen Wendong

In the Poetic Style of Siyan Shi
St. Andrew's Abbey
December 8, 1995

Perfectly suited to each other,
You both have flown side by side,
As a pair of lovebirds!
May the search for truth and goodness
Be your common ideal!

194. 瓜達蘆湃聖母
1531 年 12 月 9 日
給墨西哥璜・地亞哥的訓辭

七言詩
聖安德肋大修院
1996 年 2 月 24 日

吾兒之中汝最小，必須確知認識清：
吾乃**童貞瑪利亞**，完美無瑕永俊英；
真**天主母**余且是，萬物靠祂而生存，
遐邇萬類祂掌管，是祂主宰乾和坤。
聖殿建此吾切願，向吾致敬致崇尊，
余之愛憐助祐護，由茲顯示賜萬民。
吾乃爾之仁慈母，吾乃烝民好娘親。
凡是和睦居斯土，凡是圓顱方趾人，
一切愛我情意真，一切向我呼號慇，
舉凡尋我心火熱，舉凡對我信賴恂；
其哭其泣其悲痛，吾將於茲傾耳聽，
其苦其困其災難，吾將為療為減輕！

> 註：1996 年 2 月 20 日，當瓜達蘆湃聖母
> 像卡將在墨西哥重印時，負責發行
> 這像卡的美國康州斯坦福龔樞機基
> 金會秘書龔楊彥鴻女士，曾要求我
> 修改附在卡上的聖母訓辭無韻的中
> 譯文。我乃因之按照英文原件，以
> 有韻的七言詩予以重新譯出。

194.   Words Of Our Lady Of Guadalupe To Juan Diego

Mexico, December 9, 1531

Know for certain, least of my sons,
That I am the perfect and perpetual Virgin Mary,
Mother of the True God
Through whom everything lives,
The Lord of all things near and far,
The Master of heaven and earth.
It is my earnest wish
That a temple be built here to my honor.
Here I will demonstrate, I will exhibit,
I will give all my love, my compassion,
My help and my protection to people.
I am your merciful mother, the merciful mother
Of all of you who live united in this land,
And of all mankind,
Of all those who love me,
Of those who cry to me,
Of those who seek me,
Of those who have confidence in me.
Here I will hear their weeping, their sorrow,
And will remedy and alleviate
All their multiple sufferings, necessities, and misfortunes.

Note: On February 20, 1996, when the cards of Our Lady of Guadalupe were
about to be reprinted in Mexico, Ms. Agnes Gong (Kung), the secretary of the
Cardinal Kung Foundation in Stamford, CT, USA, the distributor of the holy
cards, asked me to do some corrections on the Chinese translation in blank verse
of Our Lady's Words attached to the card. Then, I made a retranslation in the
poetic style of Qiyan according to the English original.

195. 祝賀
上海主教龔品梅樞機鈞座
於重逢新任樞機
台灣高雄單主教鈞座時
歡慶九七高壽

鷓鴣天
聖安德肋大修院
1998 年 7 月 3 日

卅載洪爐千古名，
忠心來美享遐齡。
頂天頭上樞機冕，
照世楷模室內燈。

迎好友，
喜心靈，
燕京轉化禱同聲。
聖神但願臨華夏，
期頤舉國慶申城！

195.   Congratulations To His Eminence Cardinal Ignatius Gong Pinmei, Bishop Of Shanghai, On The Celebration Of His 97th Birthday At His Reunion With His Eminence, The New Cardinal Paul S. Shan, Bishop of Gaoxiong, Taiwan

To the Tune of Zhegu Tian
(Partridges in the Sky)
St. Andrew's Abbey
July 3, 1998

Your thirty years in the great furnace
Have tempered you and brought you an eternal fame.
Because of your ardent loyalty,
You have come to the United States
To enjoy your advanced age.
Your never subdued head is honored with a Cardinal's hat;
Your example shines in the world,
As a lamp set forth in the house.

Welcoming your dear friend,
Filled with joy,
You pray together with him,
In the union of one voice,
For the humble transformation of Beijing.
If only the Holy Spirit would descend
Upon the Chinese Mainland
So that the whole country may celebrate your centenary
In Shanghai, your native city!

196. 拜謁聖父教宗
若望保祿二世

七律
義大利羅馬
2001 年 5 月 2 日

彈指之間十五秋，

聖城偕友喜重遊。

華堂**彌撒**虔而靜，

聖父音容健且遒。

敬獻三書鴻鵠志，

稟明卅載赤牢囚。

懇求慈**主**將狼化，

華夏烝黎名永謳！

註：2001 年 4 月 30 日傍晚，我與兩位好友杰
姆、奧德麗・阿伯雷拉伉儷，在洛杉磯搭
乘德國盧漢莎航空公司的班機，於次日薄
暮到達羅馬。5 月 2 日星期三上午，我們
參加了教宗若望保祿二世在聖伯多祿廣場
的公眾接見。就在三小時之前，我榮幸地
和其他三十一位人士望了他在私人小堂舉
行的彌撒。隨後，當他在接見室個別接見
時，我向他獻上了有關自己經歷的三本英
法文書，並向他稟告了自己曾為信德於中
共監獄囚禁過廿六年。他惠賜了唸珠一串
和宗座祝福。

196.   A Private Audience With Holy Father Pope John Paul II

In the Poetic Style of Qilu
Rome, Italy
May 2, 2001

In a flash
Fifteen autumns have passed,
Once again with joy
I visit the Holy City with my friends.
In his resplendent chapel
The Holy Father celebrates Mass with devotion and quietly;
His countenance looks healthy,
His voice strong.

With reverence I present him my three books,
Showing the soaring ideals of a big mysterious bird;
And I reveal to him
Myself as a prisoner in the Red jail for thirty years.
May the merciful Lord convert the Wolf
So that
The Chinese people may sing His Name for evermore!

Note: On April 30, 2001, in the evening, Jaime and Audrey Abrera, a married
couple, my good friends, and I took an airliner from the Lufthansa German
Airlines at Los Angeles and arrived in Rome the following evening. On May 2,
Wednesday morning, we participated in Pope John Paul II's general audience at
St. Peter's Square. Just three hours earlier, I had the privilege of attending his
Mass in his private chapel with 31 other people. And then, when he received
each one of us in the audience room, I offered him my three books in English
and in French concerning my experiences and reported to him that I was imprisoned
for 26 years in Chinese Communist jails for the Faith. He gave me a rosary
and his Apostolic Blessings.

197. 贈亨利和瑪利亞·
哈杜伉儷

生查子
法國卡爾龐特臘
2001 年 5 月 12 日

讀完譯作歡，
衷曲馳函吐。
車站笑顏迎，
一見親如故。

驅車瑪院奔，
往事廳堂敘。
府第睡眠香，
辭別晨曦煦。

197.   A Poem For
Henri And Marie Ha Duy

To the Tune of Sheng Zha Zi
(Fresh Berries)
Carpentras, France
May 12, 2001

Having read the French version of my book,
You were so pleased
That you sent me a prompt letter
To unbosom yourselves.
You greeted me with a smile
At the station,
Feeling close like old friends
At the first glance.

You drove me
To the Abbaye Sainte-Madeleine.
There,
In a meeting room I recounted my past.
I had a sweet sleep in your house.
Under the warm morning sun,
I bid you farewell.

198. 向明谷聖若瑟大修院修士
談己經歷

人月圓
法國菲辛
2001 年 5 月 12 日

大廳修士排排坐，
經歷細心聆。
客先主後，
輪番朗誦，
臺上雙聲。

聽完講話，
爭相提問，
興奮群英。
來迎車站，
去而車送，
深謝恩情。

198.   A Talk On My Experiences
To The Monks Of
The Abbaye Saint-Joseph De Clairval

To the Tune of Ren Yue Yuan
(The family Reunion and the Full Moon)
Fixin, France
May 12, 2001

Sitting in lines in the auditorium,
The monks listen to my experiences attentively.
First, the visitor,
And then, the Abbot
Take turns doing the reciting;
On the platform
The two voices sound alternately.

Having listened to the talk,
The monks vie to raise questions excitedly.
Greeted at the station,
Seen off,
And driven to Mrs. Elisabeth Joliet's house,
I am much obliged to the hosts
For their kindness.

199. 作客依撒伯爾·
若利太太家

漁家傲
法國菲辛
2001 年 5 月 13 日

二月寒空飛雪片，
送來萬里君鴻雁。
叔祖來華吾院建；
蒙勖勉，
加州逃難無尤怨。

五月花都榮晤面，
田園尊宅春光滿。
他日西山冬霧散，
重建院，
讚歌堂內衝霄漢！

199.   Sojourn In
Mrs. Elisabeth Joliet's House

To the Tune of Yu Jia Ao
(Fisherman's Pride)
Fixin, France
May 13, 2001

In the cold sky of February
Snowflakes dance,
Bringing me your swan, your letter
From afar, ten thousand miles away.
Your granduncle, Fr. Prior Jehan Joliet,
Went to China
To lay the foundation of our original monastery.
Encouraged by him,
I do not resent being a refugee in California.

I feel honored to meet you
In May
In your dazzling capital;
Your house in the idyllic countryside
Is fully bathed with spring scenery.
Some day when the winter fog in Xishan vanishes,
Our monastery will be restored
And the chant in oratory will soar to the skies!

200. 拜訪天主教列日 ─
中國友愛會

卜算子
比利時邦諾
2001 年 5 月 17 日

春雨正霏霏，
邦諾堂中禱。
圖片書刊碑與亭，
教史神州表。

閱歷**赤牢**中，
如實廳堂道。
故國關心謝主人，
告別斜陽照。

200.   A Visit To The Fraternite D'Eglise Liege-Chine

To the Tune of Pu Suan Zi
(The Fortune Teller)
Banneux, Belgium
May 17, 2001

Spring rain sleeting,
We pray in the chapel of Banneux.
Pictures, books, periodicals, stele and pavilion:
All tell the history of the Church in China.

My experiences in the Red jail
Are narrated in the hall,
As they really were.
Grateful
To you,
Mrs. Anne Deprez, and all my other hosts
For your special concern about my Motherland,
I bid all of you farewell
At the glow of the setting sun.

201. 與費敏女士
同朝露德

眼兒媚
法國露德
2001 年 5 月 20 日

慈雕瞻仰艷陽天，
敬謝滿心間。
追思**母愛**，
獻呈香燭，
酌飲甘泉。

始胎無玷頑童憫，
容顯百年前。
恩情永記，
膝前哀懇：
續救塵寰！

註：2001 年 5 月 19 日到 21 日，應我的
　　法文書的譯者費敏女士的邀請，我
　　同她一起做了一次露德朝聖之旅。
　　爰填詞一闋，以誌其恩情，以敬謝
　　聖母。

201.   A Pilgrimage To Lourdes With Mrs. Frederique Barloy

To the Tune of Yan Er Mei
(The Eyes' Fascination)
Lourdes, France
May 20, 2001

On a brilliant and charming spring day,
Gazing at your loving statue, O Lady,
I am filled with veneration and gratitude.
Recalling your love,
The love of a mother,
I offer you an aromatic candle,
And drink from your sweet Fountain.

You,
The Immaculate Conception,
Merciful to us, your naughty children,
Appeared here
More than one hundred years ago.
Keeping your kindnesses in mind forever,
Kneeling before you,
I implore you
For continuing to save this world!

Note: In May 2001, from the 19th to the 21st, at the invitation of
Mrs. Frederique Barloy, the translator of my French book, and in her company,
I made a pilgrimage to Lourdes. I wrote this poem to record
her kindness and to offer my reverence and thanks to our Holy Mother.

202. 兩週客居
瑪利亞-德肋撒·托洛太太
和雅妮·托洛小姐家

采桑子
比利時昂布爾
2001 年 5 月 27 日

涼秋十五隨風逝，
喜又登門。
五月陽春，
後院前庭綠草茵。

驅車助訪五修院，
舊誼重溫。
東道慇懃，
半月關懷如至親。

202.   Two Weeks' Stay In The House Of Mrs. Marie-Therese Thoreau And Miss Agnes Thoreau

To the Tune of Cai Sang Zi
(Picking Mulberries)
Embourg, Belgium
May 27, 2001

As fifteen cool autumns have passed
With the wind,
I delight in coming to your house once again.
In the May's spring
In your back and front yards
There are carpets of green grass.

With your help and your driving,
I visit five monasteries
To relive my old friendship with them.
You, my very hospitable hosts,
Have shown me a care as for a close kin
For half a month.

203. 三晤費敏女士於巴黎火車站

踏莎行
法國巴黎
2001 年 5 月 27 日

重閱拙書，
心潮湧捲，
毅然惠譯同胞勉。
去年譯作已刊行，
濟人榮主宏圖展。

露德同朝，
尊門邀宴，
安排記者來相見；
今猶助我赴機場。
銘心刻骨君恩典！

203.   The Third Meeting With Mrs. Frederique Barloy At The Paris Railway Station

To the Tune of Ta Suo Xing
(Walking across the Meadow)
Paris, France
May 27, 2001

Rereading my book,
You felt such an upsurge of emotion
That you determined to do a translation
To encourage your compatriots.
Your translation, published last year,
Carries out your great ambition
Of saving people and glorifying the Lord.

You invited me
To a common pilgrimage to Lourdes
And to a dinner at your home.
You also arranged for me
Two interviews with journalists.
Today, you even come to the railway station
To help me to get to the airport.
Your kindness is imprinted on my heart and bones
With gratitude!

204. 辭別多默·
巴布西斯修士

玉蝴蝶
義大利羅馬
2001 年 5 月 28 日

屆時**聖座**書呈，
籌劃爾先行。
合照亮晶晶，
三遭數為增。

需求全照料，
來去送還迎。
廉票得螢屏，
五中恩德銘。

204.   Saying Goodbye
To Brother Thomas Babusis

To the Tune of Yu Hudie
(The Jade Butterfly)
Rome, Italy
May 28, 2001

To present my books to the Holy See
At the appointed time,
You anticipated the process for me.
With your assistance,
The brilliant and glittering pictures with the Pope
Are multiplied three times.

You provided me with all my needs.
You drove to the airport
To pick me up or to see me off
Whenever I came or went.
You found the cheapest air-ticket for me
Through hard work on your computer.
Your favors are engraved on my mind.

205. 題書贈
基督蒂娜・金女士

四言詩
聖安德肋大修院
2004 年 9 月 25 日

主伸臂膀，
助戰風浪：
安渡滄海，
彼岸登上！

206. 題書贈
詹妮弗・金小姐

四言詩
聖安德肋大修院
2004 年 9 月 25 日

望主慈愛，
賜爾神通：
戰勝艱阻，
進入天宮！

205.   Dedication On A Book To Ms. Christina Kim

In the Poetic Style of Siyan Shi
St. Andrew's Abbey
September 25, 2004

May the Lord stretch out His hand to you,
Helping to brave the winds and the waves,
That safely over the sea
You will reach the Heavenly shore
Of Him who saves!

206.   Dedication On A Book To Miss Jennifer Kim

In the Poetic Style of Siyan Shi
St. Andrew's Abbey
September 25, 2004

May God be so loving and benign
To grant you His strength
That you may conquer
All your difficulties and obstacles
And enter His Heavenly Palace!

207. 題書贈
阿曼達・金小姐

四言詩
聖安德肋大修院
2004 年 9 月 25 日

主乃真光，

照爾途程；

容光領瞻，

永世永生！

208. 題書贈雷內和伊梅爾達・
加西亞伉儷

四言詩
聖安德肋大修院
2004 年 9 月 30 日

爾敬**聖母**，

恩寵必蒙！

爾靠**耶穌**，

定見父容！

207.   Dedication On A Book
To Miss Amanda Kim

In the Poetic Style of Siyan Shi
St. Andrew's Abbey
September 25, 2004

May the Lord,
The Light of Truth,
Illuminate your way!
May He lead you
To see the splendor of His face
Forever and a day!

208.   Dedication On A Book
To Rene And Imelda Garcia

In the Poetic Style of Siyan Shi
St. Andrew's Abbey
September 30, 2004

Venerating Our Lady,
You will surely find grace!
Relying on Jesus,
You will see the Father's true face!

209. 題書贈
佩科米婭・金修女

四言詩
聖安德肋大修院
2005 年 12 月 28 日

獻身事主，
意誠心歡！
致聖濟世，
贏得桂冠！

210. 題書贈
帕特・漢森太太

四言詩
聖安德肋大修院
2005 年 12 月 28 日

爾恃主祐，
十架能負；
主愛永沐，
聖蹤勇步！

209.   Dedication On A Book
To Sister Pachomia Kim

In the Poetic Style of Siyan Shi
St. Andrew's Abbey
December 28, 2005

May you commit yourself
To the service of the Lord,
With a guileless spirit and a joyful heart!
May you through striving
To come to your own sanctification
And to succor others,
Win eternal laurels!

210.   Dedication On A Book
To Mrs. Pat T. Hansen

In the Poetic Style of Siyan Shi
St. Andrew's Abbey
December 28, 2005

With the Lord's aid
You are able
Your cross to bear.
So will you plunge into His love forever,
By following courageously
His footsteps!

211. 題書贈丹尼斯·
邁可拉尼斯蒙席

四言詩
聖安德肋大修院
2005 年 12 月 29 日

心焚主愛，

福音力佈；

完成任務，

天宴喜赴！

211.   Dedication On A Book
To Msgr. Dennis L. Mikulanis

In the Poetic Style of Siyan Shi
St. Andrew's Abbey
December 29, 2005

With a love for the Lord
In your heart flaming,
May you make every effort
In the Gospel proclaiming;
So that on that day
When you accomplish your duty,
You will come to the Heavenly banquet
In the spirit's beauty!